The Streetsmart Guide to

Overlooked Stocks

Other books in McGraw-Hill's Streetsmart Series include:

The Streetsmart Guide to Timing the Stock Market
by Colin Alexander

The Streetsmart Guide to Valuing a Stock
by Gary Gray, et al.

The Streetsmart Guide to Short Selling
by Tom Taulli

The Streetsmart Guide to Managing Your Portfolio
by Frank Yao, et al.

The Streetsmart Guide to

Overlooked Stocks

A Guide to Investing in the Best
Overlooked Stocks for Superior Returns

George Fisher

McGraw-Hill

New York   Chicago   San Francisco
Lisbon   London   Madrid   Mexico City
Milan   New Delhi   San Juan   Seoul
Singapore   Sydney   Toronto

The *McGraw·Hill* Companies

Library of Congress Cataloging-in-Publication Data

Fisher, George C., 1951–
   The streetsmart guide to overlooked stocks : a guide to investing in the
best overlooked stocks for superior returns / George Fisher.
      p. cm. — (The streetsmart series)
Includes bibliographical references.
   ISBN 0-07-140678-6 (hardcover : alk. paper)
   1. Stocks.   2. Investments.   I. Title.   II. Series.
   HG4661 .F478 2002
   332.63'22—dc21   2002011248

1 2 3 4 5 6 7 8 9 0 DOC/DOC 0 9 8 7 6 5 4 3 2

ISBN 0-07-140678-6

The material in Appendices 2 through 11 is reprinted by permission of S&P
Stock Guide, a service of McGraw-Hill.

McGraw-Hill books are available at special quantity discounts to use as
premiums and sales promotions, or for use in corporate training programs. For more information, please write to the Director of Special Sales,
Professional Publishing, McGraw-Hill, Two Penn Plaza, New York, NY
10121-2298. Or contact your local bookstore.

This publication is designed to provide accurate and authoritative information in regard to the subject matter covered. It is sold with the understanding that neither the author nor the publisher is engaged in rendering
legal, accounting, or other professional service. If legal advice or other
expert assistance is required, the services of a competent professional person should be sought.

> —*From a Declaration of Principles jointly adopted by a Committee*
> *of the American Bar Association and a Committee of Publishers.*

 This book is printed on recycled, acid-free paper containing a
minimum of 50% recycled de-inked fiber.

I am honored to dedicate this book to my wife, Karen, for putting up with me as I labored over this project. Late nights, missed dinners, and lonely evenings and weekends spent by herself are just a few of the sacrifices she made so that I could write this book.

Contents

Acknowledgments   xi

Introduction   xiii

CHAPTER 1   **GETTING IN THE GAME**   1
       Why Every American Needs to Be Investing
       Pay Off Your Consumer Debt
       Pay Yourself First
       Start Early in Life
       Invest Intelligently
       Historic Returns for Investors
       Time Mitigates Risk
       Stocks Outperform Bonds
       Ten Investing Mistakes to Avoid

CHAPTER 2   **THE IMPORTANCE OF A DIVERSIFIED PORTFOLIO**   21
       Bonds
       Stocks
       Stock Price Movements
       Speculation
       Market Capitalization
       Asset Allocation
       Portfolio Diversification
       Economic Sectors
       Small- and Mid-Cap Trends
       A Firsthand Lesson in Diversification

CHAPTER 3   IDENTIFYING OVERLOOKED STOCKS   **51**
What Are Overlooked Stocks?
The Life Cycle of Corporations
Fewer Restraints on New Opportunities
Nimble Management
Product or Service Differentiation
Product Innovation
Single-Market Focus
Faster Earnings Growth
Intelligible Financial Reports
Higher Insider Stock Ownership
Overlooked by the Big Companies
The Underdog Status
Sustainable Competitive Advantage
Overlooked Company Characteristics in Action

CHAPTER 4   EVALUATING MANAGEMENT   **75**
Importance of Management in Stock Selection
Return on Equity, Return on Capital, Return on Assets,
    and Long-Term Debt to Equity
Earnings per Share, Dividends per Share, Cash Flow,
    Revenues, and Gross Margins
Do Dividends Matter?
Trends
Management Efficiency Numbers in Action
Analysis
Standard & Poor's Equity Ranking
Corporate Mission Statements, Letters to Shareholders,
    and Corporate Ethics Statements
Management Stock Options
Stock Option Investigations

CHAPTER 5   UNCOVERING VALUE IN OVERLOOKED STOCKS   **111**
Finding Value
The Price-to-Earnings Ratio
The PEG Ratio
Next Year's PEG
PEG Ratios in Action
To Pro Forma or Not to Pro Forma—That Is the Question
Cash Flow per Share
The Share-Price-to-Sales Ratio
Contrarian Investing
Value Investing with a Diversified Portfolio
    of Overlooked Stocks
"You Will Never Go Broke Taking a Profit"

CHAPTER 6   **BUILDING A PORTFOLIO**   133
              Keeping Your Eyes and Ears Open
              How to Build a Diversified Portfolio of Overlooked Stocks
              Managing Volatility
              Small-Cap Stock Volatility
              The Joys and Heartaches of Being Added to an Index
              Bulls versus Bears
              The More Things Change, The More They Stay the Same
              Graham and Buffett

CHAPTER 7   **REITs AND ADRs**   149
              What Are REITs?
              Pass-Through Securities
              Types of REITs
              Historical Performance
              Evaluating a REIT
              Reported Net Earnings versus Funds from Operations
                 (FFO) and Dividends
              Examples of REITs
              REITs in Transition
              Investing Risks in REITs
              REITs, REITs, and More REITs
              What Are ADRs?
              ADRs in Action
              Examples of ADRs

CHAPTER 8   **OVERLOOKED TRENDS**   177
              Water
              Outsourcing
              The Global Accumulation and the Intergenerational
                 Transfer of Personal Wealth
              Global Resources

CHAPTER 9   **MUTUAL FUNDS**   211
              What Is a Mutual Fund?
              Mutual Fund Fees
              Mutual Fund "Phantom" Capital Gains Taxes
              Mutual Funds and Tax-Deferred Accounts
              Fund Portfolio Analysis
              "The Grand Infatuation"
              Exchange-Traded and Index Funds

CHAPTER 10   **PUTTING IT ALL TOGETHER**   227

APPENDIX 1 **STANDARD & POOR'S GLOBAL INDUSTRY CLASSIFICATION STANDARD**   231

APPENDIX 2 **OVERLOOKED COMPANY REVIEWS, ENERGY SECTOR**   237

APPENDIX 3 **OVERLOOKED COMPANY REVIEWS, MATERIALS SECTOR**   243

APPENDIX 4 **OVERLOOKED COMPANY REVIEWS, INDUSTRIALS SECTOR**   247

APPENDIX 5 **OVERLOOKED COMPANY REVIEWS, CONSUMER DISCRETIONARY SECTOR**   252

APPENDIX 6 **OVERLOOKED COMPANY REVIEWS, CONSUMER STAPLES SECTOR**   256

APPENDIX 7 **OVERLOOKED COMPANY REVIEWS, FINANCIALS SECTOR**   261

APPENDIX 8 **OVERLOOKED COMPANY REVIEWS, INFORMATION TECHNOLOGY SECTOR**   268

APPENDIX 9 **OVERLOOKED COMPANY REVIEWS, HEALTH CARE SECTOR**   275

APPENDIX 10 OVERLOOKED COMPANY REVIEWS, TELECOMMUNICATIONS SECTOR   279

APPENDIX 11 OVERLOOKED COMPANY REVIEWS, UTILITIES SECTOR   282

Endnotes   287

Bibliography and Resources   289

Index   293

Acknowledgments

I would like to extend my deepest appreciation to those who lent a hand during the writing of this book. Alex Evarts continues to be my front-line proofreader. His creative writing talents, along with his extended knowledge concerning stock investments, were invaluable to me. Robert (Opera Bob) Gibb offered his insightful view of stock investing and company evaluations. Jerry Conner focused on the flow of the manuscript—its transitions and understandability—for the novice investor. Taken together, the input of these three helped to hone the original manuscript into a precise discussion of investment strategies, research tools, and companies that fall outside the radar screen of most investors.

I would also like to thank the staff at McGraw-Hill Professional Publishing Group for their efforts on my behalf. As always, working with Kelli Christiansen, acquisitions editor, has been fruitful and rewarding.

I would like to add my appreciation to my three daughters for staying in college (and not failing their courses) during this project. Having a peaceful place to work at home helped me focus on the task at hand.

Most of all, I would be remiss not to thank my loving bride of 28 years for supporting this, and all, my projects. She has earned, and deserves, the book dedication many times over.

Introduction

There are too few Americans investing for their futures. Less than half of all households have sufficient funds invested to satisfy their eventual retirement needs. This book is written with them in mind.

Too many investors fall short in adequately researching stock investments, and, when their investments fail, they blame the fickle stock market rather than the true culprit—themselves. This book is written with them in mind.

Too many individuals consider only large-cap stocks, as they are pretty well known and are most often recommended by financial advisors. This book is written with them in mind.

Too few individuals have a defined path to their financial success. This book is written with them in mind.

First, you need to know why you are investing.

Second, you need to know how to seek out and evaluate companies and investment opportunities overlooked by other investors.

Third, you need to know where to look for these opportunities.

Fourth, you need to understand how to build a diversified group of overlooked stocks to complement other investments in your portfolio.

Fifth, you need (or may like) a list of potential candidates to begin the process.

The Streetsmart Guide to Overlooked Stocks provides all these tools to assist you in becoming a better investor. I can think of nothing more distressing than to have hard-earned money invested in underperforming mutual funds that charge fees and create undue tax liabilities. The tools in this book will assist you in breaking the chains of mutual fund investing to get you on a path of improved financial health. This book will teach you how to make smarter stock selections.

The stock market is filled with underperforming stocks. In addition, most financial advisors recommend the same large-cap, conservative stocks to all their clients, while their personal portfolios are filled with stock investments that are unknown to or overlooked by the average retail investor. I have a standard reply when I receive a broker's telephone call with a specific stock recommendation. I ask the broker if this stock is in his or her portfolio, and if not—why not?

Every now and again, a large-cap stock may creep into our discussions. *The Streetsmart Guide to Overlooked Stocks* is not just about small companies, but rather any hidden investment jewel. Many of the tools and strategies discussed are useful when reviewing big companies as well as small- and mid-sized companies.

The goal of *The Streetsmart Guide to Overlooked Stocks* is to help you find companies that are able to generate long-term shareholder value. Companies do this by embracing opportunities and managing their business to maximize profits. Evaluating management's ability to build a sustainable advantage is half the task of locating great companies. Understanding current stock price valuations will assist you in purchasing a stock when it provides the best value. There is nothing worse than to overpay for a stock, and then see the value of the investment either stagnate or go down over time. In realizing the relationship between stock price and stock value, you will be able to pinpoint reasonable stock prices. The easiest method of managing your investment risk is not to overpay for company profits. Since your goal is to maximize your investment dollars, raking the market for bargains should be your primary task. A company with excellent management, whose stock is overpriced, is no bargain. Likewise, a cheap stock price in a company with poor management is no bargain.

My brother manages his money the same way too many other Americans do. Rather than developing a disciplined saving and investing plan, he rationalizes his expenditures, and he saves and invests too little of his income. I wrote this book to help the Uncle Stephens get ahead financially.

Uncle Stephen's Windmill

I have a younger brother who is fondly known within the family as Uncle Stephen. Uncle Stephen seems to be attracted to harebrained and far-fetched ideas about saving money and investing. Like many, he keeps looking for off-the-wall money-making schemes as a shortcut to taking the methodical approach of saving and investing a portion of every monthly paycheck. Uncle Stephen is drawn to get-rich-quick schemes and grandiose sales pitches that claim huge returns on investments in short amounts of time.

I was driving by Uncle Stephen's house recently and saw something peculiar. There was some sort of erector set contraption supported by a multistory construction crane behind his house. It towered over the neighborhood. I was sure this oddity had to be a colossal screw-up and would ultimately cost someone his or her job. As I pulled into the driveway, my brother came out of the garage to meet me. He had a large grin from ear to ear.

He pointed to the steel structure and said, "What do you think of my latest investment? It's a combination windmill and cellular phone transmission tower."

"What on earth are you doing?" I asked.

"My electric bill has doubled and the end is not in sight. The talking heads on TV are scaring me with all this blackout stuff. Even last night, California Governor Davis made Jay Leno turn off all the studio lights, and I had to watch the two of them in candlelight. I want to do my part to solve this crisis and my new windmill will generate free electricity.

"Over the past year, my electric bill has gone from $115 a month to $184 a month, and it seems to just keep going up," Uncle Stephen said. "At the current rate of increase, I figure I will be paying almost $500 a month to plug in my electric razor in 2004. So, I decided to generate my own electricity. What better way than to build a windmill? The manufacturer has a deal with the local cell phone company to install and lease an antenna on top, and I get a cut of that."

"How much does this contraption cost?" I asked.

"$27,000 up front or $358 a month for 12 years, less the $100 a month payment I get from the phone company. It may seem steep, but my electricity is free."

"$358 a month? That's a total of $50,000 for your 'free' electricity," I said. "I bet that doesn't include the cost of insurance in case that thing comes crashing down on your house. Or the repairs and maintenance. Have you figured those into your cost as well? What happens if the cost of electricity stabilizes, or is even lower in a few years?

"Bro, I think you would be far better off to take that $27,000 or $358 a month and invest it for your future. You should get better returns for your investment dollars than buying into your windmill power-generating plan. Turn off your air-conditioner and unplug your motorized exercise bike if you want to cut down on your energy costs."

If Uncle Stephen had invested just 6 years ago either a lump sum of $27,000 or $358 a month (total invested $25,776) in stocks, he could have built a nice position in a well-managed company. For example, if Uncle Stephen had enrolled in the dividend reinvestment program of any one of the following companies on January 1, 1996, his stock position could have been worth on January 1, 2002:

Company (Stock Symbol)	$358 per Month	$27,000 Lump Sum
S&P 500 (SPY)	$31,800	$53,600
Northrop Grumman (NOC)	$43,700	$54,900
Equity Residential Properties (EQR)	$45,700	$78,000
Pitney Bowes (PBI)	$36,500	$65,300
Progress Energy (PGN)	$43,500	$66,700
Wm Wrigley (WWY)	$45,300	$65,900
Fortune Brands (FO)	$40,300	$50,200
Pacific Century Financial (BOH)	$42,200	$58,800
RPM, Inc. (RPM)	$48,100	$54,400
Raymond James Financial (RJF)	$53,500	$117,700
Scotts (SMG)	$44,400	$65,100
WD-40 (WDFC)	$43,500	$70,700
Cascade Natural Gas (CGC)	$41,100	$52,900

When Uncle Stephen is evaluating money-saving purchases, he should first analyze the opportunity costs of not investing those funds. Then he might realize his proposed purchase may not be such a great deal after all.

To all those Americans who are not saving enough, who are not studying investments enough, and who don't know how to find overlooked investment jewels, this book is for you.

The Streetsmart Guide to

Overlooked Stocks

CHAPTER 1

Getting in the Game

A penny saved and invested wisely is a
dollar more for your financial dreams.
—Grandfather Fisher

Each of us has financial needs, such as a rainy day fund, educational expenses for ourselves and our children, and our own retirement. Yet far too few of us regularly save and invest. Of the approximate 100 million American households, only about half have money in financial investments, such as stocks and bonds. Consumer debt and consumer spending as an aggregate are considered one of the engines for our economy. In reality, however, these slowly steal money away from our ability to save and invest for our future. Paying off consumer debt and establishing a regular savings program provide the seed money for building your financial future. Over the past 50 years, stocks have provided a far better investment return on our savings than either bonds or bank certificates of deposit. History has shown the longer the holding period for stocks, the lower their risk. Starting early and maximizing your rate of return will have a substantial impact on the accumulation of wealth.

Why Every American Needs to Be Investing

Consuming to satisfy a false sense of importance was a key element of the 1980s and 1990s, which were known as the "Me" decades. "Buy,

buy, buy" and "Charge, charge, charge" were the battle cries during those years. Delayed gratification was out of vogue, and everyone seemed to want everything on the spot. As a society of consumers, we are virtually bred to spend. For instance, there are now playrooms at most McDonald's restaurants. As one generation is brought up with the "advantages" of playtime at McDonald's as a means of occupying children's attention at mealtime, they become more apt to take their own children there. When we don't have the cash in our pocket and the urge to spend overpowers the financially prudent part of our brain, we pull the easily obtained credit card out of our wallet and charge. It is too easy to rationalize that small minimum credit card payment. Far too often the microscopic part of our brain that is satiated by new shoes, or new stereos, or the latest electronic gadget, overpowers our fiscal responsibility. In America these days, it is the person who is debt free and stashes away a consistent amount of each paycheck who is not the norm. However, doing both ensures a secure financial future. Grandfather Fisher once told me, "Earning a paycheck will pay your bills. Saving and investing will fulfill your dreams."

To obtain your financial dreams, you need a strategy. It is not possible to succeed without a plan of attack. Like a military campaign, realizing the dreams of educating your children or having a comfortable retirement require a vision and a plan to achieve that vision. You must save a bit of each paycheck and every bonus, and you must make intelligent investment decisions. This is the ammunition against going broke at some point in your life.

Financial advisors have different recommendations as to how much should be saved. My rule of thumb is that 12 percent of your net income every paycheck should be set aside. A minimum of 3 to 6 percent is for retirement, and the balance is for other needs. Nonretirement needs may include an account to pay for both unexpected as well as anticipated expenses, such as the down payment for a new car when the old jalopy finally gives up the ghost, college expenses for dependents, or funds for vacations.

There are many retirement cost calculators found on the Internet that will help you determine if you are saving enough for your retirement. Many financial advisors suggest that you will need 75 to 80 percent of your preretirement income to maintain your lifestyle into your retirement years. Using a retirement cost calculator found at Leggma-

TABLE 1-1 Annual Savings Required to Generate 75 Percent of Preretirement Annual Income, Based on 3 Percent Annual Raises, Retirement Age 60, 10 Percent Preretirement Return, and 8 Percent Postretirement Return

Age	Income	Amount Already Saved	Account at Retirement	Percent of Annual Income Needed to Be Saved
25	$30,000	$10,000	$798,800	4
35	$40,000	$25,000	$792,000	9
45	$50,000	$100,000	$737,400	15
55	$60,000	$200,000	$658,200	79

Source: Leggmason.com.

son.com, Table 1–1 outlines the amount you need to save as a percentage of income.

An individual at age 25 with a retirement savings account of $10,000 would need to save 4 percent of his or her annual income to generate $798,000 for retirement by age 60. A 55-year-old individual with $200,000 already saved for retirement would need to save 79 percent of a $60,000-a-year income to achieve a retirement savings of $658,000 by age 60.

To encourage workers to build a retirement fund, employers often offer to match contributions to a 401(k) retirement account. The matching contributions usually range from 1 to 3 percent of annual compensation. An employer-matched contribution to a retirement plan is free money. The profit from wisely investing this free money can have a dramatic impact on the quality of life during the retirement years.

As an incentive for Americans to save for their retirement, the federal government recently raised the maximum annual tax-deductible contribution to a tax-deferred individual retirement account (IRA). In 2002, the maximum contribution to a traditional or Roth IRA was raised to $3000. It will increase in 2005 to $4000. After 2005, the maximum contribution will be indexed to the compounded rate of inflation. For example, if the rate of inflation in 2006 is 2.5 percent, the maximum contribution will be raised from $4000 to $4100. In 2007, the maximum contribution will be raised to $5000. If in 2008, the inflation rate is again 2.5 percent, the maximum contribution will increase to $5125. Annual contributions to company-sponsored 401(k) retirement accounts were also raised. The maximum contribution limit will increase to $15,000 in 2007. Investors over 50 can add a bit more to their retirement accounts in an attempt to catch up for previous years' contributions that may have been too low. In an IRA, those over 50 can contribute an additional $500 until 2006, when the catch-up provision increases to $1000. Older folks can contribute to their 401(k) plan up to an extra $1000 in 2002. The catch-up provision increases to $5000 in 2006. An older individual can contribute up to $20,000 to a 401(k) in 2007 ($15,000 maximum limit plus $5000 catch-up provision). Look for the feds to continue to raise the limits as they try to wean Americans off Social Security as the primary source of retirement income.

For example, Bob, age 22, graduates from college and gets a job as a salesperson for the local Widget Company. His annual salary is $35,000, and he anticipates a 3.5 percent annual raise. Bob establishes a tax-deferred retirement account and initially funds it by making a $3000 contribution. Bob continues to contribute $3000 annually until at age 25, he bumps up his contribution to $4000. At age 28, he increases his contribution to $5000 a year. At that point, he increases his contribution by 2.5 percent a year, keeping up with inflation. His employer matches his contribution by 3 percent of his annual compensation after his first year of employment. Bob is a conservative investor and invests half his annual contribution in bonds, which return 6 percent a year. The other half is in stocks, which return 12 percent a year. At various stages in his life, Bob's retirement account may look like Table 1–2.

Although Bob never made more than $153,000 in any year over his working lifetime, he was able to amass a sizable retirement account balance. The key is that he religiously contributed to his retirement account, and his employer contributed 3 percent of his income. During his 43-year employment career, Bob invested a total of $301,600 while his employer chipped in an additional $105,200. In addition, Bob started early and stuck to his plan over his entire employment lifetime.

Pay Off Your Consumer Debt

Americans have been transformed into a society focused on immediate gratification. We don't plan ahead. We buy what we want and we

TABLE 1-2 Year-End Retirement Account, Annual Contributions Split 50 Percent Bonds, 50 Percent Stocks, 3 Percent of Income Matched Equally by Employer

Age	Salary	Employer Contribution	Annual Savings	Account Balance, Bonds	Account Balance, Stocks	Total Retirement Account
22	$35,000	$0	$3,000	$1,590	$1,680	$3,270
30	$46,000	$1,380	$6,550	$30,200	$39,700	$69,900
35	$54,000	$1,620	$7,380	$61,445	$95,000	$156,500
40	$65,000	$1,950	$8,290	$105,000	$195,000	$300,000
45	$77,000	$2,100	$9,318	$168,000	$375,000	$543,000
50	$91,000	$2,730	$10,848	$254,000	$697,000	$951,000
55	$108,000	$3,240	$11,802	$374,000	$1,269,000	$1,643,000
60	$129,000	$3,870	$13,304	$539,000	$2,038,000	$2,577,000
65	$153,000	$4,590	$15,012	$763,000	$4,073,000	$4,836,000

want it now. Only after we have satisfied our burning material desires do we hopefully figure out a way to pay for it.

The average American spends between $700 and $1150 a year on holiday gifts, but then takes 6 months to pay the bill. According to RAM Research, a credit card tracking company, Americans charge $400 billion a year on their credit cards. Thanks to easy credit terms, there are over 1 billion credit cards in circulation. That is 4 credit cards for every man, woman, and child in America.

Why are credit cards so easy to obtain? It's simple. It is very profitable for the card issuers. At an average interest rate of 15 percent, Americans pay $50 billion in interest every year. That $50 billion in annual interest is enough money to buy every professional basketball, hockey, and baseball team in America, with billions of dollars to spare. The total interest paid to all credit card companies each working day is about the same amount needed to buy one very well equipped Boeing 747 airplane.

The average balance on credit cards is $5800. At 15 percent interest, it costs $870 a year to maintain that balance. If a debtor wanted to pay it off in a year, payments would be $415 a month. The minimum the credit card companies would demand, however, would be just $106 a month, and at that pace, it would take 6 years to pay off. If a debtor paid off the balance using the minimum monthly payment, total interest charges would reach a total of $2612, or 52 percent of the original purchases. An individual could invest the same $870 (equal to just 1 year's interest to carry a credit card balance of $5800) at an 11 percent compounded annual return, and it would be worth over $56,000 in 40 years. Table 1–3 outlines the total interest you would pay if you made only the minimum payments each month.

If you cut out your credit card debt, you will probably find seed money for saving and investing. To see how sound this advice is, consider the different financial paths taken by Alex and Andrew. At age 20, Alex decides that one of his financial principles is never to incur credit card debt. His neighbor Andrew, in contrast, carries an average credit card balance of $4000 for which he is willing to pay $50 a month in interest. Alex is an astute investor and picks great companies as investments. Each year, Alex is able to generate a 13 percent return on his investments. Since Alex has no credit card debt, he takes the same $50 a month Andrew pays in interest and invests it. Over his lifetime, this $50 a month contribution to his investment plan pays off rather handsomely. At age 70, Alex has increased his wealth by $2,638,600. Andrew, on the other hand, has a substantially smaller retirement account and still carries his $4000 credit card balance.

TABLE 1–3 What You Pay in Total Interest When You Pay Only the Minimum Monthly Payment, Based on a 2 Percent Minimum Payment

Interest Rate	19%	15%	11%
$1500 balance	$4298	$1956	$1018
$2000 balance	$6198	$2789	$1441
$2500 balance	$8098	$3622	$1864

Source: myvesta.com.

Pay Yourself First

All income comes from either capital at work or people at work. Capital at work usually generates a return on the capital—that is, a profit. People at work usually earn a paycheck. Businesses thrive and prosper by taking their profit—the return on previously invested capital—and reinvesting it in their businesses. Similarly, individuals need to take a portion of their paychecks, or their personal profit, and reinvest it for their future.

Successful companies reinvest their profits to develop new products, build new factories, or market their existing products better. Individuals also need to reinvest their personal profit back into themselves in order to prosper. Companies that squander their profit or fail to continually reinvest in their businesses eventually fail. Individuals who fail to invest on a regular basis will find that funds will not be available when needed for retirement or their dependent's education.

We must pay ourselves first; we must build our financial future with the same seriousness as we pay the water or electric bill. No one will do it for us. We have to have the fortitude to do it for our family members and ourselves. The consequences of not saving enough are a reduction in the quality of our retirement years, though that may be decades from now. If we don't pay our mortgage payment, the bank will take our house. If we don't pay our phone bill, Ma Bell will turn off our phone service. If we don't save and invest, we will not realize our dreams and desires. The most important component of financial success is to pay ourselves first.

Many families try to budget their income to the penny. They develop a precise cash flow model—cash in from their paychecks and cash out to pay their bills. They meticulously plot out the weekly or monthly paycheck, followed by a matrix of expenses. According to their ledger, the monthly budget should have a specific amount left over for savings and investing. However, the reality in twenty-first century America is that this approach is doomed to failure.

In his book *Money for Life*, Robert Sheard talks about an obscure and uncelebrated property of money called the "elastic rule of monetary expansion." This rule applies regardless of income or social status, and it is unavoidable except by the most astute individuals. Simply put, the rule states that "no matter how much money you earn, your expenditures will automatically expand to meet that level." The corollary monetary theorem, the "impossible nature of specific budgeting," also holds true. This corollary states, "No amount of earnings is ever adequate to provide you with any money 'left over' at the end of the month if you try to plan your entire budget ahead of time." Together, these monetary facts of life are the major reason Americans don't, or can't, save. Most of us make New Year's resolutions that include having more money to save each month. However, much like our resolutions to lose weight, by February, resolutions to save more this year end up in the ever-growing New Year's resolution trash heap. The unforeseen birthday present, the new flowering bush for the garden, or the latest dress in the shop window get the cash mentally allocated to the resolution.

The best way to overcome the devastating effects of the elastic rule of monetary expansion and the impossible nature of specific budgeting rule is to make the first payment from the first check of the month to you. Rather than trying to survive on the monetary leftovers, your financial future takes its rightful place among other creditors.

Set a goal of a specific dollar amount to save and invest each pay period. It could be as little as $10 or $20 a week, or as much as several thousand dollars a month. Again, I recommend that 12 percent of your net income be diverted to accounts specifically established for your financial future. There are many *direct stock purchase plans* (DSPPs) or online stockbrokers who would be pleased to establish an automatic withdrawal from your bank account scheduled to coincide with your pay periods. As your income grows over time, so will the dollars set aside for your future. This is a painless means to build wealth. Most company-sponsored retirement plans offer automatic contributions deducted from your paycheck. You should also save a portion of the occasional windfall, such as a company bonus or an inheritance. The bottom line is putting money away for your future needs to be as habitual as getting up in the morning.

Start Early in Life

Every financial guru espouses the benefits of starting to save and invest early in life—and rightfully so because the benefits of starting early cannot be understated.

For example, Hank begins investing $1000 a year at age 20, and he realizes an 11 percent annual return. At age 30, Hank stops investing, but he lets his account accumulate. At age 50, Hank's $10,000 investment has grown to $149,000. Harry starts investing at age 30, 10 years after Hank started, saves $2000 a year and also realizes an 11 percent annual return. Harry invests $2000 a year until age 50. He has invested $40,000, or four times the amount Hank has. However, Harry's account is worth only $134,000, which is $15,000 less than Hank's account. The difference is Hank's much smaller contribution compounded over a longer time than Harry's.

Invest Intelligently

Many people are paralyzed with fear of losing their hard-earned money. This paralysis prevents them from even getting started. With the stock market decline of 2000 and 2002, many investors found their brokerage accounts shrinking by 25 percent or more. In the 1990s, the stock market seemed headed straight to the moon. Then the realities of investing hit home hard.

Stock prices go down as well as up, and there will be times when specific positions in any portfolio will show a loss. But investors must stay focused on the long term and "stay the course." Over time, investing in well-managed companies has rewarded those who are willing to remain invested and who continue to invest through tough market cycles.

Phil and Paul were roommates and fraternity brothers in college, and both took up the same career—long-term-care insurance sales. Phil was conservative with his income while Paul liked to live the good life. As their incomes rose over the years, Phil stashed away more of his income than Paul did. Phil brought his lunch to work, and he often feasted on peanut butter sandwiches and rice cakes for dessert. Phil purchased only late-model used cars and drove them until they were virtually antiques. Phil was known to drive out of his way to fill up with cheaper no-name gasoline, and he was a stable client of the local junkyard where he bought parts to fix his car. He purchased a small beach home and rented it out when he was not vacationing there. Phil even cut down his own Christmas tree because it was cheaper. Phil was known as a skinflint, and many thought he had the first dime he ever earned. Above all, however, Phil saved a minimum of 12 percent of his income, and some months he saved much more. He invested in well-managed company stock. Phil, through his research, picked companies with a record of increasing company profits and, over time, increasing shareholder dividends.

Paul, on the other hand, loved his exotic beverages. His daily routine included a Sri Lankan double latte for breakfast, a Nicaraguan Segovia mocha for lunch, an Ethiopian cappuccino for dinner, and a cup of organically grown decaf Yamamotoyama tea before bed. Paul had a habit of purchasing only automobiles that had waiting lists, and the longer the list, the better. One of his personal goals in life was to explore every Club Med on the face of the planet. Paul was a favorite of every door-to-door salesperson and telephone solicitor. Many a Girl Scout needed only to pay a visit to Paul to make her annual cookie quota. Paul managed to save only 6 percent of his income, and he invested in only safe, secure government bonds.

Phil and Paul made a pact when they were in college. Each would retire once he had saved $1 million. Phil retired before Paul and was able to move permanently to his beach home at the early age of 52 because he had saved more than Paul and had earned a larger return. Paul had saved less and had a lower return of 6 percent on his bond portfolio. He had to toil at his job until age 65, a full 13 years longer than his fraternity brother.

According to Dwight Lee and Richard McKenzie in their book *Getting Rich in America,* "The amount you save may be less important than the rate of return and the period of time over which you allow your net worth to build in determining your net worth at retirement." Table 1–4 outlines various scenarios concerning savings rates and rates of return.

Historic Returns for Investors

The stock market has proven to be the best place to grow your hard-earned money. There are many investment choices. The major asset categories are stocks, bonds, or cash (like money market accounts or short-term government treasury notes, also known as "T bills"). Table

TABLE 1-4 How Compounding Interest Works under Different Savings and Retirement Plans

One-Time Savings of $2000 at Age 22

	Rate of Appreciation of Assets		
Retirement Age	15%	8%	5%
65	$817,700	$54,700	$16,200
75	$1.64 million	$80,400	$20,800

Savings of $2000 Each Year from Age 22

	Rate of Appreciation of Assets		
Retirement Age	15%	8%	5%
65	$6.23 million	$713,800	$302,200
75	$12.55 million	$1.06 million	$396,000

Saving 10% of Income, Starting Annual Salary of $30,000 at Age 22 and Receiving 1% Real Annual Increases Thereafter

	Rate of Appreciation of Assets		
Retirement Age	15%	8%	5%
65	$10.01 million	$1.20 million	$525,500
75	$20.16 million	$1.79 million	$696,900

Source: Dwight Lee and Richard McKenzie, *Getting Rich in America,* HarperBusiness, New York, 2000.

1–5 lists 10-year compounded annual returns by decade according to Ibbotson Associates, *Stocks, Bonds, Bills, and Inflation, Edition 2000* (SBBI). The data are based on investments made at the beginning of the decade and held until the end.

With the exception of the 1970s, the compounded return for the S&P 500 Index over a decade period outpaced government bonds, corporate bonds, and inflation. The average annual 10-year compounded return, adjusted for inflation, for the S&P 500 Index was 9.6 percent over each of the past 5 decades. When adjusted for inflation, bonds experienced negative returns in the decades of the 1950s, 1960s, and 1970s. In other words, bond investments failed to maintain

TABLE 1-5 Compounded Annual Percentage Rate of Return by Decade

Dividends and Interest Reinvested

	1950s	1960s	1970s	1980s	1990s
S&P 500 Index	19.4	7.8	5.9	17.5	18.2
Small-cap stocks	16.9	15.5	11.5	15.8	15.1
Long-term corporate bonds	1.0	1.7	6.2	13.0	8.4
Long-term government bonds	0.1	1.4	5.5	12.6	8.8
Government T bills	1.9	3.9	6.3	8.9	4.9
Inflation	2.2	2.5	7.4	5.1	2.9

Source: Ibbotson Associates, *Stocks, Bonds, Bills, and Inflation, Edition 2000,* Chicago.

purchasing parity of the principal plus interest received because the rate of inflation was higher. During the past 50 years, only in the 1980s and 1990s did bonds provide investors with positive inflation-adjusted returns.

In the decades of the 1960s and 1970s, the value of stock in smaller companies substantially outperformed the value of stock in larger companies. There have been cycles in the stock market when large companies have outperformed smaller companies, such as in the decades of the 1980s and 1990s. When evaluated in the longer term, however, smaller companies have generally provided better returns. For the 25-year holding period 1975 to 2000, small company stocks returned 17.6 percent annually while large company stocks returned 15.5 percent. While that may not seem to be much of a difference, over a 25-year holding period, the difference surely adds up. For example, a $10,000 investment in 1975 in small company stock could have been worth $575,600 in 2000, at 17.6 percent annual return. The same $10,000 invested in large company stock could have been worth $366,900 at 15.5 percent annual return. Owning stock in small- and mid-cap companies is more profitable even though it also carries a higher risk. When researched properly and purchased as a portion of a diversified portfolio, small- and mid-cap stocks can provide the boost every investor is seeking.

Time Mitigates Risk

The longer an investor holds an investment, the higher the probability that he or she will ultimately earn a profit and the lower the risk that he or she will lose the capital. The longer a shareholder retains his or her shares, the higher the chance there will be a capital gain.

Ibbotson Associates is well known for its studies of the benefits of long-term investments. According to Ibbotson, since 1926, there has never been a negative return in a 20-year holding period for investments in the S&P 500 when dividends have been reinvested. There have been negative returns on 10-year holding periods from 1929 to 1938 and from 1930 to 1939. Since 1931, during every 10-year holding period, investors have made money. Some periods saw higher earnings than others, but in the end an investor with a 10-year horizon has almost always come out ahead. For 5-year holding periods, there have been negative compounded investment returns only seven times. Those periods were 1927 to 1931, 1928 to 1932, 1929 to 1933, 1930 to 1934, 1937 to 1941, 1970 to 1974, and 1973 to 1977. Four of the seven negative return periods were during the Roaring Twenties and the Great Depression. History is never a guarantee of the future, but the results from these holding periods are compelling.

Stocks Outperform Bonds

A diversified portfolio should contain both stocks and bonds although historically bond returns have failed to keep up with stock returns. Bonds are usually purchased not for their returns but for their capital preservation features. Bonds can be an integral part of a portfolio as the need to liquidate the funds gets closer and the level of acceptable risk decreases, as when an investor nears retirement. U.S. government bonds are considered the benchmark for investment safety. Unfortunately, they provide a lower return than stocks.

One of the monetary tools the Federal Reserve has to manage economic cycles is the control of interest rates. When the economy grows too fast and is overheated, the fed will raise interest rates to slow the rate of economic growth. When the economy stalls and begins to contract, the fed will lower interest rates to generate more economic activity.

There have been short-term periods, such as in 2000 and 2001, during which bonds have outperformed stocks. However, those times are usually when interest rates are declining after being raised to cool the economy, along with a short-term declining stock market. These conditions have existed during only a few brief periods. Stocks have outpaced both bonds and inflation the rest of the time. The average annual return for the S&P 500 Index since 1925 has been around 12 percent. The average annual return for bonds has been less than half that.

However, rate of return is not the only concern for investors. As the need to withdraw invested funds gets closer, capital preservation becomes a larger concern. For example, if you will need to access your investments for college or retirement within 60 months, you should begin to consider moving assets from stocks to bonds. The goal is to reduce the risk that your stocks will take a header, which happened to some stocks during the declines of 2000 and 2001. For example, some U.S. government bonds purchased at the interest rate peak of 2000 returned 19 percent over the ensuing 12 months while the S&P 500 declined by more than 20 percent.

Ten Investing Mistakes to Avoid

Many individuals invest in a random way, which often leads to their losing money. These investors often attribute their losses to luck, believing that the stock market cards are stacked against them. People who make random investments on impulse have not developed an investment strategy or a predetermined investing plan. They plunge willy-nilly into the financial markets. When they make bad decisions, they blame the system rather than the true culprit for their misfortunes: themselves.

According to Paul Merriman, founder of Merriman Capital Management, common personal finance mistakes can be grouped into the following categories:

- Procrastinating
- Lacking a written plan
- Taking too much risk

- Taking too little risk
- Paying investment fees
- Overreacting to media hype
- Taking amateur advice
- Relying on recent market performance
- Focusing on the wrong things
- Expecting perfect performance

By identifying and studying these often-made mistakes, an individual can avoid them and increase the chance of earning long-term capital gains.

Procrastinating. Procrastination takes many forms. Delaying the establishment of, or contribution to, their retirement plan is a common and costly mistake many Americans make. For example, waiting until the end of the year to make a contribution to your retirement account, rather that contributing at the first of the year, could cost you as much as $450,000 over 40 years. The difference is the result of 40 years of compounding of the initial investment. The sum of $2000 invested every January 1, with an aggressive annual return of 15 percent, would be worth $4,091,000 after 40 years. The same $2000 annually invested on December 31, however, would be worth $3,558,000. Investing is like voting in Chicago. Do it early and often.

Many investors also procrastinate when it comes to annually reviewing their investments or making additional investments. An investor who waits for the "right time" or for a market correction usually doesn't invest at all. I do not advocate a blind investing technique, as investors should always seek value in their purchases. But when they find it, they should act. Too many rationalize their procrastination tendency by believing they will catch up when the market is better, when they are making more money, or when they have a bit more time. Every day they delay, however, is one less day they have until they need the funds to meet their financial goals.

Lacking a Written Plan. Would you consider driving to Igloonick, Canada, without a road map and a sense of direction? Would you consider sailing from Buzzards Bay to the Bay of Bimini without an oceanographic chart? I would hope not. However, many investors, both young and old, just throw money at the market without a written plan or understanding of their investments. According to *Fortune* magazine, people with a written plan with which they direct their investments on average have five times as much money at retirement than those without. The investment plan should contain well-thought-out concepts, such as asset allocation desired, types of stocks, and specific criteria for choosing management and stock value.

I have a friend, Dude, who invests in stocks. Dude is a relatively conservative investor, and he won't buy any stock unless the issuing company has very little debt, the management owns a lot of its own company stock, and the cash flow has steadily increased during the past 3 years. Most importantly, they have to pay him to own their stock—Dude buys only those stocks that pay dividends. Are Dude's criteria better or worse than yours are? The answer is not important. What is important is that Dude has a plan and sticks to it. If he feels comfortable with his plan and realizes an acceptable rate of return on his investment, then he is head and shoulders above those without a plan. Having a written plan also lets you know when you have deviated from the plan. This allows you to get back on track.

How do you develop an investing plan? If you are a do-it-yourself investor, reading finance books and surfing the Internet will allow you to learn the basics of developing a sound financial road map. You could ask a professional for assistance, but make sure that he or she is not paid to sell you financial products. Estate lawyers, accountants, or even bankers could be of benefit, as these professionals should be well versed on the subject of developing an investment plan.

Taking Too Much Risk.   Investment risk is not just a theoretical concept; it is a real-life event. All investing involves taking some risk, and each investor must understand the relationship between risk and reward. Typically, the more the risk, the higher the potential reward. However, taking too much risk could be devastating to your financial future. Just think about investors who had the vast majority of their portfolio in Internet stocks in early 2000. Many of those stocks are now worth just a few pennies on the dollar of their previous valuations. People who assume too much risk become speculators, not investors. There are successful speculators, but they all have one thing in common: They actively manage their risk and know how much money they can afford to lose.

Taking Too Little Risk.   It is easy to stuff your mattress with dollars or to keep your funds in a money market account. In contrast, investing in stocks is neither perfect nor guaranteed. But historically the long-term returns in the stock market have been unmatched. Very low risk often equates to very low returns. A money market account will likely never lose money, but the annual interest return is much lower than it would be for stocks. For example, $10,000 invested in a money market account with a compounded rate of 5 percent would be worth $238,000 after 65 years. That same $10,000 returning 12 percent in the stock market would be worth $15.6 million after 65 years.

Paying Investment Fees.   I will discuss this in detail later in the book, but as a teaser, follow this example: The top five mutual funds control about $310 billion in assets for their investors. The average mutual fund charges its investors an annual management fee of between 1.0 and 1.5 percent. Each and every year, investors pay these top fund families around $3 billion in fees. That amounts to about $3 billion that these investors no longer have for their financial future, and the compounded return on these fees over decades can add up to tens of trillions of dollars of reduced assets.

Overreacting to Media Hype.   We have all seen the covers of national finance magazines. They usually read "Best Funds for 2002 and Beyond," "Turn $10,000 into $1 Million with These Stocks," or "Must-Have Investments for the Next 10 Years." However, study after study has shown these media-hyped stocks underperform going forward. These headlines, however, do sell magazines. The talking heads on cable finance programs should be forced to tattoo on their foreheads that their investment advice is not necessarily designed to make you money but rather to increase their television ratings. It is far better to take these articles and programs as a source for investing ideas to be further researched. Do not take them as the gospel for your hard-earned investment dollars.

Taking Amateur Advice.   Too many investors buy stocks based on a tip they have received from their friends, relatives, or even their stockbroker. The lure of hot tips and the dream of replicating the wealth of

Warren Buffett are almost irresistible. "I know somebody at the company" or "This stock will make you a ton of cash" are not sound reasons to invest in a company. Remember that there is no easy shortcut to building wealth.

Relying on Recent Market Performance. It is human nature to believe that good things will always continue. The other side of the coin is also true, that a stock that has dropped will be a loser until the end of time. Many investors believe that a stock that has doubled in price will continue to do so forever, and they will blindly buy it. Many investors also believe that once a stock drops, it may never recover. It just does not work that way. While excellently managed companies will return a respectable long-term profit for their shareholders, there will be times when its stock becomes overpriced and times when it is undervalued. It is very important to follow the advice of Benjamin Graham, the father of value investing and the teacher of Warren Buffett: "Rake the market for value."

Focusing on the Wrong Things. It is human nature to focus on our winning ways in the stock market, but it is extremely important to evaluate the entire portfolio. One or two stocks may double or even triple in price, but a portfolio that is underwater as a whole is still a losing proposition. It is important to continually review the overall performance of an entire portfolio.

Expecting Perfect Performance. There is a vast difference between acceptable returns and perfection. Some people can't stand to have anything but the "best," including their stocks. There will always be "better" stocks than the ones you choose, stocks that will outperform your choices. There will also be many more stocks that underperform the ones you choose. Keep your focus on generating acceptable long-term returns based on the risk you are willing to accept. Your goal should be to make a profit on your investment over the long term by finding stocks currently trading at prices that are reasonable in relation to their long-term potential, rather than buying what you believe will be the next fad in investing. Perfectionists often flit from one stock to another, trying to find that one stock that will rise from $1 to $100. The prudent long-term investor, on the other hand, locates stocks that are currently undervalued based on the quality of company management and their ability to grow shareholder value over the next decade or two.

Individuals, young and old, need to be on a focused course of accumulating personal wealth over time. The best source of personal investment capital is your current payment to credit card companies. Paying off consumer debt and redirecting those funds into a savings and investment plan will allow you to build your wealth faster. After every weekly or monthly paycheck deposit, make sure the first check you write is to yourself. The stock market has provided individual investors the best returns, and the longer an investor holds onto a stock or bond, the lower the investment risk. Avoid making common, and sometimes costly, investment mistakes.

As an individual investor assembles a consortium of assets, investment choices grow. Companies overlooked by most investors should be included in the stock selections that make up a diversified portfolio.

CHAPTER **2**

The Importance of a Diversified Portfolio

*Annual income twenty pounds, annual
expenditures nineteen pounds nineteen
six, result happiness. Annual income
twenty pounds, annual expenditures
twenty pounds ought six, result misery.*
—MR. MICAWBER TO DAVID IN CHARLES
DICKENS'S *DAVID COPPERFIELD*

Every portfolio should include cash, bonds, and stocks. Branching out across all asset classes is a time-tested investment strategy to reduce portfolio risk. Diversification may not only reduce portfolio risk; it may also increase overall returns. When evaluating stock selections, investors should focus on management's ability to generate profits. Long-term corporate earnings growth alone is the determining factor that will lead to higher stock prices. Small and mid-sized companies, operated by proven managers with a history of increasing revenues and profits, are investment vehicles many individuals use to increase their overall portfolio returns.

Bonds

The two major classes of investments are stocks and bonds. Each has unique attributes and drawbacks, and each deserves a place in every investor's portfolio. Stocks usually offer higher returns over the long term, but they are considered a higher risk. Bonds offer a lower return over time, but they are considered a safer investment.

Bonds are like loans to companies, countries, and municipalities. There are two types of U.S. government bonds: savings bonds sold through the banking system and U.S. treasury bonds usually bought and sold through brokers. Savings bonds are almost like government-issued certificates of deposit (CDs). Popular with small investors due to their low denominations, many investors start by buying savings bonds, then move on to U.S. treasury bonds as the dollars invested grow. When investors buy a bond, they are, in essence, buying a promissory note from the issuer who promises to repay the bond at a specific time in the future, known as the *maturity date*. If, in January 2003, an investor buys a $10,000 U.S. government bond due in 30 years, the U.S. government promises to repay the investor $10,000 in January 2033. Most bonds pay interest on the face amount of the bond, or loan. The amount of interest the investor receives varies based on the prevailing market interest rates at the time of purchase. For example, in early 2000, the Federal Reserve was raising interest rates to cool down an overheated economy. Market rates rose, and newly issued bonds were paying investors around 6.5 percent. As more expensive credit took its anticipated toll on the economy, the Federal Reserve began to reduce interest rates, and newly issued bonds were paying 5.4 percent interest by the winter of 2001. Over my investing lifetime, I have seen 30-year-bond interest rates as high as 15 percent in the 1980s and as low as 5.4 percent in the spring of 2002.

Bonds are usually purchased as part of a diversified investment portfolio. Considered to have less risk than stocks, bonds are bought when investors are more concerned about capital preservation than capital gains. As people get older, the need to spend their savings and investments comes closer, and savvy investors want to make sure their capital will be available when they actually need it. For instance, a couple establishes a college savings and investing plan for their child upon birth. The time frame for the financial need is 18 years. Initially, the couple invests in stocks in order to realize a higher appreciation of their capital. Starting in year 14 or 15, the couple may begin moving money out of stocks and into bonds. Their focus has changed to making sure the funds will be available when they need them to pay tuition bills.

Once issued and initially purchased by an investor, bonds can be resold and traded on the open market. If I were to buy a 30-year bond and decide 25 years later that I want to cash it in, I could sell it through the bond market. Bonds are issued in denominations of $1000, and they are usually bought and sold in groups of five for $5,000. The market prices of bonds rise and fall based on the interest paid on the bonds versus the current market interest rates. Bond prices move inversely with movements in the general interest rates. When interest rates rise, bond prices fall, and when interest rates fall, bond prices rise. In the bond market, bonds are traded and quoted based on units of $100. A bond with a face value, or value at maturity, of $10,000 would be quoted as one hundred $100 units. If I bought a $10,000 face value bond and paid $10,000 in the bond market, I would pay a market price of $100 each and have 100 units.

For example, suppose I buy a newly issued U.S. treasury bond for $10,000 that will pay a fixed annual interest of $600, yielding 6 percent at the time of purchase. If interest rates fall to 5 percent, investors would be willing to pay me $12,000 for my $10,000 face value bond to receive a 5 percent interest payment. I continue to receive $600 in interest, but the prevailing interest rate is now 5 percent. A 5 percent return on $12,000 is $600. The bond will be quoted in the marketplace at $120. Likewise, if interest rates climb to 7 percent, investors would be willing to pay me only $8,571 for my $10,000 face value bond so that they could receive a comparable 7 percent interest payment. My bond would be quoted in the marketplace at $85.71. Upon maturity, bonds are redeemed by the issuer for their face value or their original loan amount, regardless of the market price.

No one can predict the future of interest rate movements. It is prudent to buy bonds with maturities matching the financial need. For retirement needs 30 years in the future, 30-year bonds should be purchased. For college needs bonds should be bought with a 5- or 10-year maturity. Another approach to long-term bond investing is to ladder the maturity dates, or in other words, purchase a series of bonds with a range of maturity dates. For example, suppose you purchase equal amounts of bonds due to mature in 1 year, 3 years, 5 years, and 10 years. When the 1-year investment matures, you would reinvest it into new 10-year bonds. When the 3-year note matures, you would buy more 10-year bonds, and continue to do so whenever a note matures. The advantage of laddering an overall bond investment is that you reduce the risk that interest rate changes will affect your portfolio. If rates increase, you can take comfort knowing that soon you will have capital from bond maturities available to take advantage of the change. If rates decline, you will have a portion of your portfolio at above market rates.

Unless rates are excessively high, don't purchase bonds with maturities beyond the time you anticipate that you will need to spend the capital. If interest rates are higher at the time you sell your bond, the market price may be lower than what you paid.

I recommend that a minimum of 15 percent of your total portfolio be invested in bonds that are held to maturity.

Buying bond mutual funds as an alternative is a poor choice as they are more sensitive to interest rate changes. Bond mutual funds do not mature like the bond assets they hold, and their price is based solely on the current yield. As interest rates rise, bond mutual fund prices decline; the value of the underlying bond assets they hold also declines. It is possible for an investor to buy a bond mutual fund during times of low interest rates, and it may take a very long time before the investor recoups the initial investment. During the winter of 2001, in response to the recession, interest rates reached their lowest level in almost 40 years. I believe new bond fund investors in late 2001 and early 2002 will not recoup their capital for many, many years as interest rates will rise to more normal levels along with an improving economy. This rise in rates will create a decline in the value of bond mutual funds.

In addition, bond mutual funds charge their investors annual management fees. The average long-term bond fund followed by Morningstar charges an annual fee of 1.05 percent. For example, the Equitrust High Grade Bond Fund was listed as a low risk and above average for returns. The fund has returned an average of 6.37 percent over the past 10 years. However, the fund charges an annual fee of 1.68 percent. Had an investor been able to match the 6.37 percent return on his or her own without using the Equitrust Fund and saved the annual management fee, the return would have increased to over 8 percent. Chapter 9 concerns the pitfalls of mutual funds.

TIPS and Inflation.   The U.S. government in the 1990s introduced a new type of bond called a *treasury inflation protected security* (TIPS). The scourge of bond investing is the impact of inflation. *Inflation* is defined as the gradual increase in price over time of the same goods or services. For example, when watching old reruns of *The Andy Griffith Show,* it always amuses me to watch scenes from the local coffee shop with Sheriff Andy and his sidekick, Barney Fife, sitting around the coffee shop counter. When the check comes, they sometimes argue over who will pay the cost of their 15 cent coffee. Today, they would be arguing over who would pay the cost of their $1.00 to $1.50 cup of coffee. That is inflation.

Put another way:

What cost $10,000 in 1961 would cost $59,032 today.

What cost $10,000 in 1971 would cost $43,573 today.

What cost $10,000 in 1981 would cost $19,417 today.

What cost $10,000 in 1991 would cost $12,958 today.

Inflation impacts bond investors because the principal of the bonds is repaid in static dollars. For instance, a $10,000 30-year bond purchased in 1971 would have repaid $10,000 at maturity in 2001. However, the purchasing power of the $10,000 in 1971 would have been worth only $2334 in 2001 due to inflation. To compensate for the deflated principal dollars, bond investors usually demand an interest rate return higher than the current inflation rate. Thus, if inflation is at 2.5 percent, bond investors may seek fixed-interest-payment returns of around 5.5 percent.

Unlike typical bonds, a TIPS indexes both the principal and semi-annual interest paid on the principal to the current inflation rate. This difference is significant: Had TIPS bonds been offered in 1971, a $10,000 30-year TIPS bond would have matured in 2001 with a value of around $43,000. TIPS bonds pay a lower interest yield, but that yield is paid on the inflated amount of the principal, called the *accrued principal.* For example, a TIPS bond may have an interest rate of 3.5 percent, while a traditional bond may have a fixed 6.0 percent interest rate. However, as the accrued principal in a TIPS bond increases with inflation, the interest received also increases. For example, if 30-year TIPS bonds had been offered in 1971, the interest the bond would have paid in 2001 would have been $1505 (accrued principal of $43,000 times the interest rate of 3.5 percent). In late 2001, the Treasury Department saw the error of its ways. Realizing that TIPS bonds were too good of a deal for investors, the Treasury announced that it was no longer issuing TIPS bonds with less than a 30-year maturity. TIPS bonds can be purchased in denominations of $1000 either directly from the government or from a stockbroker. For more information, call 202-874-4000 or visit publicdebt.treas.gov. In my opinion, TIPS bonds are great investments for the bond allocation of your portfolio.

Corporate Bonds.   Corporate bond investors usually earn higher interest than government bond holders. However, corporate bonds do not guarantee repayment. Corporate bond issuers may file for bankruptcy protection and default on their obligations. Recent examples are Global Crossing, Kmart, Celotex, and, of course, Enron. While a bankrupt company may not completely default on its bonds, investors who hold bankrupt bonds may realize only pennies on the dollar of their investment. To offset the risk that a company may fail, corporate bond investors demand a higher return. For short-term maturities, when corporate viability is quite high and repayment at maturity seems likely, corporate bonds may be appropriate.

Stocks

Companies generate capital for the businesses by borrowing money from banks and other financial institutions, issuing bonds, or selling pieces of their businesses to the general public. Rather than lending money to companies, many investors desire to become part owners and will take an equity position in a corporation. The vehicle used for this asset transfer from corporations to investors is called *common stock*. When companies make the decision to move from holding their own stock, that is, from being *privately held,* to offering their stock for sale to the general public, that is, to being *publicly held,* they become *public companies.*

Investors who buy *stocks,* or *shares,* in public companies are purchasing some of the assets and future profits generated by the company. These investors are then considered *stockholders,* or *shareholders,* in those companies. Stockholders own a specific percentage of all net assets and can lay claim to a portion of company profits. Stockholders receive *stock certificates* representing their ownership of corporate assets. The first time companies offer their stock for sale to the general public is called an *initial public offering* (IPO). The company may subsequently sell additional shares to the general public to generate additional capital. This is called a *secondary public offering*.

For example, American Capital Strategies (stock ticker symbol ACAS) is an industrial venture capital firm that went public in August 1997. American Capital Strategies specializes in offering financing for small industrial companies. The company has invested nearly $1 billion in venture capital in 60 companies since its own IPO. In exchange for its financing, ACAS acquires senior debt and an average of 36 percent equity. American Capital Strategies also usually receives at least one seat on the board of directors of the companies they finance. The average interest ACAS received on its portfolio of investments in the fourth quarter of 2001 was 15.2 percent, and the average age of the companies it financed was 44 years. American Capital Strategies holds investments in an array of industries; their holdings include a canoe manufacturer, a fighter jet cockpit hatch manufacturer, an industrial gas distributor, a pneumatic valve manufacturer, and a food service equipment manufacturer. ACAS generates additional capital for new investments either by selling stock or by packaging and reselling portions of its loan portfolio. When it resells loans, American Capital Strategies makes a profit by charging a servicing fee for collections. In addition, it profits from the interest rate spread between what is charged the borrower and the terms of the resale. This spread is usually several percentage points.

As of December 31, 2001, American Capital Strategies had 35.6 million shares outstanding, up from 27.6 million at the end of 2000. During the year, management had sold 8 million shares, for which it received an additional $213 million in capital to expand its venture portfolio. American Capital Strategies had assets of $905 million and liabilities of $263 million as of December 31, 2001. Corresponding book value, or shareholder equity, was $641 million. Net operating profits for 2001 were $71.6 million, up 60 percent from the $44.7 million reported in 2000. In 2001, the company paid dividends and returns of capital to shareholders totaling around $81 million.

As a shareholder of one share, I own 1/35,600,000 of the company. Net operating earnings for my one share in 2001 were $2.24, up from $1.96 in 2000, for a gain of 14.2 percent. Although net operating dollar profits were up 60 percent for the year, ACAS issued additional shares, and my portion of the company shrunk from 1/27,600,000 to 1/35,600,000. As of December 2001, my one share of American Capital Strategies assets was worth $25.43, and my portion of its liabilities was $7.41, leaving a net book value of $18.02. In 2001, I received $2.30 in dividends for each share I owned, and the stock traded between $23.68 and $29.89. Based on this trading range, ACAS offered a dividend yield of between 9.7 percent and 7.6 percent.

If American Capital Strategies happens to fail and goes bankrupt, my one share will be worthless. If the company is liquidated, its assets are distributed to bondholders and banks ahead of equity investors. When a company files for bankruptcy, stockholders usually receive only pennies on their dollars, if anything at all. The most recent example is Enron. At their zenith, Enron stock sold for almost $90 a share. In bankruptcy, their current share price is $0.20. A $9000 investment is now worth just about $20.

Stock Price Movements

The action of Wall Street can be summed up in one sentence: Long-term corporate profit potential moves markets and stocks. As actual earnings grow on a consistent basis, share prices will follow. The ability of management to deliver consistent earnings growth is a major contributor to increasing share prices over the long term. Don't let anyone convince you otherwise. The value of shares is based on old-fashioned supply and demand. With a finite number of shares available, share prices move up if there are more buyers than sellers. Share prices move down if there are more sellers than buyers. What causes investor interest? Long-term investors seek companies with good prospects for increased earnings and dividends over time. If a company is increasing earnings quickly, there will be a lot of interest in owning its stock. However, if earnings momentum stalls or the prospects of the company are not as good as previously thought, investors may lose interest.

Speculation

"The mob is easily led and may be moved by the smallest force, so that its agitations have a wonderful resemblance to those of the sea"— Publius Cornelius Scipio, Roman statesman and warrior, 162 B.C.

The basics of mob mentality have not changed in the 2164 years since that statement was made. Likewise, the basics of successful investing have not changed in more than 400 years. Novices and even some of the most sophisticated investors, however, at times get caught in a speculative investing trap. There have been and will always be short-lived fads in investing, but corporate profits will be the only economic factor that will move markets higher over time.

There have been surges of excessive speculation dating from the tulip bubble of 1637 to the Internet bubble of 2000. Speculators and naïve investors will occasionally call the shots for short spurts of time. But these fads have little to do with the basics of business (making a profit), and they are doomed to eventual failure. Fads have withered and died in the past and will fail again in the future. Only the ability of corporations to increase profits quarter after quarter, year after year, decade after decade matters. Period.

Long before the crash of Internet startups crushed the dreams of stock-market-investors-turned-speculators, Semper Augustus was at the center of a similar financial downfall for many. Semper Augustus is a midnight-blue tulip topped with a band of pure white and accented with crimson flares. In 1637, the Dutch were infatuated by this rare tulip, and due to a horticultural short squeeze and excessive hype, there was much more demand than supply. The bulb itself takes 7 years to grow from seed, and the mother plant will last only a few years while producing just two or three *offsets*, or clones, annually. Holland was in the midst of an economic boom, and cash was plentiful. Money that had just a few years before gone toward fighting Spain for Holland's independence now flowed into commerce. The Dutch merchants were getting very rich because they were at the center of a booming East Indies trade. At the height of its popularity, one single Semper Augustus tulip bulb could cost as much as a wealthy merchant's annual income. In the winter of 1636 to 1637, some bulbs were changing hands up to 10 times a day, each time at a higher price. Soon after, the tulip market crashed when, at a routine bulb auction, speculators stopped offering such high prices. Within days, panic had spread around the country, and the market for rare and high-priced tulips evaporated. What had only days before fetched over 5000 gilders was now worth less than 50. People who purchased the bulb near the peak of the tulip bubble would not have recouped their investments—4 centuries later.

In the 1920s, the Radio Corporation of America (RCA) was the hot momentum stock. It rose 2600 percent in 3 years; then it crashed to just 30 percent of its all-time high. Those who bought RCA at its zenith had to wait over 30 years (when Radio Corporation of America began to manufacture televisions) to break even. In the 1970s, when the U.S. government decoupled the dollar from the gold standard, the price of gold skyrocketed more than 2000 percent to over $800 an ounce. Soon afterward, the price of gold crashed to around $300, and it has yet to recover to its highs of 1972. Similar tales of woe surround the Japanese stock market between 1982 and 1990. The Japanese stock market index, the Nikkei, rose over 1000 percent, but it then crashed to nearly one-third of its all-time high.

These yarns of sorrow all have two basic and common themes. The first is that prices paid for these investments had little fundamental underpinning of value. The second is that individuals who bought these investments did so without analysis of the underlying fundamentals. If investors had bothered with basic research, the problems with these investments would have been apparent. Investors became speculators with Publius Cornelius Scipio's mob mentality.

Over the long term, increasing corporate profits produced by companies with proven management will be the driver to increasing stock gains. Corporate profits have been the fuel for long-term increases in shareholder value. Nothing more, nothing less.

Market Capitalization

Companies are grouped by market size, which is known as *market capitalization,* or *market cap.* Market cap is calculated by multiplying the total number of outstanding shares by the price per share. *Outstanding shares* are all the shares a company has issued minus those shares that the company has repurchased and is retaining. Microsoft (MSFT) has 5.385 billion shares outstanding, and it trades at $60 a share. Its market cap is $325.3 billion. Money manager Eaton Vance (EV) has 69.3 million shares outstanding, and it is trading at a share price of $40.71, for a market cap of $2.836 billion. Pennichuck Corp. (PNNW), a small water utility company, has 2.382 million shares outstanding, and it trades at around $26.50 a share. It has a market cap of $63.123 million.

Companies are usually separated into these categories using the following guidelines. These market cap ranges have been widely accepted throughout Wall Street:

Large cap: Market capitalization greater than $10 billion

Mid-cap: Market capitalization between $1.5 billion and $10 billion

Small cap: Market capitalization smaller than $1.5 billion

Large-cap companies usually have name recognition. General Motors, IBM, AT&T, Honeywell, and Alcoa are examples of large caps. The 30 companies making up the Dow Jones Industrial Average are all large-cap companies. Mid-cap companies are slightly smaller, and examples include the grocery store chain Albertsons (ABS), defense contractor Raytheon (RTN), industrial basic chemical producer Air Products and Chemical (APD), and banking concern KeyCorp (KEY). Small-cap companies include a local bank, Seacoast Financial (SCFS); a water utility, Philadelphia Suburban (PSC); a lawn fertilizer manufacturer, The Scotts Company (SMG); and a credit card processor, Global Payments (GPN).

Many people assume that small caps are mainly high-risk, technology, or biotech startup companies with unproven management. That is not always the case. Small caps come in all industrial flavors and ages. Every industrial sector of the economy contains large, medium, and small companies. There are small companies in the basic chemical products sectors, in the utility sector, and in the financial sector.

Many small- and mid-cap companies have been around for generations. For example, Scotts was founded in 1868, Philadelphia Suburban in 1902, Raytheon in 1922, KeyCorp in 1927, Albertsons in 1939, Air Products in 1940, and Raymond James in 1962.

Sometimes a larger company will spin off certain divisions and assets into separate independent companies. For example, in 1970, National Data Corporation (NDC) founded a financial processing division. In 2001, National Data spun off this division, and it is now known as Global Payments Inc. (GPN). While this credit card and check processor has a short public history, its roots and management date back over 30 years.

The goal of every company is to rise through the ranks of its competitors. Over time, many business concerns traverse the financial landscape, going from a startup to a small cap to a mid-cap, ultimately

joining the ranks of the select few large caps. Some will rise only to the
mid-cap level and remain in this category for their business lifetimes.
Others will ascend to the large-cap ranks, where their businesses then
stall, their market cap declines, and their ranking slips back into the
mid-cap category. Some businesses, though excellently managed and
profitable, have geographic or industry constraints that may prevent
them from expanding past small-cap status. As an investor, individuals
should be seeking companies with above-average business prospects
and a history of excellent management. That will allow revenues, profits, stock prices, and market capitalization to grow over time. There is
nothing more rewarding than to conduct your due-diligence research,
locate and invest in well-managed companies, and then see your investment choices grow in value over the decades.

Asset Allocation

One of the guiding principals of investing is that the assets in a portfolio be allocated among diverse investment options. As discussed earlier, there are three major classes of assets: cash, stocks, and bonds.
Asset allocation is the investment strategy of separating financial
investments into these basic categories. Each investment decision we
make impacts our asset allocation. Every stock we purchase from our
cash savings reduces our low-risk cash. The theories, benefits, and
risks associated with asset allocation are consummated with every
trade. Asset allocation is implemented either by design or by default.

For instance, Walter is an overly conservative, long-term investor.
Walter was just 25 when his rich uncle died and left him a $100,000
inheritance. Walter decided to invest his windfall 50 percent in cash, 25
percent in bonds, and 25 percent in stocks. Walter realized a 3 percent
annual return on his cash position, 6 percent on his bonds, and 12 percent on his stocks. He reinvested the interest and dividends back into
the same asset classes. Walter retires at age 60. The total value of his
portfolio is $1.632 million. Much to his surprise, however, the asset
allocation had changed over time from 50 percent cash, 25 percent
bonds, and 25 percent stocks to 8 percent cash, 12 percent bonds, and
80 percent stocks. Due to a higher return on the bond and stock asset
allocations, these grew at a faster pace than the cash. Table 2–1 reviews
the transformation of Walter's portfolio allocation over time.

TABLE 2-1   Asset Allocation Changes Over Time Based on Annual Returns of 3 Percent from Cash, 6 Percent from Bonds, and 12 Percent from Stocks ($100,000 Initial Investment Allocation: 50 Percent Cash, 25 Percent Bonds, 25 Percent Stocks)

	Cash	Percentage of Portfolio	Bonds	Percentage of Portfolio	Stocks	Percentage of Portfolio
Initial	$50,000	50%	$25,000	25%	$25,000	25%
Year 5	$56,200	46%	$31,400	25%	$44,000	33%
Year 10	$65,200	35%	$44,700	24%	$77,600	41%
Year 15	$77,800	28%	$59,900	22%	$136,800	50%
Year 20	$90,300	22%	$80,100	19%	$241,100	59%
Year 25	$104,800	16%	$107,200	17%	$425,000	67%
Year 30	$121,300	12%	$143,400	14%	$748,900	74%
Year 35	$140,600	8%	$192,100	12%	$1,319,900	80%

Asset allocation has a greater impact on the overall performance of a portfolio than any other factor in long-term investing. In a study published by Ibbotson Research, the allocation of assets was found to be responsible for 91 percent of the performance of a portfolio. Actual stock selection was responsible for about 5 percent, and market timing 2 percent. Other factors accounted for 2 percent.

Portfolio Diversification

Every investor should diversify his or her purchases within each asset class among many different investments. The basis of adequate diversification is that no one single stock or bond performance will overly impact the performance of the portfolio as a whole. An investor may have good asset allocation among cash, bonds, and stocks, based on his or her personal risk level. However, the portfolio holdings may still not be diversified enough within each asset class to truly implement the risk strategy the investor desires. For example, Walter wanted to reduce his risk initially by having 50 percent of his assets in cash, 25 percent in stocks, and 25 percent in bonds. Had he chosen only one or two stocks within the asset class, his risk profile would have been high.

If one of the two companies he chose went bankrupt, his portfolio would have lost 12 percent of its entire value. The same is true of Walter's bond assets. If he only had a few different bond maturities from the same bond issuer, he would have had a much higher risk. By owning several stocks in several industrial sectors, Walter reduced his risk that one sector or specific stock selection would have undue influence on the entire portfolio.

Not all stocks or industrial sectors rise and fall at the same time. Good economics for one company may be devastating for another. For example, high oil prices are good for the energy sector because the price of the oil rises above the cost of producing it. But higher oil prices puts the squeeze on airline and trucking company profits because their costs of doing business increase. A portfolio with investments in both sectors has a reduced risk of overexposure to just the underperforming sector.

There has been a lot written about the number of investments needed to achieve quality portfolio diversification. In 1949, Benjamin Graham, considered the father of value investing, published *The Intelligent Investor*. Graham stated that diversification is adequate when the number of stocks (or bonds) in a portfolio ranges between 10 and 30. J. L. Evans and S. H. Archer reduced this number in their quantitative study "Diversification and the Reduction of Dispersion" in 1968. The study found that with as few as 10 to 15 selected stocks, a portfolio could achieve adequate diversification. The study also stated that having more than 15 stocks does not add to the benefits of diversification and is a waste of time in terms of quantitative risk. For 30 years, either the 10- to 15- or the 10- to 30-stock diversification thresholds were widely accepted.

The most recent study on diversification, "Have Individual Stocks Become More Volatile?" is by John Campbell, Burton Malkiel, and Yexiao Xu. This study was published in *The Journal of Finance* in February 2001. According to these academics, it now takes up to 50 "randomly selected" individual stocks to achieve the same diversification advantages as 10 to 15 stocks gained in the mid-1980s. Their position is that money managers control more stock assets and have the ability to greatly influence stock prices. With the explosion of mutual funds and managed accounts, money managers hold 50 percent or more of most publicly traded stocks. As companies meet or fail their quarterly earnings growth targets, money managers clamor to buy or sell stock, which causes volatility in the price. To satisfy short-term-thinking money managers, company management takes higher business risks to generate higher earnings growth. The researchers believe that eventually every business product will become a commodity, which forces management to continually reinvent themselves, exposing shareholders to higher levels of risk.

My feeling on this subject is that professional money managers do control a greater percent of individual stock assets than before. But I don't believe well-managed companies are willing to accept speculative risks just to satisfy short-term investors. Most well-managed companies have a clearly defined business strategy, which they implement with precision. The goal of proven managers is to expand their respective businesses either through attaining a greater share of the market or a better position in the market.

Some companies will deviate from their historic products and services when they realize their primary business activity happens to be in an industrial sector that is declining in profitability. The new business focus may or may not be fruitful for investors. For example, AT&T (T) has been unsuccessfully trying to reshape itself. The profitability of its basic business—telephone services—has experienced a dramatic downward shift over the years.

Founded in 1919, Nokia (NOK), the large cellular phone manufacturer in Sweden, was once a stodgy paper- and-steel making company. In the early 1980s, its management was taken over by a few young visionaries who believed in the opportunities of the cellular telephone business. The new management proceeded to transform the almost-bankrupt company and refocus its assets on an entirely new business. Nokia is a classic example of a company that successfully reinvented itself.

Small- to mid-cap companies develop and implement a focused business plan and grow earnings over time through better market penetration. Campbell, Malkiel, and Xu's study also uses a random selection process for determining optimum levels of diversification. There should be nothing random in stock selection. Only after an investor evaluates the management's ability to increase earnings and dividends over the long haul and understands the price valuation should he or she add or delete a company from a portfolio.

I will stick with the masters and their time-tested approach of having between 10 and 30 stocks to achieve diversification. This would correlate to an investment position of 10.0 percent to 3.3 percent of the stock allocation dollar amount evenly distributed to each individual stock.

As a portfolio increases over time, stock allocation can become overweighted in a specific stock or economic sector. No single company stock should represent more than 12 to 15 percent and no single economic sector more than 20 percent of a portfolio.

Investors who are starting out may not have sufficient funds to purchase this many stocks. A minimum ownership goal should be between $5000 and $7000 in each stock position. This amount gives the investor meaningful dollar returns. If a stock doubles in 7 years, then redoubles in another 7 years, a $5000 investment would create capital gains of $15,000, and a $7000 investment would create a capital gain of $21,000. A $5000 goal is also easily obtainable. A $100 monthly investment with a return of 12 percent a year would equal $5000 in 41 months, or less than 3.5 years. Sometimes a stock's performance is greater than 12 percent a year. If it is, then the $5000 goal is reached faster. For instance, in March 1997, I started a dividend reinvestment and stock purchase plan (DRIP) with Chicago Bridge & Iron (CBI). CBI is focused on the oil infrastructure construction business. I had $100 automatically withdrawn from my savings account every month. The stock price fluctuated between $18 and $10 until late 1999, when it started to climb. By May 2000, I had accumulated 325 shares at an average cost of $12.30 each. The stock was trading at $16, and I had achieved my goal of $5000 worth of CBI. However, I invested only $4000 of capital. I then canceled the automatic investment program and started over with another stock selection. I kept the CBI shares I purchased in their DRIP program. CBI continued to trade higher, and, in 2001, it hit an all-time high of $36. My 325 shares were worth over $11,000. Since then, the stock has retreated to the high $20s, and my position is worth a bit more than $9000.

The minimum number of stocks in a portfolio should be 10, and the minimum number of economic sectors represented in a portfolio should be 5. From this base, companies in different industrial sectors can be added.

A well-diversified portfolio may underperform in a bull, or rising, stock market. A bull market is usually limited to only a few sectors at a time. However, sectors will rotate in and out of favor, and each will have its turn in the spotlight. In a bear, or declining, market, a well-diversified portfolio will usually outperform. Stock market declines, like bull markets, will have some sectors that are not as affected, and these will decline less than the overall market.

Economic Sectors

Standard & Poor's, a firm that provides data and information on individual companies as well as stock market trends, many years ago devised a system for classifying all companies into economic sectors. Securities analysts rely heavily on the S&P Global Industry Classification Standards (GICS) in monitoring market activity among the economic sectors. Economic sectors react differently to the same economic events, and sectors expand at different rates. For instance, technology is usually associated with high earnings growth. Utilities are associated with more stable earnings. Generally speaking, a group of competitive companies within an industrial sector will move together in the stock market.

In 1999, Standard and Poor's expanded their list of economic sectors from 8 to 10. In addition, they also expanded and realigned industry and subindustry categories. Table 2–2 lists the major economic sectors along with major industry groupings. A more detailed listing is provided as an appendix at the end of this book.

Just as it is important to diversify a portfolio across economic sectors, it is also important to diversify across market capitalization. As discussed earlier, there have been times when small-cap stocks have outperformed large-cap stocks. No one has a crystal ball clear enough to predict what companies will be the stellar performers over the next 10 years. What our crystal balls can tell us is that well-managed and aggressive small- and mid-cap companies should get larger and should reward shareholders with higher share prices. A portfolio that has both large-cap stocks, like Merck (MRK), and small-cap stocks, like Omnicare (OCR), may outperform a portfolio of just large-cap drug companies. As Omnicare continues to gain market share and increase profits above the drug industry averages, their stock price should continue to climb higher, also above industry averages. If you invest in five different sectors with no less than a total of 10 individual stocks, you will reduce your risk that any one stock or sector tanks.

TABLE 2-2   Standard & Poor's Global Industry Classification Standards (GICS)

Energy

Materials

Industrials

>   Capital goods
>   Commercial services and supplies
>   Transportation

Consumer discretionary

>   Automobiles and components
>   Consumer durable and apparel
>   Hotels, restaurants, and leisure
>   Media
>   Retailing

Consumer staples

>   Food and drug retailing
>   Food, beverage, and tobacco
>   Household and personal products

Health care

>   Health care equipment and services
>   Pharmaceuticals and biotechnology

Financials

>   Banks
>   Diversified financials
>   Insurance
>   Real estate

Information technology

>   Software and services
>   Technology hardware and equipment

Telecommunication services

>   Telecommunication services

Utilities

Source: Standard & Poor's.

Small- and Mid-Cap Trends

In the 1990s, the boom in mutual funds, the growth of 401(k) retirement accounts, and the increase in the globalization of business favored investments in large-cap stocks. According to *Mutual Fund* magazine's March 2002 issue, in the 1990s, well over half of all mutual funds were invested in large-cap stocks while only 5 percent of fund assets were in funds focused on small caps. As defined contribution retirement plans became more popular, many individuals were making investment decisions for the first time, and they were choosing mutual funds. Many of these funds invested in large-cap companies with familiar names. Large companies were also finding that untapped overseas markets were growing faster than our domestic market and that they were fertile ground for added revenues and profits. This fueled the drive for globalization by large-cap companies.

These factors created an environment in which large-cap stocks outperformed small- and mid-cap stocks. Between 1990 and 1999, the Russell 1000 Index of large-cap companies returned an average of around 18 percent a year. The Russell 2000 Index of small-cap stocks returned an average of 13 percent. Other small-cap indexes returned upward of 15 percent for the decade.

However, in eight of the nine major recessions since World War II, small-cap stocks outperformed large-cap stocks in the 1-year periods beginning 3 months prior to the official end of the recession. Only in the 1961 to 1962 recession did large caps outperform. The average gain for small-cap stocks over this period was 45 percent while the average return for large-cap stocks was 30 percent.

The major contributing factor in their competitive advantage is their relative small size vis-à-vis large-cap companies. Thus small caps have greater percentage revenue and profit gains in part because it is easier to double profits from a base of $150 million than to do so from a base of $20 billion. As the economy turns around in 2002 and 2003, small- and mid-cap companies should have the highest percentage earnings gain.

History has shown in real-dollar terms that small-cap companies have provided long-term investors with the best returns. Based on Ibbotson's research shown in Table 1–5, Table 2–3 outlines real-dollar gains based on a $1000 investment at the beginning of each decade and held until 1999.

TABLE 2-3 $1000 Invested at the Beginning of the Decade and Held Until 1999

	Value in 1999 of Small-Cap Stocks	Value in 1999 of Large-Cap Stocks
$1,000 invested in 1950	$1,058,100	$591,200
$1,000 invested in 1960	$222,000	$100,392
$1,000 invested in 1970	$52,200	$47,300
$1,000 invested in 1980	$17,600	$26,700
$1,000 invested in 1990	$4,000	$5,300

Large-cap, mid-cap, and small-cap stocks move in cycles. Sometimes large-caps lead in offering higher investor returns; at other times it is small- and mid-caps. What causes these cycles? One factor is that small- and mid-cap companies rely more heavily on their specific markets, and they are not as diversified as larger companies. Smaller companies may therefore feel the effects of a sectional downturn in the economy faster than large companies do. Small companies are also more nimble and respond to improving economic conditions faster than the larger companies. Most small- and mid-cap companies are still focused on the domestic markets and derive a majority of their earnings from the United States. The lack of foreign market exposure helps smaller companies during times of economic stress overseas. For example, during the virtual depression conditions that gripped Asia in the late 1990s, multinational companies, such as Citigroup (C), were experiencing earnings weakness as previous profits from this region evaporated. Investors Financial Services (IFIN), however, had little exposure to the Asian markets and did not experience similar earnings pressures.

Based on current valuations, small- and mid-cap stocks may provide better value than their large-cap brethren. As of December 31, 2001, the P/E ratio for the S&P 500 Index was 21, and earnings growth for the index companies for 2002 was estimated at 18 percent. The S&P 600 Small-Cap Index was selling at a P/E ratio of 18, with earnings growth anticipated to be 32 percent. On a value basis, the large-cap index was trading at 1.16 times the underlying earnings growth rate (P/E of 21 divided by growth rate of 18). The small-cap index was trading at 0.56 times the underlying profit growth rate (P/E of 18 divided by growth rate of 32). In other words, large-caps stock prices were at a 16 percent premium to the profit growth rate, while small-cap stocks were trading at a 44 percent discount to its profit growth rate.

From 1990 to 1998, small-cap trailing P/E ratios were usually higher than large-cap trailing P/E ratios. Small-cap stocks traded at a P/E ratio of between 1.0 times (in 1992) to over 1.3 times (in 1990, 1991, 1995 to mid-1996) the large-cap ratio. In January 1998, the relative P/E ratio of small-cap stocks dropped to 0.8 and has not risen over 1.0 since. If small-cap stocks traded up to parity to the P/E ratio of the large-cap indices, it would represent a rally of 15 percent. If small-cap stock were to strengthen to the relative highs experienced in the 1990s, it would represent a rally of at least 50 percent.

Are Small- and Mid-Cap Companies Outside the Investment Spotlight? Large-cap stocks fueled the stock market boom of the 1990s. Many funds and investment advisors focused on these well-known companies. Small caps may be considered higher risk because the companies, and their management, have less history. Less known perhaps is that more investment home runs are hit using small-cap stocks. Mid-cap stocks, those that have a market capitalization of between $1.5 billion and $10.0 billion, sometimes also lack the investor visibility they deserve. A few mid-cap companies worthy of investors' attention are listed below:

Tyson Foods

HealthSouth Corp.

Electronic Data Systems

Beckman Coulter

Dole Foods

Washington Mutual Banks

Dun & Bradstreet

Payless Shoes

Ocean Energy

Manpower

Sonoco Products

Mid-cap stocks may lag their small-cap cousins in a strong bull market, but they typically retain more of their previous gains in a downturn. Well-managed mid-cap companies will continue to demonstrate their ability to build shareholder value for long-term investors. As earnings increase over the years, so should their stock price.

Can Diversification with Small- and Mid-Cap Stocks Increase Returns? As outlined in Table 1–4, small-cap stocks outperformed the S&P 500 in the 1960s and 1970s and were neck and neck with large caps in the 1980s. During the 1960s and 1970s, small-cap returns were twice the S&P 500. These trends should reappear in the current decade. Small- and mid-cap stocks can have a very positive impact on portfolio returns.

For example, Alex hits the jackpot and wins $60,000. In January 1997, he buys $60,000 of the S&P 500 Index, using the S&P 500 Exchange Traded Fund (SPY). Five years later, Alex's S&P 500 investment is worth $89,000 for a gain of $29,000, or 48 percent. This equals a 9.6 percent annual gain. As we know, the stock market performed poorly in 2000 and 2001. At its peak, Alex's portfolio would have been worth $109,500—a gain of 82 percent. In January of each year, his S&P Index fund would have been worth the following:

	1997	1998	1999	2000	2001	2002
S&P 500	$60,000	$73,800	$96,700	$109,500	$97,800	$89,000

However, if Alex had developed a diversified portfolio of mid-cap stocks, he could have done much better. Although there is no guarantee that Alex will pick 10 winning stocks, if he does his company research and understands stock value, his chances of picking winners increases. For example, Alex could have chosen the following companies:

Apache Corporation (APA, energy) is an oil and gas exploration and production company with onshore and offshore operations in Australia, China, Egypt, Indonesia, the Ivory Coast, North America, and western Canada. More than 50 percent of Apache's total reserves are natural gas. Apache operates almost 3300 gas wells and nearly 6000 oil wells. Apache is well known for buying oil reserves from other companies when oil prices are low. Then Apache increases well production and cuts costs.

Plum Creek Timber (PCL, materials) is a real estate investment trust. It owns over 7 million acres of timberland and nine wood products conversion plants in the Pacific northwest, northeast, and southern United States. PCL's resource unit harvests and exports timber, and the manufacturing unit produces lumber, plywood, and fiberboard. Plum Creek is the second-largest timber owner in the United States.

Kennametal (KMT, industrials) manufactures and distributes a broad line of metalworking, mining, and highway construction tools and equipment. It makes cutting, milling, and drilling tools used in the metalworking industry; drums, bits, and accessories used in mining; and bits, grader blades, and snowplow blades used in construction. The company markets its Kennametal, Hertel, Kendex, Kenloc, Kyon, Drill-Fix, Fix-Perfect, and other products in the United States and internationally.

Federal Signal (FSS, industrials) is a global manufacturer of leading niche products in four operating groups: environmental vehicles and related products, fire rescue vehicles, safety and signaling products, and consumable industrial tooling.

Hormel Foods (HRL, consumer staples) is best known for its Spam canned meat, which sells worldwide at a rate of 3.8 cans per second. Hormel Foods is actually a diversified food producer that makes a variety of ethnic, convenience, and health-oriented foods. Its processed foods include Jennie-O turkey products, Dinty Moore beef stew, Hormel and Stagg chili, Chi-Chis Mexican foods, Always Tender pork products, and Hormel fat-free hot dogs and vegetarian chili. Meat products generate the most revenue and account for over half of Hormel sales. The company operates processing and packaging facilities in 11 states and sells its products in 50 countries around the world.

Omnicare (OCR, health care) is the number 1 independent provider of pharmacy and related services to the nursing home market. It serves more than 445,000 residents in over 5500 long-term elder care institutions in 37 states. The company purchases, repackages, and dispenses drugs for nursing homes. Omnicare also provides computerized medical recordkeeping and third-party billing for patients in its clients' long-term-care facilities. Omnicare also offers consultant pharmacist services such as monthly patient drug-therapy evaluation, monitoring of drug administration procedures within a nursing facility, and compliance with state and federal regulations. Other related services include infusion therapy and medical supply provisions.

Investors Financial Services (IFIN, financial services) provides asset administration services for mutual fund managers, investment advisors, insurance companies, and banks. More details are provided about IFIN in the next chapter.

Symantec (SYMC, information technology) is a world leader in Internet security technology. It provides a broad range of content and network security solutions to individuals and enterprises. Revenues reflect strong sales growth in virus protection solutions.

Telephone & Data Systems (TDS, telecommunications services) is one of the largest non-Bell telephone companies in the United States. The company has more than 3 million customers in 35 states. Its TDS Telecom subsidiaries consist of over 100 small phone companies providing plain old phone service to mostly rural and suburban customers in 28 states. TDS service subsidiaries provide computing services and custom printing, and they offer cell phone service through United States Cellular Corp.

Philadelphia Suburban Corporation (PSC, utilities) is one of the nation's largest investor-owned water utilities. Philadelphia Suburban's two subsidiaries, Philadelphia Suburban Water and Consumers Water Company, serve nearly 2 million residents with water operations in Pennsylvania, Ohio, Illinois, New Jersey, and Maine. Since 1992, the company has pursued a disciplined growth-through-acquisition strategy. Philadelphia Suburban has completed 68 acquisitions. There are currently 50,000 municipal and community water systems in the United States (85 percent serve fewer than 3300 people). Approximately 6400 of these systems are in states where PSC operates. Acquisitions combined with natural growth have allowed the company's customer base to grow at a rate of 4 percent—among the best in the water utility industry.

Chicago Bridge & Iron (CBI, industrials), founded in 1889, builds steel tanks, pressure vessels, cryogenic storage facilities, and other steel-plate structures for the petroleum, pulp and paper, mining, and chemical industries. Chicago Bridge & Iron recently has acquired companies specializing in oil refinery construction and repair. Praxair purchased the company in 1996, absorbing one division and spinning off Chicago Bridge & Iron. The company has offices in five states and operates in Canada, Asia, South America, Europe, South Africa, Australia, and the Middle East. A leading U.S. provider of steel-plate structures, Chicago Bridge & Iron is expanding its global markets by pursuing energy and other industry clients in China, India, Mexico, and Russia.

Harley-Davidson (HDI, consumer discretionary) is the only major U.S. maker of motorcycles and the nation's number 1 seller of heavyweight motorcycles. Harley-Davidson offers 23 models of touring and custom cycles (the larger ones affectionately known as "Hogs") through a worldwide network of more than 1200 dealers. The company's legendary, high-powered Harley motorcycles include the Electra Glide, the Sportster, and the Fat Boy. Besides its bikes, Harley-Davidson also sells attitude. Goods licensed with the company name include a line of clothing (MotorClothes), toys, and other items such as deodorant and throw pillows.

Had Alex invested $5000 in each of these companies, his portfolio would have been worth $117,200 in 2002, instead of the $89,000 in his index investment. His portfolio would have grown at the following pace:

	1997	1998	1999	2000	2001	2002
Portfolio	$60,000	$68,800	$65,000	$86,100	$101,100	$117,200

But what if Alex did not have a windfall and had simply invested $12,000 each January in either his S&P 500 Exchange Traded Fund or $1000 annually in each of his stocks? The following would have been his results if he had dollar cost averaged the same $60,000 over five years:

	1997	1998	1999	2000	2001	2002
S&P 500	$12,000	$26,700	$47,000	$65,200	$70,200	$64,000
Portfolio	$12,000	$26,600	$40,000	$63,000	$95,200	$115,900

The prices Alex would have paid for each stock position in January is shown in Table 2–4, adjusted for stock splits. While some of the stocks have done exceptionally well, such as Investors Financial, others have lagged. In a diversified portfolio, such as the one above, not all selections will be winners all the time. Occasionally, our stock selection process will fail us and we will choose a real loser.

TABLE 2-4   Portfolio Purchase Price, Adjusted for Splits

	1997	1998	1999	2000	2001	2002
S&P 500	$792	$975	$1277	$1446	$1291	$1176
Apache	$35	$34	$24	$36	$65	$48
Plum Creek Timber	$28	$30	$27	$25	$25	$28
Kennametal	$41	$51	$23	$32	$28	$40
Federal Signal	$25	$21	$25	$14	$19	$22
Hormel	$12	$16	$16	$20	$17	$26
Omnicare	$28	$30	$36	$13	$18	$24
Investors Financial	$7	$12	$15	$22	$69	$69
Symantec	$15	$21	$20	$51	$35	$68
Telephone & Data	$36	$45	$47	$107	$99	$90
Philadelphia Suburban	$9	$14	$18	$13	$17	$22
Chicago Bridge & Iron	$18	$16	$12	$16	$17	$25
Harley-Davidson	$10	$13	$23	$30	$36	$54

A Firsthand Lesson in Diversification

Enron's bankruptcy is a great example of how diversification protects investors when things go wrong. Enron will be studied in business schools for decades to come, not only as one of the largest bankruptcies in U.S. history but as a company with a fleeting yet stellar rise in an emerging field of deregulated energy.

From its origins as a natural gas pipeline company, Enron became a leader in trading energy in the 1990s. As deregulation of the electricity markets took hold, the traditional, vertically integrated electric utilities started to break up. Power plants were combined and sold to form one company. Major transmission lines formed another, and end-user services formed a third. To reconnect the three to create seamless electric service for users, an opportunity for an intermediary emerged. Enron became that intermediary and developed a huge business buying and selling electricity. It was the first company to offer a national network of electric and natural gas products, and it was able to develop utility contracts with major U.S. corporations. For example, Ford Motor Company, with manufacturing facilities nationwide, now had the ability to negotiate long-term contracts with a single utility provider. Enron also established a broadband trading business for excess broadband capacity. In addition, Enron began developing trading markets for coal, pulp, paper, plastics, and metals. At its prime, Enron had evolved into a market maker for up to 1800 different products and services.

Enron emerged as one of the largest energy-trading-intermediary companies in the world, and it became more esoteric as its success blossomed. Through a complex formula, Enron even bet on the weather and offered "weather-risk-management" products to utilities, energy distributors, agricultural companies, and financial institutions. In exchange for a premium, the company would compensate a utility for every day the temperature exceeded a certain level as a hedge against higher temperatures resulting in lower heating-related revenues. Enron became a darling on Wall Street, and its stock was a must-have for just about everyone's portfolio. Share prices skyrocketed from $30 in 1998 to $90 in 2000 as revenues grew from $31 billion to more than $100 billion. Enron executives became known as industry visionaries, and many utility companies were seeking to duplicate Enron's trading success.

Then the house of cards began to unravel. The stock price sank to under $10 a share in the fall of 2001. On December 2, 2001, Enron filed for bankruptcy. By March 2002, Enron stock was trading at less than $1.00 per share.

At the root of Enron's failure was its immense need for capital. As a trader, Enron needed cash to continually buy contracts, or options, for product in the future. To fund this cash need, Enron resorted to little-used loopholes in accounting regulations. Shareholders and current debtors would not have approved large capital infusions using traditional means of selling more shares of stock or borrowing more money. So Enron used "off-the-books" transactions to generate upward of $30 billion in additional cash. Current accounting regulations do not require debts of subsidiaries that are less than 50 percent owned by the parent company to be included in the company's financials. Enron began to aggressively use unconsolidated subsidiaries as a vehicle to generate huge amounts of capital by issuing debt instruments. Enron, however, was the primary recipient of the loan proceeds, and it was the financial powerhouse backing up the creditworthiness of the loans. When the dust finally settles, Enron may have as much as $30 billion in unconsolidated subsidiary liabilities. According to its financial statements, Enron's total reported liabilities were around $13 billion, but its actual liabilities were over $40 billion. The most troublesome aspect of this case is that some of Enron's top management were also partners in these unconsolidated subsidiaries, and rather than the company shareholders who in reality held the liabilities, the management would have reaped the rewards of any profits.

Several off-the-books partnerships began to run into trouble and were unable to pay their outstanding loans. This required Enron to step in to make good as the loan guarantor, and after just a few deals went sour, the entire scheme unraveled.

Many believe the management of Enron was at fault for the bankruptcy. In this view, the management knew, or should have known, that although their off-the-books dealings were skirting the letter of accounting laws, their actions could be viewed as defrauding both bondholders and shareholders.

From a portfolio viewpoint, the lessons of Enron's shareholders are many. The most important lesson is that Enron shareholders lost their entire investment. For investors who had a large percent of their overall portfolio in Enron stock, the loss was devastating. Many employees have lost the vast majority of their retirement account value. The second lesson is that as Enron's stock price climbed and revenues grew, there was less and less scrutiny of their annual reports. While extremely complex, most shareholders spent more time counting their stock profits than reviewing financial numbers they found difficult to understand. This lesson is a replay of an old investing adage that people should invest only in those companies they understand. If you can't read its financial statements and in a few simple sentences describe what the company does, you should look elsewhere for your stock selections. The third lesson should be to take systematic profits when an investment selection performs extremely well. My rule of thumb is to take some profits whenever a company's stock doubles in price. The sales proceeds allow you to rebalance your portfolio and to continue to diversify. The fourth lesson is that there is truly no adequate means of protecting yourself against potentially unethical business practices. This fact, however, should not be a reason for you to discount the advantages of building wealth over time by investing in the stock market.

My father tells a story from the early 1960s of the Ainger Chemical company, a small, local chemical manufacturer. Ainger had invented the then-latest combination of materials that would revolutionize the budding plastics and polymer business. My father believed investing in Ainger Chemical stock would surely generate the capital gains needed to send five children to college. The company grew quickly and needed to hire a new treasurer and a chief financial officer. The stock rose along with earnings growth. After a particularly strong quarter of cash flow growth, it appeared the treasurer and chief financial officer absconded with all the cash and liquid assets of the company and fled the country. Within days, Ainger filed for bankruptcy, and its stock became worthless.

Another example of the need for portfolio diversification is the fall of AT&T (T). Over the past 10 years, the long-distance telephone business has changed dramatically. There is more competition, and prices for telephone services have decreased substantially. AT&T has struggled with profitability. In 1992, AT&T generated $1.92 a share in profits, while in 2001, it lost $1.33. AT&T's share price has also fallen. In 1992, AT&T's high was $35, and the stock reached a high of $66 in 1999. However, the stock currently trades below $15 a share. For years, AT&T was considered a "grandmother-and-widow stock," as the company's stability and steady earnings growth was appropriate for conservative investors with a long-term horizon. However, as history has shown once again, nothing in the stock market is for certain, and even grandmother-and-widow stocks have risk.

The bottom line is that if you don't diversify, you could lose a substantial amount of your investment value if a few of the limited number of investments you chose fail. For investors with even the minimum equal diversification of 10 stocks, a total loss on one position in the portfolio should not be a bank-busting event. While it hurts, over time it is possible to make up this loss. For example, a $50,000 portfolio with $5000 invested in Enron at its zenith would still have a value of $45,000. At the historic return of 12 percent a year for the market as a whole, the portfolio would regain its $50,000 value in about a year.

Unfortunately, those investors who had less than the minimum diversification of stocks may not see their portfolio recover for many, many years.

One of the pillars of most trusted investment advice is that portfolio assets should be diversified. Bonds and TIPS should be included in every investor's portfolio. Long-term corporate profit growth is the single most important factor in determining a stock's current and future share price. Portfolio diversification should be analyzed for economic sectors and market capitalization. A well-diversified portfolio should have a few overlooked small- and mid-cap companies. The potential for higher returns from overlooked stocks may assist in giving your portfolio a boost over the long term.

There are a few common attributes overlooked stocks have in common. Finding smaller companies most investors miss can be easier than most investors believe.

CHAPTER 3

Identifying Overlooked Stocks

I've been rich and I've been poor;
believe me rich is better

—GLORIA GRAHAME

Good overlooked stocks provide investors with better returns than their more widely held and much larger competitors. Good overlooked companies are usually well-managed firms in the earlier stages of a corporate life cycle than larger capitalization companies. There are very specific stages a company goes through, and there are corporate alterations from one stage to another. These alterations have a large impact on the company's ability to sustain profit and grow shareholder value.

What Are Overlooked Stocks?

When discussing stock selection with a broker or financial advisor for the first time, most investors receive the advisor's boilerplate recommendations. The recommendations most likely will include companies that are quite large and well-known. Johnson & Johnson, Home Depot, AOL Time Warner, Wal-Mart, General Electric, Cisco Systems, Nortel Networks, and Microsoft are all names that roll off the tongue of most investment advisors. During the heyday of technology stocks in 1999 and 2000, Amazon, CMGI, and Yahoo were some of the mainstays of a broker's recommendations.

But what do advisors discuss over happy hour at the end of a hectic day? I bet some of those names are hardly mentioned. As they down their third martini and munch on free finger food, the topic probably moves to good overlooked stocks. These are companies that don't usually show up on the radar screen of the common investor, but they are excellently managed and have great future prospects. They are just smaller and less well-known than others in their industry. Overlooked stocks can usually be categorized as small- and mid-cap companies, and they are found in all economic sectors.

For example, Johnson & Johnson (JNJ) is one of the biggest drug companies in the world. Shire Pharmaceuticals (SHPGY) is one of the smallest. Johnson & Johnson has a market cap of $179.438 billion and revenues of $33 billion. Shire Pharmaceuticals has a market cap of $8.450 billion and revenues of $516 million. Does this mean that Johnson & Johnson is a "better" company with "better" future prospects? Not necessarily. Large-cap companies usually have larger cash flow because of higher revenues, and this allows more flexibility to expand their market position. Smaller companies, with smaller cash flow, are sometimes hindered in their ability to grow their business—but not always.

In 2000, Johnson & Johnson had cash on hand of $6.757 billion, operating cash flow of $6.905 billion, and free cash flow (operating cash flow less capital expenditures) of $5.216 billion. Shire Pharmaceuticals had cash on hand of $186 million, operating cash flow of $78 million, and free cash flow of $12 million. Johnson & Johnson dwarfed Shire Pharmaceuticals in most respects. Shire's strength is specializing in niche drug markets where they can achieve substantial market share.

With the 2000 and 2001 slowdown in profits at Merck (MRK) and Schering Plough (SGP), along with the asbestos litigation concerns of Pfizer (PFE), Shire Pharmaceuticals is bucking the industry trend. Shire Pharmaceuticals is a mid-cap international specialty drug company with a focus on four therapeutic areas: Alzheimer's disease, attention deficit hyperactivity disorder (ADHD), kidney failure, and HIV. The company is based in the United Kingdom, and it is the result of merging six small specialty drug companies over the past five years. The United States accounts for 75 percent of revenues. Shire Pharmaceuticals announced that third quarter 2001 results were up 54 percent over

2000. Long-term earnings growth is estimated at 26 percent a year. Their top three selling drugs and the markets served are Adderall (ADHD), 46 percent of revenues; Agrylin (excessive platelet production), 11 percent; and Pentasa (ulcerative colitis), 10 percent. Other niche drugs account for 33 percent of revenues. The FDA recently approved a once-per-day version of Adderall, and the company is introducing the drug Reminyl for the treatment of mild to moderate Alzheimer's disease. Johnson & Johnson will market Reminyl in the United States and pay Shire Pharmaceuticals 12 percent to 15 percent royalties. The company currently markets 8 drugs and has 22 more in the pipeline. In addition, Shire Pharmaceuticals recently received FDA approval for its "Second Look" computer-aided detection system for mammography.

Shire Pharmaceuticals' management has a unique approach to the drug business. The company has grown by acquiring niche drug companies and by smart marketing of good brands. The company motto is "Search, develop, market." Management searches for specialty drug discovery firms that have new products with proven potential that are ready for preclinical testing or human trials. Shire then develops the clinical trials and aggressively markets the product. Most manufacturing is outsourced, which allows management to concentrate on continued research and marketing.

As a foreign company, Shire trades American depository receipts (ADRs) on the Nasdaq. The earnings growth rate over the next five years is anticipated to be 26 percent (compared with an anticipated earnings growth rate for Johnson & Johnson of 13 percent) with an earnings per share (EPS) of $1.30 per ADR for 2002 and $1.50 for 2003. Based on its current stock price and potential earnings growth, Shire may be considered an overlooked value investment in the pharmaceuticals sector.

The Life Cycle of Corporations

Corporations are like people; they are born, they grow to middle age, and eventually they die. Like Ponce de León's mythical fountain of youth, however, excellent management can extend the corporate life cycle virtually forever by reenergizing the company through restructuring and product changes. There are several ways the life cycle of a company is categorized. Some say there are 4 stages: innovation, franchise building, globalization, and decline. Others say there are 5 stages: introduction or startup, expansion, maturing, standardization, and restructuring. Others use a 10-stage life cycle. Whatever terms are used, however, the theories are the same. Successful companies move from one stage to another as their success grows, and each stage is very definable. Within each stage, there are management traits that will set the stage apart from the other stages. As the company grows, so should revenues, profits, share prices, and market capitalization.

The *startup stage* is also known as the *IPO stage,* the *introduction* or the *courtship stage, infancy,* or the *go-go stage.* It is characterized as a company at its birth and just after. The founders are honing their business idea, searching for startup capital, and hiring a few employees. Product ideas and services are being field-tested to evaluate acceptance in the market.

Equity financing is usually the major source of funding. Startups have extreme risk, and banks are reluctant to step in with assistance. Operating losses are normal, as critical mass in revenues is a long way off. The founders are the major decision makers, and everyone wears multiple hats to get the job done. Increasing revenues is virtually the only focus for the company. Annual revenue growth can be explosive. If even marginally successful at this stage, top managers sometimes begin to believe they are infallible, and their pomposity can breed failure. Many companies, especially high-tech and Internet firms, issue stock through initial public offerings at this stage.

The *small-cap stage* is also known as the *innovation, expansion,* or *adolescence stage.* It is characterized by a ripening of the company. Professional managers who have backgrounds in specialized areas such as finance, marketing, and manufacturing are brought in to take the founder's vision into the next phase of development. The company begins to make money, and its internal focus switches from strictly sales to management and finance systems. Sometimes there are conflicts as the founder is required to give up some decision-making powers and the need to delegate becomes apparent. Original products and services are improved, and the original business idea expands to encompass more innovations and customer support. As profits increase, financing turns from less equity and secondary offerings to more traditional bank lending and bond offerings. When the corporate engine is firing on all cylinders, there can be substantial growth in sales and revenues. Competitors are beginning to take notice of the new company's market share. Revenue growth is still strong but not as explosive as during the startup phase. Strategic acquisitions centering on the company-specific industrial subsectors are considered as a means of quickly adding market share and customers, but they are still within the narrow business focus. At this stage, most businesses won't venture too far from their area of expertise.

The *mid-cap stage* is also known as the *maturing, franchise building,* or *prime stage.* It is characterized by a strengthening of market share with clarity of business vision. Companies develop a balance among business control, corporate nucleus, and flexibility in innovation. Everything comes together: customer needs, financial needs, and management needs. New business ideas are encouraged, and expansion may be outside the original focus of the company. Management may utilize a decentralized approach to create new profit centers within the company without losing its entrepreneurial spirit. In many companies, the founder is no longer in charge, and the original corporate vision has been somewhat altered based on the realities of sustained revenue and profit growth. Seasoned professionals are strong members at every level of the management team. Research and development are actively funded through internal cash flow. Revenue and profit growth have slowed, but they should still be above industry averages. Cash flow allows for substantial amounts of debt, and investor interest creates a viable secondary market for company shares.

The *large-cap stage* is also known as the *globalization, stability, standardization,* or *maturity stage.* It is marked by a reduction in innovation and entrepreneurial spirit. Product markets stabilize and risk diminishes as profits become steadier but less explosive. Plant and equipment are expanded to produce more of similar products. As current domestic markets reach sales saturation, overseas markets are approached. Joint ventures and overseas factories are established. Equity as a portion of total assets is reduced as internal cash flow and debt finances more asset growth. Management's focus is on not making waves, and innovation is discouraged due to relative revenue and profitability needs. While welcoming new ideas, the reception is couched in terms of overall substantial contributions rather than incremental contributions. Acquisitions of smaller companies replace internally incubated startups. Corporate leaders begin to rely on what has been done in the past to lead them into the future.

The *decline stage* is also known as the *obsolete* or *recrimination stage*. It is characterized by waning customer importance, old or obsolete products, and management stuck in its ways. The corporate focus and vision are in decay. Management points fingers and witch-hunts rather than attempting to uncover what went wrong. A lack of corrective measures foretells the corporation's pending downfall. Declining sales and cash flow can create problems if the company has a large amount of debt. Much like the buggy whip manufacturer in the early 1900s who refused to realize the importance of the automobile, companies in the decline phase are in a perpetual state of denial concerning their products and customers. Unless the company reorganizes, restructures, and reenergizes, it is doomed to extinction. The downsizing and delayering of management, along with a new strategic mindset and corporate vision, are frequently essential in turning around a corporation in decline.

Overlooked stocks are usually found in the small-cap and mid-cap stages of corporate life cycles. Although they are lesser-known companies, they have several positive business traits that differentiate them from their larger competitors. As more aggressive companies, overlooked stocks have advantages, characteristics, and attributes that may make them better stock investments over the long term.

Fewer Restraints on New Opportunities

Back in the 1970s and 1980s, I worked in management for the largest division of a *Fortune* Top 50 manufacturing and distributing company (annual revenues back then in excess of $12 billion). Some of my responsibilities were to locate new products for our divisional sales team, develop new markets for existing products, and conduct initial research into potential acquisitions. As the company grew in size, so did the minimum revenue levels for each potential opportunity. Before my departure, the minimum project to be considered by upper management had to generate at least $100 million in revenues. The theory was that projects of smaller size would not have sufficient impact on overall sales and profits to warrant the expenditure of capital and personnel. If a proposal could not justify this level of revenue within 18 months, it was not seriously considered. In the mid-1980s, it became more difficult to generate this type of revenue gain in our specific industry. As a result, division revenue growth began to decline, along with division profit growth. Then the corporation began to expand in other industries and the company moved away from its historic strength. Many large U.S. corporations have similar problems with finding adequate opportunities for new growth.

Smaller companies, on the other hand, may not have the same restraints concerning the minimum size of new opportunities. Combined revenues for Shire Pharmaceuticals' Agrylin and Pentasa drugs are approximately $108 million, which is 21 percent of company revenues. These are also very profitable for the company, contributing approximately $16 million, or 7.5 percent to its bottom line. For Johnson & Johnson, these same drugs would amount to less than 0.3 percent of revenues and less than 2.8 percent of profits.

Nimble Management

Overlooked stocks may also be more nimble than their much larger competitors. As smaller companies, they usually have the ability to react more quickly to customer needs and market changes. Overlooked companies usually have flatter management organizations. This means senior managers are closer to the trenches where customer opportunities arise and problems are resolved. Fewer managerial layers translate into faster market response times and higher customer satisfaction, which leads to better market penetration and higher profits. In a lean organization, both management and staff have their ears to the ground so they can hear the grumbling of clients and prospective clients. In many instances, this method of accumulating customer feedback leads to better business intelligence than the high-priced research that larger companies throw at their problems. Some large companies suffer from a "silo mentality" which has the effect of isolating the top executives from grassroots problems and their employees as well. Overlooked companies tend to have a higher level of entrepreneurial spirit. It's OK to make mistakes if the employee is hustling and is productive. Employees know their contributions and efforts will be seen and recognized by their managers. This leads to higher employee morale and greater employee productivity. These attributes eventually improve the company's bottom line.

A good example is Nantucket Bank, a small micro-mini bank on the island of Nantucket, Massachusetts, and a subsidiary and recent acquisition of Seacoast Financial Services Corporation (SCFS). Nantucket Bank has three offices and fewer ATM machines than you have fingers. It has been very profitable, however, and it has a loan-loss ratio that should be the envy of the industry. For years, there were two banks on this little island located 30 miles off the coast of Cape Cod: Nantucket Bank and the other bank. Historically, bank loan decisions were made right there on the island. In the late 1990s, FleetBoston Bank purchased the other bank. To cut overhead, loan decisions were transferred to loan committees in Boston, 90 miles away. With a history dating back to the beginning of the whaling days, native Nantucketites are known for their independence and Yankee spirit. The other bank's customers did not like the fact that loan decisions were being made by the city folk in Boston, and so they moved their accounts in droves to the Nantucket Bank. A few years later, the Nantucket Bank was purchased by Seacoast Financial. The management of Seacoast Financial realized that the strength of the Nantucket Bank was in its local roots. Seacoast Financial decided to structure the acquisition as a subsidiary rather than merging the smaller bank as Compass Bank branches, the flagship bank for Seacoast. Loan decisions are still made on the island, and the Nantucket Bank continues to be the local bank of choice.

Product or Service Differentiation

In order to survive, all but the largest corporations need to find a successful business strategy not exclusively based on product cost and selling price. Many overlooked companies are not the low-cost leaders in their industries. Much larger competitors may have the advantage of lower cost of capital, lower manufacturing costs, and lower raw materials costs. In order to overcome these deficits, successful smaller companies have to develop product or service differentiation. Al Trout has written many books concerning this topic, and his best one is *Differentiate or Die*. With mass amounts of product duplication on retail shelves and in new-car lots, it is extremely important for smaller companies to develop a market plan centered on the qualities of their products and/or services that differentiate them from their larger competitors. Differentiation strategies come in many shapes and styles. Some of them are the following:

- Manufacture custom orders and short production runs.
- Produce products or services that are of higher quality.
- Produce products that are innovative and better meet the clients' needs.
- Offer better customer service, both before and after the initial sale.
- Offer better or more lenient credit terms.
- Develop a marketing and distribution strategy that is supported by the client base.

Product Innovation

Smaller companies have historically been the hotbed of product innovation. Although many large companies have very active and well-funded research and development (R&D) departments, smaller firms usually have more of an entrepreneurial spirit and a greater willingness to assume risk.

Illinois Tool Works (ITW) is an unusual company, and its management has an entrepreneurial approach to the business. With revenues approaching $10 billion and a market cap of $21 billion, Illinois Tool Works is a small large-cap company. As a leading diversified manufacturer with an 85-year history, Illinois Tool Works operates 592 businesses. Each business unit is operated in a decentralized style, and the unit managers are fairly autonomous and retain the bulk of decision-making responsibilities. Illinois Tool Works is overhead lean with just 200 staff personnel at their home office. Their products include industrial fasteners, metal components, machinery consumables such as machine cutting tools, and food equipment systems. The company serves mainly the construction, general industrial, automotive, food, paper, and electronic markets. Illinois Tool Works operates in over 40 countries. International sales represent around 30 percent of total revenues. The company is customer driven and strives to improve its clients' competitive positions by increasing productivity and product quality, which reduces the clients' operating costs. Profits and new-product development responsibilities are given to the head of each business unit. The local business team is very focused on the performance of its specific business. This intense focus on grassroots profitability and innovation has aided the company in achieving a 5-year average return on assets 25 percent above its competitors. Illinois Tool Works is an extremely nimble company and is structured to respond to changing market forces as a business one five hundredth of its size would respond.

Single-Market Focus

Overlooked companies are usually focused on the task at hand. As a company grows in size, it tends to lose focus and to become complacent in meeting its customers' needs. In contrast, overlooked companies usually have a single clear business target at which corporate resources and management efforts are deployed consistently. These companies are not distracted by the type of clutter that accumulates in a larger, more diverse operation. Being able to home in on a single or select few markets and focus on a few products and services, the management in the overlooked companies has the advantage of being able to put its full weight of the company's capital and expertise into the tasks of building market share, revenues, and profitability. Many times, these smaller companies are the experts in their specific field, while their larger competitors are more generalists.

The founder or the individual who had the original idea for the company may lead overlooked companies. There is rarely anyone more motivated to generate success than the individual who had the initial vision for the company. The further a company gets from its founding vision, the more distracted its management becomes. Branching out into new businesses having nothing to do with the original success of the company often leads to its downfall. A good example is Conseco Financial's (CNC) purchase of Green Tree Acceptance, a shaky mobile home financing company. Conseco built its business in insurance, and it was unfamiliar with the pitfalls of this higher-risk venture in mobile homes. The acquisition failed, and the company lost billions of dollars of shareholders' money on the acquisition. Clayton Mobile Homes (CMH), a long-time vertical manufacturer and financier of manufactured housing, has been extremely successful in the identical market where Conseco failed. The main difference is that Clayton Mobile Homes has a thorough understanding of the specific quirks of the mobile home financing industry because it is an integral part of their business focus. Successful small- and mid-cap companies usually expand through acquisition, centering on their expertise and single-market focus.

CenturyTel (CTL) is a good example of a company with a single-market focus. With 2001 revenues of $2.2 billion, net earnings of $225.7 million, and a market cap of $4.5 billion, CenturyTel is overshadowed by the likes of AT&T (T), Verizon (VZ), and BellSouth (BLS). Based on access line count, the company is the eighth-largest local exchange telephone company, and based on population, it is the eighth-largest cellular company in the United States. CenturyTel focuses strictly on small city and rural markets. It was formed in 1930 when William Clark and Marie Williams purchased the Oak Ridge Telephone Company in Oak Ridge, Louisiana. Headquartered in Monroe, Louisiana, the company has grown through 18 acquisitions. It serves nearly 3 million customers in 21 states. As the larger telephone companies beat up each other trying to gain market share in metropolitan areas such as Boston, Dallas, and Los Angeles, CenturyTel continues to expand its reach in rural America. The large competitors believe rural customers are too expensive to service, and they focus on more densely populated areas. CTL has been successful by implementing a business strategy that maximizes profits based on the market attributes of a less densely populated area.

According to the company, the advantages of focusing on the rural rather than metropolitan markets are a greater potential for high growth and low risk, stronger customer loyalty, more opportunities to provide multiple services to the same client, and higher barriers of entry for competition. CenturyTel's key strategies to achieve future growth are the following:

- Be a dominant rural service provider.

- Offer high-quality local networks to drive incremental revenue streams.

- Achieve excellent margins and strong cash flow.

- Leverage core competencies into expanded operations.

The company has a proven track record of outperforming the telephone industry. Five year revenue growth is 13 percent versus the industry average of negative 9 percent, the operating margins are more than twice the industry average, and the net profit margins are two and a half times the industry average.

Faster Earnings Growth

More revenue dollars in the overlooked companies end up on the bottom line due to slimmer overhead and less corporate debt. Products and services offered by smaller companies tend to fill the needs of niche markets that are too small for the big companies to consider. However, that does not necessarily mean these niche markets are less profitable. On the contrary, many niche markets can be more profitable than the commodity-oriented products offered by much larger competitors. In addition, profit margins can be higher as the company's strength is not based solely on offering the lowest price but also on creating value for the client. The company that builds the most customer value, either perceived or actual, gets to charge the highest price. Furthermore, building value in the eyes of clients has the added benefit of creating higher customer loyalty. Companies that inspire high loyalty in their customers usually have the ability to generate higher profit margins.

Intelligible Financial Reports

Small- and mid-cap companies usually generate financial reports that are much less complicated than those of large caps. Investors can readily see where earnings growth comes from in small- and mid-cap corporations. If a company is focused on only a few markets and offers only a few products, accounting presentations to individuals and professionals are simpler. In contrast, it is sometimes difficult for investors to interpret the elaborate financial reports of large caps. General Electric (GE) is a multifaceted behemoth made up of very large and diverse divisions. For several years, as General Electric diversified into new businesses, its financial statements became increasingly harder to understand. The accounting of its numerous acquisitions and its growth in the financial services sector have complicated GE's financial statements compared to its statements during the earlier period when it was mainly a manufacturing company. In another example, the debacle of Enron is being considered an accounting scandal, in part due to extremely complex accounting practices. Due to simpler account reporting it is usually easier for investors to understand the earnings and earnings growth of smaller companies.

Higher Insider Stock Ownership

Small- and mid-cap stocks usually have a higher percentage of management stock ownership. Although controversial, high insider stock holdings ensure that management and shareholders have the same goal: increasing shareholder value through higher revenues, profits, and share prices.

An example is Equity Office Properties Trust (EOP), the nation's largest real estate investment trust (REIT) and publicly held owner of office properties. The company has a market capitalization of $11 billion and revenues of $2.3 billion. Equity Office Properties owns and manages 128 million square feet of primarily Class A office space in 774 buildings in 37 major metropolitan areas across the country. The company offers solutions to customers with local, regional, or national office space needs. Equity Office Properties' origin dates back to 1976. Billionaire Sam Zell, the current chairman, founded the company. The company's portfolio was consolidated and taken public in July 1997. Since that time, Equity Office Properties has nearly quadrupled in size, growing from 32.2 million square feet to 128 million square feet through strategic acquisitions including the Beacon Properties, Cornerstone Properties, and Spieker Properties. Officers and directors own 18.037 million shares, or 6.8 percent of all outstanding shares, which represents a dollar value of stock in excess of $505 million. Sam Zell owns the largest share of insider stock worth nearly $490 million. As the chairman, Mr. Zell should be motivated to grow shareholder value. By doing so, his personal wealth will increase.

Sometimes insiders own virtually all the shares. Tyson Foods (TSN) is one example. Tyson has sales of $10.75 billion and a market cap of $4.45 billion. Tyson Foods is the nation's leading poultry processor, operating more than 50 food production facilities in 22 U.S. states and

17 countries. The company breeds, raises, processes, and markets chickens and Cornish game hens. Almost half of sales are to food service companies and nationwide clients. It also sells tortillas and chips under the Mexican Original brand. In late 2001, Tyson Foods purchased large beef packer IBP. Tyson Foods also produces seafood, raises swine, and produces animal feed and pet food.

Tyson Foods has two classes of common stock, Class A and Class B. The major difference between the two is that the B class confers shareholder voting rights on issues such as shareholder proposals and members of the board of directors, while the A class does not. By offering only the nonvoting class to the public in exchange for their capital, many companies offer two classes of stock as a means of retaining complete voting control of the company. Don Tyson, founder, owns 99.9 percent of the voting Class B shares and 80.5 percent of Class A and B combined. Shareholders, as owners of the company's equity, should have a vote on how their company is operated. When management has too much ownership, they have the ability to do whatever pleases them, which may not necessarily be what is in the best interest of building shareholder value. Some companies have been criticized by many for doing just that.

For example, Tecumseh Products Company (TECUA) is a mid-cap manufacturer of small gasoline engines, compressors, and pumps. The company has two classes of stock, Class A (nonvoting) and Class B (voting). The majority of voting shares outstanding is owned by the Herrick family, and the company is managed by Todd Herrick, grandson of the founder. Tecumseh has a history of overly conservative management, entrenched due to an inherent corporate structure that does not allow for adequate outside shareholder representation. Since 1995, TECUA has maintained a high level of liquidity with between 30 and 37 percent of current assets held as cash. This cash has been invested in extremely short maturities of U.S. treasury notes, yielding a very small return. Tecumseh has consistently maintained a cash balance of between $261 million and $317 million. As outside investors are limited to owning nonvoting shares, all corporate decisions, including election of the board of directors, are effectively controlled by the family. Even large shareholders have little opportunity to voice their opinions as to the future direction of the company. It would seem to me that astute management would be uncovering business expansion opportunities that would have returned a substantially better return for shareholders. At the least, outside directors should be evaluating the strong cash position of TECUA and questioning if low return investments are in the best interest of all shareholders.

As a rule of thumb, investors should seek companies in which management and directors own between 3 and 5 percent as a minimum and between 40 and 50 percent as a maximum of outstanding shares. Less than 3 to 5 percent ownership could indicate that management may not be making decisions in the best interest of shareholders. The same is true of companies in which management owns virtually all the outstanding shares. To find out how much stock is controlled by management and directors, refer to the annual proxy statements. Proxy statements can be requested from a company's investors relations department, or they may be available online at the company Web site, or they may be obtained from the Securities and Exchange Commission (search SEC archives for filing DEF 14A) at www.sec.gov/edgar/searchedgar/formpick.htm. Table 3–1 lists the percentage of stock owned by management in some typical companies.

Investors should feel comfortable that management has their best interests at heart. With the exception of Cinergy, management has sufficient holdings of company stock so that their interests should align with those of the shareholders. Enterprise Products has a larger than desirable percentage of management ownership and would deserve further investigation.

TABLE 3–1 Management Ownership of Stock as a Percentage of Outstanding Shares

Copart Industries	32%	Medicis	57%
Illinois Tool Works	13%	Hudson United	6%
Barra Software	26%	Florida Rock	31%
McCormick	7%	Cinergy	2%
Enterprise Products	76%		

Source: Securities and Exchange Commission, sec. gov.

Overlooked by the Big Companies

Big companies often may not pay much attention to smaller niche players in the belief that their smaller counterparts are inconsequential. The biggies in the marketplace tend to be a bit arrogant when it comes to estimating the ability of others to steal their existing business. Several times in my business career I have brought the actions of much smaller competitors to the attention of management. The reply was usually something along the lines of "They don't count" or "Competitor X couldn't possibly do that." This complacency breeds outstanding opportunities for niche players, and their growth can proceed unimpeded until it reaches a point where they are more than a burr under the saddle.

In markets dominated by a few big players, this type of attitude seems to be prevalent. The giants just don't seem to care about the smaller companies with 5 percent of the market. Inevitably, the smaller player continues to gain market share at the expense of the large company until the large company decides to buy out its competitor. Many acquisitions are the result of complacency on the part of the dominant player who allows smaller companies to prosper until they become sufficient problems that need to be taken out once and for all.

The Underdog Status

Americans love the story of David and Goliath. As a nation, we are always rooting for the underdogs. Many times we will favor them with our business just because they are the underdogs. In our society, there is an image that smaller is better. You see it all the time in many different industries and products. Examples are ICB Root Beer, MicroBrewers, Avis Rental Car, and Southwest Airlines. Many small- and mid-cap companies successfully compete with their larger competitors by focusing closely on their clients' needs. Some smaller customers can relate to the trials and tribulations of smaller suppliers as they, too, tackle the problems of competing with the biggies. These companies may favor and work closer with smaller suppliers in part because they appreciate the challenges of competing with larger companies.

Sustainable Competitive Advantage

John Price, financial author and promoter of the "Sherlock Holmes approach to investing," wrote in an article entitled "Three Little Words of Successful Investing," dated October 1999, that he believes the three most important words in successful investing are "sustainable competitive advantage." This phrase refers to a company's ability to develop and exploit year after year a competitive advantage in its industry. The advantages that can be exploited are found mainly in products and services, ability of management, sales organization, brand recognition, and location. Excellent managers are able to generate profits from these business advantages.

Companies that consistently offer leading products and services that are preferred in their specific marketplace should have a base for consistent earnings. The ability of management to operate the company in a fiscally sound manner, while still expanding its business and market reach, should create added shareholder value over time. A top-notch sales organization, focused on the needs and prospects of its customers, should maximize revenue opportunities. Many times the location of a business is important to its success, especially if delivery costs are high.

Innovative products have a sustainable competitive advantage only as long as they are innovative. Patents and intellectual property have the ability to generate sustainable competitive advantages. The problem is that without an entrepreneurial spirit and the research and development budget to consistently develop new innovations, the competitive advantage is only sustainable until it is copied or improved upon by the competition.

Strong brand names within a particular industry are also elements of sustainable competitive advantage. While we may think of the mega consumer brands, such as Pepsi or Volvo, within each industrial sector, many smaller companies have developed strong brand recognition. This brand awareness equates to quality, leadership, and honest business relationships. In the fire truck and rescue vehicle business, Federal Signal (FSS) has developed a leading position, and, although it is not known to many outside the industry, the company has a substantial competitive advantage. Pitney Bowes (PBI) has a sustainable advantage due to its well-known brand name in the mailing machine business as does Investors Financial Services (IFIN) in the mutual fund custodial services business. Overlooked companies with a sustainable competitive advantage will produce outstanding results for their long-term shareholders.

Overlooked Company Characteristics in Action

In March 2002, I had the opportunity to chat with Kevin Sheehan, CEO and president of Investors Financial Services (IFIN). It was a relaxing interview at his home on Cape Cod. Away from his hectic work and travel schedule, Mr. Sheehan was very candid and informative concerning IFIN's characteristics as a small- and mid-cap company.

The following is a business summary of Investors Financial Services published in the S&P stock reports, March 2002:

> Investors Financial Services, through its wholly owned subsidiaries, Investors Bank & Trust and Investors Capital Services, provides asset administration services for the financial asset management industry. Clients include mutual funds, investment advisers, banks, and insurance companies.
>
> IFIN seeks to differentiate itself from its competitors and gain market share by bundling core services, such as custody and accounting, with value-added services. In addition, the company focuses on maintaining technological expertise; developing expertise in complex products, such as multimanaged funds, limited partnerships, and exchange-traded funds; and delivering superior client service.
>
> In addition to its core services—global custody and multicurrency accounting—the company provides value-added services, such as mutual fund administration, securities lending, foreign exchange, cash management, performance management, and institutional transfer agency services. IFIN combines its products into a single integrated technology platform, allowing the company to assign a single dedicated client team, providing a full suite of services, to each account.
>
> Global custody entails overseeing the safekeeping of securities for clients and settlement of portfolio purchases and

sales. Domestic net assets under custody have grown from $22 billion in October 1990, to $285 billion in December 2000. Multicurrency accounting entails the daily recordkeeping for each account or investment vehicle, including calculations of net asset value per share, dividend rates per share, and the maintenance of all books, records, and financial reports required by the SEC and other regulatory agencies.

Investors Financial Services began in 1969, when Eaton Vance, a large money manager, began offering custodial services. Around the same time, a similar business was established as a part of the now-failed Bank of New England. The bank's decline began when it fell victim to the savings and loan problems of the late 1980s. In 1990, the Bank of New England sold its custodial services business to Eaton Vance, combining the two competitors. Current bank and U.S. securities regulations require that many of the financial services offered to asset managers be structured under the auspices of a banking company. Since Eaton Vance is not structured as a bank but rather as a financial management firm, revenue and earnings growth potential of IFIN was severely hindered. In 1995, management persuaded Eaton Vance to spin off these services as a separate company. With its new bank structure, Investors Financial has a corporate advantage that was missing when it was a part of Eaton Vance.

Even though the current company has only 5 years of financial and stock trading history, the top 10 executives have a minimum of 10 years with the company. Mr. Sheehan was hired in 1980 and has over 20 years experience with the company.

When asked what the corporate mission of IFIN was, Mr. Sheehan replied, "To make money for our shareholders at the exclusion of just about everyone else, even employees. To make money at IFIN, employees need to own our shares. There is no substitute for tying personal wealth to management performance." Investors should take note of the priority IFIN's management gives to its shareholders.

Management at IFIN is pretty good at making money for shareholders. Earnings per share have risen an average of 40 percent annually during the past 5 years. Mr. Sheehan believes management has a fiduciary responsibility to generate exceptional long-term shareholder value. "Value is driven by consistently growing earnings per share.

Share valuation will follow. In addition to growing earnings, management has a responsibility to position the company in the long term as a potential acquisition. One does this by gaining credibility with clients and shareholders."

IFIN has several sustainable competitive advantages. Large banks such as Citigroup (C), JP Morgan Chase (JPM), and State Street (SST) mainly serve the industry. Within the traditional bank management structure, each service is designated as an operating unit, and there is little interaction between operating units. For instance, custodian services are usually separate from accounting services. IFIN, however, has built a unified management organization offering an integrated platform of services, centered on increasing technological productivity. IFIN leads their industry in technology-based services combining all aspects of their clients' needs. This technology edge also creates a higher level of service to clients. In the past, economies of scale were drivers of profit margins in this niche financial business. The larger the value of assets under management, the lower the cost to provide the service. The industry has changed dramatically to a technology-based cost structure that no longer favors the large competitor. IFIN's technology leadership expands client services while reducing costs, creating their sustainable advantage.

When asked to describe his management team, Mr. Sheehan replied, "No bureaucratic dance going on here." IFIN has a horizontal management style. The 10 top executives are responsible to run the company. IFIN's managers interface with client organizations on several different levels, improving efficiencies of their multitask management style. Each executive is actively involved with all aspects of services for their clients or potential clients. IFIN's unique business of focusing on the investment community creates interesting opportunities. As management looks to raise capital through private placement of stock within the asset-managed community, their investors have the potential of being clients. In addition, clients have an obvious potential to be future investors.

Historically, the business focused on the low-margin core service of providing custodian services, and this remains the base product IFIN offers. From this base, IFIN offers clients additional, higher-margin services such as tax report preparation. IFIN started its relationship with Barclays Bank by providing custodian services. With the complexities of new exchange-traded funds (ETFs), Barclays Bank began to outsource ETF accounting services, and it has increased its business with IFIN. With their technology advantages, IFIN now has the ability to develop more complex services, which it can use as a client building block. For example, Goldman Sachs was looking to outsource a complex and esoteric asset management service they were performing in house. IFIN provided the advanced solution to meet Goldman Sachs's needs, and they acquired the business. From this higher level of corporate interaction, building on this initial relationship should mean greater business opportunities for IFIN.

A common market focus across the company has aided in client development. With a strong corporate focus on the services IFIN provides, there are fewer distractions. While the efforts of larger competitors may be diverted to satisfy the needs of a large organization, IFIN has remained focused on the task at hand, building company profits and client business.

Due to its smaller size, IFIN can acquire strategic businesses that are "too small" for the larger companies. For example, in February 2001, IFIN purchased the advisory business of Chase Manhattan Bank for $42 million. The advisory unit provided services to individual retirement account and individual portfolio managers. This business was not very important to the overall success of giant Chase, but the new clients fit nicely into IFIN's strengths. A similar acquisition was made from the Bank of Boston a few years before. Both acquisitions allowed IFIN to expand client services and increase the profitability of the accounts. What had been considered as having little opportunity for larger companies was a great fit for Investors Financial Services.

Mr. Sheehan agreed that small- and mid-cap companies can often expand earnings at a faster rate than their larger competitors. "From our smaller asset base, it is easier to generate meaningfully higher revenues and profits. Our assets total around $800 billion, while our large competitors handle $6 trillion and higher. It is easier for us to double our assets to $1.6 trillion than for them to double theirs to $12 trillion." An increase of $800 billion in assets under management would double the assets for IFIN but represent an increase for their larger competitors' assets of only 12 percent.

Directors and officers own 13 percent of IFIN's shares. According to Mr. Sheehan, "We are true believers in the company and its opportunities. That's why we own it." IFIN also has strong employee participation in their employee stock purchase plan.

Investors Financial Services is riding the wave of two very powerful yet overlooked trends: outsourcing and the growth in global financial assets. Overlooked trends are discussed in more detail later in the book. As the costs to perform certain tasks in house become higher, outsourcing of services becomes more attractive. With IFIN's integrated platform of services and technology, they are able to provide cost-effective solutions to their clients. The back-office costs for professional money managers are escalating. Recent events have added pressure on the cost to operate a back office to efficiently move the paper flow—for example, Y2K expenses, the change to decimals in stock trading, and the conversion of the euro. Many are finding that outsourcing these services is less costly in the long run and that their clients do not care who conducts the back-office paperwork.

According to Mr. Sheehan, within the market IFIN serves, custodian services are 100 percent outsourced by their clients. Simple accounting, such as net asset value and multicurrency accounting, are 23 percent outsourced. Administrative services, such as tax preparation and regulatory compliance, are 17 percent outsourced, and actual stock trading is 5 to 9 percent outsourced. Investors Financial Services has much room to grow within the outsourcing trends of the financial industry.

The World Trade Center terrorist attack on September 11, 2001, demonstrated fundamental weaknesses in our current financial systems. Reliance on single-site, paper-driven back-office systems is too vulnerable to disruption. As the World Trade Center collapsed, the image of tens of thousands of pieces of paper floating to the ground became etched in the minds of every manager of back-office financial operations. Millions of paper documents containing vital financial information were lost in a matter of minutes. To remedy this flaw in the system, multisite, technology-driven systems—IFIN's specialty—will be the new standard for back-office financial operations.

In June 2005, new Securities and Exchange Commission regulations will become effective, and they will dramatically impact the back-office operations of all money managers. Known as "T+1," one of the new regulations will require that all *settlement*, or *pay, dates* be one day after a stock or bond trade. The current regulation allows three business days to settlement. The trend is to eventually require real-time settlement. According to Mr. Sheehan, the T+1 and eventual T regulations will require more system integration and will quicken the pace of the outsourcing trend. The shortened time cycle between the current batch approach to processing based on real time will favor those companies with the best, most integrated technology. IFIN is positioning itself to take advantage of this opportunity, offering the most efficient platform integration in the business. The deadline of June 2005 has already been pushed forward by one year. The original date of June 2004 was recently changed under pressure from asset managers who complained about the cost of implementation. To comply with the 2005 deadline, companies need to address the necessary system upgrades and make decisions concerning compliance in 2002 and 2003.

As a firm believer of the cost advantages of outsourcing, Investors Financial Services has a strong relationship with Electronic Data Systems (EDS). EDS is one of the largest computer software and hardware consulting services firms in the United States. This relationship supports IFIN's technology leadership.

Not only is IFIN well positioned to take advantage of the outsourcing trend, it also has the advantage of a growing client base. According to ING Bearing, a large European financial services company, global assets managed by professional money managers is valued at $47 trillion. In the past 5 years, global opportunities for professional money managers have grown at an annual rate of between 12 and 20 percent depending on the country. The personalization and privatization of retirement accounts and a need for investors to diversify their investments have fueled the expansion. This growth should continue, offering IFIN an ever-increasing potential for new clients and higher revenues from existing clients.

Mr. Sheehan provided some insight into the company's dividend policy. IFIN has a very small 5 percent payout ratio. IFIN pays 5 percent of net earnings in dividends to its shareholders. When asked if the dividend will be increased, Mr. Sheehan explained management's philosophy. As long as the company is seeking outside capital to grow the business, mainly through the private placement of new shares of stock, it would make little sense to increase the dividend. IFIN currently uses all available capital internally generated through their cash flow to expand the business.

Investors Financial Services is a well-managed, and mostly over-looked, company poised to continue rewarding shareholders through increasing earnings and higher stock prices.

Most companies progress along relatively similar lines. Identifying where a specific company lies in its life cycle will assist investors to better understand the prospects for the future. Small- and mid-cap companies have many advantages over their larger competitors. How management utilizes and capitalizes on these advantages will directly impact corporate earnings, and stock prices, over the long term. Overlooked companies should excel in turning their complete sustainable corporate advantage to the highest profit level achievable. The ability of management to develop and execute a focused business plan that increases shareholder value is critical to the success of overlooked companies.

CHAPTER 4

Evaluating Management

It is Enterprise which builds and improves the world's possessions. . . . If Enterprise is afoot, Wealth accumulates whatever may happen to Thrift; and if Enterprise is asleep, Wealth decays, whatever Thrift may be doing.

—JOHN MAYNARD KEYNES

Accurately assessing management's ability to consistently generate a profit is one of the key ingredients of successful stock selection. To better gauge management's ability, an investor can review a few key financial ratios. Comparing a company's ratios with those of their competitors may reveal interesting aspects of the quality of management. These ratios are called *efficiency ratios,* and they assist investors in evaluating how efficiently management has used its capital to generate profits. Corporate mission statements and letters to shareholders also will reveal the commitment management has to its shareholders. Although management stock options can be a successful tool in motivating managers to increase shareholder value, their use is controversial and may, at times, provide an opportunity for abuse.

Importance of Management in Stock Selection

Some companies' advertising themes are about their most important asset. It is not their factories, not their land, and not their fancy office buildings. Their most important asset is their people. This type of advertising is not only effective; it is also truthful. When investing in a company, the major value investors are purchasing is the ability of management to grow their business in a profitable manner. The ability of management to use corporate assets and turn them into consistent profit growth will separate great companies from mediocre companies. Excellently managed companies have the competency to turn investment capital into revenue-generating assets and revenues into the highest profit possible. To raise the capital necessary to purchase the assets used to generate their profits, managers either borrow money or issue stock. Shareholders are then the beneficiaries of these efforts through higher stock values.

With the cash flow generated from the profitable operation of their businesses, managers either pay off their debt, reinvest in their current business, purchase new businesses, or return a portion to their shareholders in the form of dividends and stock buybacks. Over the years, as operating cash flow grows, so do the future prospects of the company and its stock prices.

The goal in studying management and their effectiveness in generating profits and cash flow is to identify the best long-term candidates for your investment dollars. The best candidates should be established companies with proven management in industries that are expanding. The industries served need not be large, and the companies need not be the industry leaders.

The best managers have the ability to use the assets at their disposal and generate sustainable competitive advantages. They have the desire to realize the company's fullest potential and are almost fanatical about protecting their competitive advantage. Exceptional managers will take the assets they are given and consistently produce excellent profits for their shareholders. The best companies generate increasing cash flows over time and reinvest the cash into their businesses. Product development and asset expansion are keys to maintaining a competitive edge. The better managers will always figure out a way to increase profits, regardless of the hurdles they face, and they will figure out ways to make more profit than their competitors.

Managers should also be worthy of your trust. When you invest in their company, you are becoming an owner and effectively the boss of the CEO. Managers should be honest and fair and should work diligently to expand shareholder value. While it may be difficult to uncover alleged fraudulent managers (such as in the case of Enron), eventually their illegal dealings will come to light. Fear of potential fraudulent management should not be the excuse that prevents you from investing for your future.

No shareholder will begrudge a chief executive officer (CEO) who becomes wealthy through ownership of company stock. However, the issuance of stock options that unduly favor management by not requiring substantial increases in share price is unfair to all shareholders and is paramount to giving the store away.

The American economic style of free markets will produce business cycles of overall business growth and retrenchment. This is a business fact of life. Economic growth comes in cycles. Some last just a few years and others last many. During the 1990s, the United States experienced the longest period of economic expansion in our history. Times of economic contractions also vary, with some lasting a few months and others several years. The Great Depression of the 1930s was the longest period of economic contraction in our history. Against an ever-changing economic backdrop, the best managers will find a way to build their businesses profitably.

Management has a fiduciary responsibility to their shareholders. As the keeper of corporate assets, it is management's responsibility to use those assets wisely. According to "New Concepts of Fiduciary Responsibilities" by Edward Tasch and Stephen Viedeman:

> In 1830, a Massachusetts court offered a definition of prudence that has, through decades of subsequent re-examination and re-definition, survived in the canon of fiduciary responsibility as "the prudent man rule." All that can be required of a trustee to invest is that he shall conduct himself faithfully and exercise sound discretion. He is to observe how men of prudence, discretion and intelligence manage their own affairs, not in regard to speculation, but in regard to the permanent disposition of their funds, considering probable income, as well as the probable safety of the capital to be invested.

Successful managers focus on these principles and, in doing so, amply reward their shareholders. The key is that successful managers are prudent with shareholder assets, while at the same time generating higher investor returns. For instance, managers may use the credit available to the company to make timely and sensible acquisitions, and then use the increased cash flow from the acquisition to pay down the debt used to acquire it.

Management's other fiduciary responsibilities include that of not conducting personal business in situations in which there may be a conflict of interest. The interest of the company should be paramount when compared to the interests of individual managers. Managers should not realize personal gain outside their compensation package, with the exception of any gain that accrues from the company stock increasing in price.

The importance of management to the success of a business is like that of the captains in an America's Cup yacht race. The competing yachts are basically the same style, size, and shape. The yachts' power, the wind, is a consistently changing force, but it is the same for all contestants. The course set to be raced is also identical for all contestants. The major difference between the winner and the loser is the captain and crew's ability to tweak their yachts to generate more speed. Teamwork is critical. The minute differences between how the sails are trimmed and the seconds saved between taking down the genoa jib and setting the spinnaker may be the determining factors in winning the race. The outcome of the America's Cup is determined by the captain and crew's ability to take advantage of the slightest wind change and their ability to outthink and outmaneuver their competition. The America's Cup is usually won by the smartest and most talented crew.

Overlooked stock selection is similar. Companies with the best managers will win the race of increasing shareholder value over time.

There are several indicators used to evaluate the effectiveness of management. There is revenue and EPS growth, return on shareholder equity, return on assets, operating and free cash flow generation, and the budget for research and development. Investors should review each of these prior to purchasing a stock. Many investors lose sight of these evaluation tools and get caught up with the excitement of new-fangled products or short-term movements in stock prices. In the long term, however, investor excitement will not have as much impact on stock gains as will excellent management.

Many investors are skittish when it comes to management evaluation and stock research. It is far easier to take the stock tip from your neighbor, the antics of a dart-throwing-monkey-turned-stock-picker, or the suggestions of the talking heads on TV. Many investors pass their money off to mutual fund managers because they don't want to spend the time or trouble to conduct their own research. Many other investors, however, discover that stock research is not too tough and with the help of a few comparisons, the research process can be simplified.

Detailed financial information is readily available today, but it may be confusing to new investors. To simplify the research process, we will discuss in detail the following management efficiency ratios in terms of their importance and how they can be easily compared:

- Return on equity (ROE)
- Return on capital (ROC)
- Return on assets (ROA)
- Long-term debt to equity
- Earnings and dividends per share
- Cash flow
- Revenues
- Gross margins

The appearance of startup Internet companies and the bull market of the 1990s made stock selection for short-term gains almost as easy as pin the tail on the donkey. However, history has demonstrated once again that successful stock selection and proper portfolio management are not necessarily easy and that the risks of investing are many. For those who bought stocks willy-nilly, the decline of stock prices in 2000, 2001, and 2002 could have been very painful. However, through the development of a personal investing plan and careful research, most investors find they are able to minimize the risks. The astute investors know that in the long term, there is no better place for exceptional returns than the stock market and that adequate research will protect him or her against the pitfalls of fads and trendy investing.

Keep in mind the old adage that exceptional companies attract exceptional managers. Investing in companies with proven managers is a time-tested method of achieving exceptional capital gains. Much of this management talent, however, is overlooked by the Wall Street pros.

Return on Equity, Return on Capital, Return on Assets, and Long-Term Debt to Equity

Three of the most common evaluation tools are return on equity (ROE), return on capital (ROC), and return on assets (ROA). These are efficiency ratios, and they tell investors how efficiently management is utilizing company assets. The higher the ROE, ROC, and ROA, the more money management is earning for its shareholders. The lower the debt to equity, the less debt the company carries.

The formula for *return on equity* is net income before nonrecurring charges divided by the book value, or shareholders' equity. *Nonrecurring charges* may include things like sales of assets or charges to close facilities. *Shareholders' equity* is calculated by subtracting liabilities from assets. For example, Company A makes a net profit of $120 on shareholders' equity of $1000, which would generate an ROE of 12 percent (12 = 120 / 1000). High return-on-equity ratios may be the result of excessive use of debt, a high return on assets, or both. This ratio measures how much profit the company is making from every dollar of investors' capital. The higher the ROE, the more profits management generates on equal dollars of investors' equity.

$$\text{Return on Equity} = \frac{\text{Net Income}}{\text{Book Value}}$$

Return on capital is computed by dividing the net income by shareholder equity, or book value, plus long-term debt. For example, if Company A has $500 in debt, the ROC would be 8 percent (8 = 120 / (1000 + 500). The ROC is a measure of how effectively management employs all its capital, both borrowed and invested by shareholders. Effectively managing debt is critical to the growth of a company. When debt levels are added to an ROE analysis, a clearer picture of management's ability to generate a profit from all available capital becomes clearer. Management with higher ROC ratios are generating more profits on equal amounts of total capital.

$$\text{Return on Capital} = \frac{\text{Net Income}}{\text{Book Value} + \text{Long-Term Debt}}$$

The formula for the *return on assets* is net income, before nonrecurring charges, divided by total corporate assets. For example, if Company A has $1500 in assets, its ROA would be 8 percent (8 = 120 / 1500). The ROA evaluates how effectively management produces profits from all its assets, such as factories and equipment. A higher return on assets can be attributed to higher profit margins or higher asset turnover, such as inventory. Older assets that have depreciated over the years are carried on the financial statement at below market value and may skew the ROA. A higher ROA demonstrates the ability of management to generate higher profits on equal amounts of assets.

$$\text{Return on Assets} = \frac{\text{Net Income}}{\text{Assetts}}$$

Long-term debt to equity is calculated by dividing long-term debt by book value. For example, Company A has a long-term debt-to-equity ratio of 0.5 (0.5 = 500 / 1000). This ratio indicates the leverage the company has. The higher the ratio, the more leverage and potentially higher risk for the company. The best managers generate increasing profits while reducing debt-to-equity levels.

$$\text{Long-Term Debt to Equity} = \frac{\text{Long-Term Debt}}{\text{Book Value}}$$

For example, Greg and Peter each open separate and competing landscaping businesses with $10,000 each from their savings accounts. Greg and Peter contributed their savings as equity in their respective businesses. Each bought $10,000 worth of landscaping equipment. After one year, Greg had earned $5000, and Peter had earned $4000. Greg's return on equity was 50 percent while Peter's was 40 percent. You would think that Greg was a better businessperson and had done a better job of managing his business because he made more profit on equal amounts of equity and his ROE was higher (see Table 4–1).

If you stop researching here, you may not have sufficient information to determine who has been the better manager. Further research covers that after they started, Greg took out a loan of $20,000 while Peter borrowed about a third of that, or $7000. Since capital is defined as equity and debt, the capital for the two companies would be figured as $30,000 for Greg and $17,000 for Peter. Greg's ROC was 16 percent ($5000 divided by $30,000), while Peter's ROC was 23 percent ($4000

TABLE 4-1 Management Efficiency Ratios for Greg's and Peter's Landscape Businesses

	Greg	Peter
ROE	50 percent	40 percent
ROC	16 percent	23 percent
ROA	20 percent	23 percent
Debt to equity	2.0	0.7

divided by $17,000). One could now assume that Peter was a better manager because his return on capital was higher.

But, we still do not have enough information to determine who is the better manager. Looking further, we see that Greg used the proceeds of his loan to buy $15,000 in new equipment and $5000 for local radio advertising. Peter, on the other hand, used the proceeds from his loan only to buy additional equipment. Greg's total assets were $25,000, and Peter's total assets were $17,000. Greg's ROA was 20 percent while Peter's ROA was 23 percent. Greg's long-term debt-to-equity ratio is 2.0 ($20,000 divided by $10,000) while Peter's debt-to-equity ratio is 0.7 ($7000 divided by $10,000).

While Greg made more cash dollars from his initial $10,000 in equity, Peter managed his business better. Peter generated more profit from his capital and his assets and incurred less debt. If you were to invest $1000 in Greg's business and he continued to manage it with the same fiscal responsibility, you could expect to realize a $160 profit. The same $1000 invested in Peter's business, on the other hand, should generate $230 in profit. In addition, Greg's business is higher risk because he has a higher debt-to-equity ratio.

Many financial reporting agencies don't offer return-on-capital ratios, but they do offer return-on-equity and debt-to-equity ratios. The easiest method of calculating the ROC is with the following formula: Return on capital equals return on equity divided by (1 plus debt-to-equity ratio). Greg's formula would be ROC = 50 / (1 + 2.0), or ROC = 16. Peter's formula would be ROC = 40 / (1 + 0.7), or ROC = 23.

$$\text{Return on Capital} = \frac{\text{Return on Equity}}{1 + \text{debt-to-equity ratio}}$$

Why does this matter? Many financial analysts believe the most accurate way to evaluate the future earnings growth potential of a company is to evaluate the ROC. This ratio illustrates management's ability to generate profits from all available capital. For every dollar of capital the company generates, either through cash flow generation, additional debt, or shareholders capital, the ROC will forecast how much profit can be produced. The higher the return on capital, the higher the future profits can be. Some financial analysts even believe that a company cannot generate sustainable profit growth faster than its return on capital. Logically, it makes sense. Long-term profits are created from revenues generated from the use of assets. Assets are generated from internally generated cash, borrowed capital, and shareholder equity. Sustainable long-term profits are based on the efficient use of all capital available.

Earnings per Share, Dividends per Share, Cash Flow, Revenues, and Gross Margins

There are four additional financial numbers that are commonly used to evaluate management's performance. These are earnings per share, dividends per share, cash flow, and revenues.

Earnings per share is the amount of net profit divided by the number of shares outstanding. There are two ways in which earnings per share increase: net earnings increase or the number of outstanding shares decreases. As corporate earnings exploded in the 1990s, companies used their excess cash to buy back shares of their own stock from the general public. This reduced the number of shares outstanding and increased the earnings per share. According to Michael Sivy, columnist for *Money* magazine, in 1998 alone, U.S. corporations bought back $209 billion worth of their stock.

As the economy slumped in 2000 and corporate profits began to evaporate, corporations scaled back their share repurchase programs. Although share buyback programs are somewhat controversial as the best use of corporate cash, they can be an effective means of increasing earnings per share. To be effective, the shares that are repurchased must not recycled back to management to satisfy stock options that are exercised. The shares must be retired from circulation. Many companies in their small- or mid-cap stage will issue additional shares through secondary offerings as a means of generating additional capital. This is usually accomplished during periods of strong profit growth. Investors can easily tell when more shares have been issued as the percentage growth in net dollar income is higher than the percentage growth in earnings per share. An excellently managed company will not only demonstrate consistency in long-term earnings growth but its earnings-per-share growth rate should exceed that of its peers.

$$\text{Earnings per Share} = \frac{\text{Net Profit}}{\text{Number of Shares Outstanding}}$$

The *dividends per share* and the *dividend payout ratio* are other tools investors use to evaluate stocks. Many companies return to shareholders a portion of corporate profits in the form of dividends. Paying dividends can be a powerful method of retaining and rewarding shareholder loyalty. The amount of dividends paid varies based on several factors, the largest of which is the specific industry in which the company competes. For example, utilities are known for distributing a large percentage of annual earnings while high-tech companies are more apt to retain their earnings and to reinvest them back into the company.

The *payout ratio* is the percent of net income paid to shareholders in the form of dividends. Knowing the payout ratio can assist investors in understanding the dividend policy of companies. This ratio is calculated by dividing the dividend by net income. For example, if a company earns $1.00 per share and pays a $0.20 dividend per share, the payout ratio is 20 percent. Most companies try to maintain a steady payout ratio so as earnings per share rise, so does the dividend. If earnings in the previous example increase to $1.50 a share, investors can anticipate the dividend to increase to $0.30.

$$\text{Payout Ratio} = \frac{\text{Dividends}}{\text{Net Income}}$$

Cash flow is the amount of cash created by managing and financing the business. Many investors believe this is a truer measure of profitability than net earnings. Keep in mind that cash flow is the cash created by the business before accounting charges required to calculate net earnings. Net earnings include noncash expenses, such as depreciation and charges for future expenses. Cash flow has several components: operating cash flow, cash flow from investing activities, cash flow from financing, and free cash flow.

Cash flow information is available in the company annual report. Annual reports are accessible either online at the company Web site or by request from the director of investor relations. Many Internet financial Web sites, such as Zacks.com, offer the most recent company financial information along with a recap of cash flow growth rates.

Operating cash flow is the amount of cash generated from business operations. As businesses live or die by this one financial number, it should be reviewed carefully for consistent growth. The basic operating cash flow is calculated by adding net income to noncash expenses such as depreciation, provisions for credit losses, and deferred income taxes. Excellently managed companies will always have positive operating cash flow, despite net earnings that are occasionally reduced by such factors as noncash merger expenses.

Cash flow from investing activities is the amount of cash generated or consumed for investing in the future of the business. This may include capital expenditures for new plants and equipment, accounts receivables that are sold as part of a finance package, or the sale of company assets. Acquisitions made with cash are also reported in the cash flow from investing activities.

Cash flow from financing is the cash generated or used in financing the business. This includes additions to or subtractions from debt, secondary offerings of stock, stock buyback programs, dividends paid to shareholders, and issuance of stock to employees.

Free cash flow is defined as the amount of extra cash the company has generated after deducting capital expenditures from operating cash flow. Some investors include expenses for debt service as a component as well. The belief is that while capital expenditures are part of cash flow from investing activities, it is crucial for the long-term survival of the company. A business that is not updating equipment and facilities on a consistent basis quickly falls behind its competitors. Capital expenditures should rise at about the same rate as revenues. Many investors believe that the calculation of free cash flow is the truest indication of the ability of management to generate unencumbered cash from operating their business.

Revenues are the dollar value of goods or services sold by the company. There are several internal and external factors that affect overall revenues and revenue growth. The most basic external factor is the economic background of the company's industry and the economy as a whole. For example, the chemical industry began its recession in 1999 as industrial customers, seeing a potential slowdown on the horizon, began to cut back on their raw materials purchases. The economy in general, however, remained strong until early 2001.

Gross profit margin is the amount of profit generated by the company before operating expenses, expressed as a percentage of revenues. Gross margin is the first level of profit analysis, and it is one of the rawest profit numbers. Excellent managers will generate gross profit margins at least in line with their competitors, and probably better. Rising gross margins will indicate that management is doing a better job of generating profits from each dollar of revenue.

$$\text{Gross Margins} = \frac{\text{Revenues} - \text{Cost of Goods Sold}}{\text{Revenues}}$$

Do Dividends Matter?

Many companies pay their shareholders a quarterly or annual dividend, thereby returning a portion of corporate cash flow. Many investors like the steady flow of income a dividend represents. Some industries attract income-seeking investors by offering a higher dividend. Utilities, for example, have historically returned a large percentage of cash flow and earnings to shareholders. Payout ratios in the utility industry usually range from 65 to 90 percent. Many small- and mid-cap companies don't pay any dividend or a dividend that is very small in relation to earnings. These companies retain the earnings for investment back into the business.

The investing world is split between those who believe paying a dividend matters and those who do not. Some believe that paying a dividend, which reduces the internally generated capital available for reinvestment into the company, hampers a company's growth. If management is prudent with its investment of excess cash flow, the business should continue to expand, increasing shareholder value over time. One of the biggest challenges to success a company faces is how to finance business expansion. A company growing revenues at a 25 percent annual rate will generate additional cash needs. More customers buying more goods or services requires higher inventories and accounts receivables. If demand is sufficient, additional factory capacity and equipment may be needed. Additional employees may need to be hired. Increased expenses such as business travel and marketing, usually accompany an increase in business activity. All this takes capital. It may not make sense to pay current shareholders a dividend, reducing available corporate capital, and to then issue more shares or borrow capital to finance additional business growth. However, to many investors, a dividend, no matter how small, is a sign of management's confidence in future profitability. A dividend may also increase shareholder loyalty to the company.

In addition, management should have demonstrated its ability to earn above-average returns from the company's available capital. Allowing them to retain more cash flow by paying a smaller dividend increases the pool of money available for management to invest.

Recent tax law changes have increased the pressure on management to review dividend policies. Dividends are included as part of earned income for personal tax calculations. Twenty years ago, the first $700 of dividend income was excluded from personal income tax, and capital gains taxes were higher than earned-income taxes. This provided preferential personal tax treatment of dividend income over capital gain. However, over the years, the exemption disappeared and capital gains tax rates plummeted. Currently, the lowest capital gains rate is 18 percent for a stock investment bought after January 1, 2001, and held for a minimum of 5 years. Earned-income tax rates are higher for many individuals, with some in a 35 percent or higher tax bracket. For these individuals, every dollar of dividend triggers a minimum 35 cent tax bill while the same dollar from capital gains triggers an 18 cent tax bill. Large shareholders began to pressure management to reduce dividend payout ratios and to increase share prices instead.

Some companies responded in the 1990s by using excessive cash flow to buy back large blocks of shares rather than increase the dividend. In theory, if these shares were permanently retired from circulation and not reissued to satisfy management stock options, the corresponding reduction in shares outstanding would increase earnings per share. Even with net earnings unchanged, the EPS can be driven higher by reducing the number of shares. This leads to higher share prices and additional capital gains.

There are others who believe that a high dividend payout is better. Sometimes, a dividend can provide a yield floor for the stock price. If the dividend is large enough in relation to the stock price, investors may be attracted to the income of the dividend rather than to the growth prospects. If the S&P 500 Index is offering a 1.5 percent dividend yield, investors could be more attracted to a stock offering a much higher yield of 3.5 percent. Especially in a bear market when most stocks are under selling pressure, a dividend could be important in providing a price at which a stock may stabilize. Some investors believe the dividend provides a minimum annual return. For example, a stock is bought at $10 and offers a $1 dividend, for a yield of 10 percent. If the stock does not increase or decrease in price, the annual return to the investor would still be 10 percent from the dividend. Investors also may seek out companies with a history of increasing the dividend. For example, if a company raises its dividend by 7.2 percent a year, the dividend will double in 10 years. Investors would be receiving twice the income on their original capital investment.

Some investors believe that too much cash flow in the hands of management can lead to abuse. The temptation to expand into non-core ventures becomes greater if there is too much cash in the bank. This is called "empire building." Management may be so successful that they virtually have more cash flow than they know what to do with. The company may expand into new businesses that are quite different from their expertise, and the anticipated profit gains may fail to materialize. More times than not, it results in the squandering of shareholders' capital. In addition, a large cash balance in the bank usually generates smaller returns and may not be the best use of corporate assets. By distributing cash flow to investors in the form of a dividend, management is left with much less temptation to wander off into uncharted territory.

Since no manager wants to be associated with the cutting or elimination of a dividend, a dividend can represent a minimum floor for earnings. While sometimes earnings will falter, investors demand at least the maintenance of an established dividend. There is no stronger sign of confidence in the future of a company than for its management to raise the dividend. This signals to investors that earnings growth should be sustainable to afford a higher payout.

Small- and mid-cap companies usually have a smaller payout ratio and smaller dividends than their larger competitors. Since many are growing faster, their capital needs are greater, and they tend to retain more of their cash flow. However, investors should not overlook the importance and value of a dividend. Dividend growth that exceeds industry averages is another positive sign for an overlooked company.

Trends

Earlier, we reviewed Greg's and Peter's landscaping businesses on a 1-year basis. However, it is important for investors to review these key management efficiency and performance ratios over time. The astute investor is looking for trends that may suggest the future. Internet financial sites provide a wealth of information concerning return-on-equity, return-on-assets, and debt-to-equity levels. Many will furnish specific company information along with comparisons for industry and sector averages.

The goal is to find above-average management, so it is important that these ratios are reviewed for 5-year and 10-year trends, along with comparisons against the competition. The best companies will have current ratios above their 3- and 5-year averages and above industry averages as well. During economic slowdowns, it is especially important to review these trends. Ten-year trend analysis is preferred. This time frame will usually include at least one economic downturn. Since the economy was in a recession in 2001 and 2002, most businesses experienced a difficult economic environment. For the next several years, 5-year comparisons will include the recession of 2001. The inclusion of company performance in a poor economic climate assists investors in making better evaluations. If the latest ratio calculations are below the recent 5- or 10-year averages, the company may not be using its capital to the best advantage in generating profits for shareholders. Keep in mind, however, that a slowdown in the economy will put pressure on any positive financial trend.

There will be overlooked companies that have a stock trading history of less than 10 years and financial information may not go back 10 years. In this case, focus on 5-year financial information, but make sure the company has been in existence for more than the 5-year time frame. For example, Copart Industries (CPRT) was formed in 1982, but it did not go public and begin trading until 1995. In situations like Copart, management has a 20-year history in the business, but financial information will be available for the period starting in 1995. When there is less than a 10-year history of financials, make sure you review the year the company was founded and the year the company went public. This will give you a better understanding of the length of time management has been around. Sometimes companies will merge, forming a new corporate entity. With the merger may come a new stock symbol and a new trading history. Previous financial information may become obsolete. These companies are like startup IPOs in that they don't have any financial "history" even though they may have been around for decades.

Management efficiency ratios vary widely by industry. Industries that are highly capital intensive, such as the utilities, will have lower returns than a less-capital-intensive industry, such as a service industry. Financial companies, such as banks and financial services businesses, will have much higher levels of debt because they borrow money to generate capital for lending activities. Banks make their money on the spread between their cost to borrow and the interest they receive by lending.

Well-managed companies will increase earnings and cash flow faster than revenues. If they accomplish this feat, they are producing more cash profits for their shareholders for every dollar increase in sales. Sometimes their revenues will not grow as quickly as revenues for their competitors. Higher profit margins that squeeze more profits can offset slower gains in revenues. Since profits and cash flow are what drive stock prices higher, investors should focus their attention on these financial numbers as well as on return ratios.

Management Efficiency Numbers in Action

There are many companies from which to choose from when conducting stock research. The following are a few companies from the S&P 400 Mid-Cap Index and the S&P 600 Small-Cap Index.

Copart Industries (CPRT, consumer discretionary, market cap $3.405 billion) focuses on services to process and sell salvaged automobiles. The company auctions salvaged vehicles, which are damaged vehicles, deemed a total loss for insurance purposes, or recovered stolen vehicles. Insurance settlement has already been made with the owners of the vehicles, and the insurance company owns the automobile. The company operates 77 locations in 36 states. More than 90 percent of the company's vehicles are obtained from insurance company suppliers. Revenues are from auction fees as well as related storing and towing fees. Copart was founded in 1982.

Medicis Pharmaceuticals (MRX, health care, market cap $1.684 billion) develops and markets dermatological products. It markets over-the-counter face creams and a moisturizer under the Esoterica name. The company also manufactures prescription pharmaceuticals that treat conditions such as acne, fungal infections, psoriasis, eczema, and hyperpigmentation. Medicis Pharmaceuticals uses brand names such as Dynacin, Lustra, Triaz, Lidex, Synalar, Loprox, Topicort, Novacet, and Ovide. Sales to Cardinal Health account for about 21 percent of the company's total revenues. Medicis was founded in 1988 and went public in 1990.

Illinois Tool Works (ITW, industrials, market cap $22.620 billion) is a diversified manufacturer, operating almost 600 largely autonomous subsidiaries. Industrial segments include engineered components, such as fasteners, metal and plastic parts, and specialty industrial machinery systems. ITW's customer base is similarly diverse. Management targets the automotive, food service, construction, and general manufacturing industries. Foreign sales constituted 35 percent of revenue. Illinois Tool Works was founded in 1917.

Hudson United Bancorp (HU, financial services, market cap $1.442 billion) is the holding company for Hudson United Bank, operating more than 200 branch offices in Connecticut, New Jersey, Pennsylvania, and New York. The bank offers retail individual retirement, money market, checking, and savings accounts. Hudson United also makes commercial real estate, business, and consumer loans. HU is very active in small business loans that are funded by the Small Business Administration. Real estate loans account for approximately 65 percent of the bank's loan portfolio. Hudson United was founded in 1890.

Barra Software (BARZ, information technologies, market cap $1.209 billion) provides computer software and services for global investment firms. Its core software products analyze and conduct risk evaluation on equity, fixed-income, currency, and other financial instruments in international financial markets. The company offers consulting services, information services, and trading-related software. Its client base in over 40 countries includes equity managers, global managers, fixed-income managers, pension funds, investment consultants, and securities traders. Founded in 1975, Barra Software went public in 1991.

Florida Rock Industries (FRK, materials, market cap $1.192 billion) manufactures rock. The company mines limestone and granite from its quarries in Florida, Georgia, Maryland, North Carolina, Virginia, and Washington, D.C. Its main products include sand, gravel, crushed stone, and ready-mixed concrete. It manufactures concrete block used in the construction industry and concrete products used in highway construction. Florida Rock conducts business in the southeastern United States at facilities that include 97 ready-mix concrete and concrete-block plants, and it operates 962 delivery trucks. Florida Rock was founded in 1945.

McCormick & Company (MKC, consumer staples, market cap $3.577 billion) manufactures food products and plastic packaging. The company's major business is to produce and market food spices and seasonings. They focus on retail, industrial food services, and food processing markets, primarily using the McCormick and Schilling brand names. The Setco and Tubed Products subsidiaries produce plastic packaging for the food industry. Sales outside of North America account for approximately 25 percent of the company's total sales. McCormick was founded in 1889.

Cinergy (CIN, utilities, market cap $5.671 billion) provides natural gas and electricity in southwestern Ohio, Kentucky, and Indiana. Its main operating unit, Cincinnati Gas and Electric, services 1.4 million customers. Electricity sales account for 73 percent of revenues, and natural gas sales represent 27 percent of revenues. Cinergy was formed in 1994 by the merger of Cincinnati Gas and Electric and PSI, Inc., a neighboring electric utility.

Enterprise Products Partners (EPD, energy, market cap $3.405 billion) provides processing and transportation services to producers of natural gas. The company processes gas liquids into their component products: ethane, propane, isobutane, normal butane, and natural gasoline. EPD transports its products to end users by pipeline and railcar. The company has long-term agreements with Burlington Resources, Texaco, and Union Pacific Resources. Enterprise Product Partners was formed in 1968.

Tables 4–2 to 4–4 provide examples of financial analysis for each of these companies for the trailing 12 months as of February 2002. Industry averages are in parentheses.

TABLE 4-2   Return on Assets, Return on Equity, Debt to Equity, and
Return on Capital for Selected Companies (Industry Averages
in Parentheses)

	Return on Assets		Return on Equity		Debt to Equity	Return on Capital	
	Current	5-Yr Avg.	Current	5-Yr Avg.		Current	5-Yr Avg.
Copart	15.0	4.5	18.1	12.3	0.00	18.1	12.3
	(4.5)	(5.9)	(17.3)	(15.5)	(0.55)	(11.2)	(10.0)
Medicis	9.0	8.5	9.8	9.7	0.00	9.8	9.7
	(2.2)	(−0.4)	(6.3)	(4.0)	(0.29)	(4.8)	(3.1)
Ill. Tool	8.2	10.8	14.2	20.0	0.21	11.7	16.5
	(5.8)	(8.0)	(11.4)	(17.8)	(0.65)	(6.9)	(10.7)
Hudson	1.3	0.9	25.0	15.3	NM	NM	NM
	(1.5)	(1.5)	(15.9)	(18.2)			
Barra	15.4	14.7	22.4	11.2	0.00	22.4	11.2
	(7.2)	(14.1)	(24.7)	(25.2)	(0.08)	(22.8)	(23.8)
FL. Rock	10.4	9.4	17.6	15.3	0.28	13.7	11.9
	(5.6)	(9.6)	(12.0)	(18.0)	(0.59)	(7.5)	(11.3)
McCorm.	7.5	7.4	36.5	29.6	0.98	18.4	14.9
	(7.0)	(9.1)	(25.4)	(30.6)	(1.40)	(10.5)	(12.7)
Cinergy	3.5	3.7	15.4	14.0	1.22	6.9	6.3
	(2.6)	(3.3)	(10.4)	(11.6)	(1.61)	(3.9)	(4.4)
Enterprise	10.6	9.0	23.9	18.5	0.74	13.7	10.6
	(7.0)	(3.4)	(18.6)	(10.9)	(0.79)	(10.3)	(6.0)

Analysis

Copart Industry. Return on capital over the past 5 years has been 20
percent above the industry average and 50 percent above the industry
average during the past 12 months. Although return on equity was
slightly below the industry average for the past 5 years, management
has improved on their own average and their average versus the industry average over the past year. Combine this improvement with no
long-term debt and Copart has demonstrated the ability to smartly use
their capital. Gross margins are at least 20 percent higher than industry
averages. Revenues and earnings have risen steadily over the past 5
years, with earnings showing the most dramatic growth. It appears

TABLE 4-3 Gross Profit Margins for
Selected Companies, Percent (Industry
Averages in Parentheses)

	Gross Margins	
	Current, %	5-Y Avg., %
Copart	40.5	36.8
	(29.9)	(29.5)
Medicis	82.6	81.7
	(66.3)	(65.5)
Ill. Tool	33.3	34.6
	(31.1)	(31.9)
Hudson	NM	NM
Barra	95.7	94.3
	(77.5)	(77.0)
FL. Rock	23.9	22.0
	(20.7)	(24.8)
McCorm.	40.9	36.8
	(39.4)	(38.2)
Cinergy	11.9	23.8
	(26.4)	(36.0)
Enterprise	9.2	8.5
	(46.8)	(45.2)

Copart has reached its critical mass from an internally generated cash flow viewpoint as operating cash flow doubled in fiscal year 2001.

Medicis Pharmaceuticals. Efficiency ratios are substantially above industry averages across the board. Management has shown their ability to outperform the financial results of its competitors, with return on capital an impressive three times the industry average. Gross profit margins are substantially higher than industry averages. Revenues have climbed at twice the industry average, and profitability is in line with its competitors. Cash flow increased an average of 73 percent a year for the past 5 years.

Illinois Tool Works. Management has consistently outperformed their competitors. Return on capital for the past 5 years has been

TABLE 4-4   Revenues (Millions), Earnings per Share, Operating Cash Flow (Millions), Capital Expenditures (Millions), and Free Cash Flow (Millions) for Selected Companies (Industry Averages in Parentheses)

	Fiscal Year 2001	Fiscal Year 2000	Fiscal Year 1999	Fiscal Year 1998	Fiscal Year 1997	5-Yr Annual Growth, Percent	
Copart Industries							
Revenues	$253.9	$190.0	$141.8	$114.2	$126.3	20.2	(28.1)
EPS	$0.51	$0.36	$0.27	$0.19	$0.15	48.0	(20.4)
Cash flow	$56.9	$26.2	$30.7	$22.8	$24.9	25.7	
Cap expenditures	$49.7	$51.0	$22.7	$19.6	$11.2		
Free cash flow	$7.2	−$24.8	$7.0	$3.3	$13.7		
Medicis Pharmaceuticals							
Revenues	$167.8	$139.1	$116.9	$77.6	$41.2	61.4	(30.5)
EPS	$1.64	$1.48	$1.27	$0.44	$0.87	17.7	(16.3)
Cash flow	$70.6	$41.2	$25.4	$20.0	$15.1	73.5	
Cap expenditures	$36.6	$37.4	$25.8	$5.8	$29.1		
Free cash flow	$34.0	$3.8	−$0.4	$14.2	−$14.0		
Illinois Tool Works							
Revenues	$9292.8	$9511.6	$9333.2	$8387.0	$7627.3	4.3	(11.4)
EPS	$2.86	$3.47	$3.12	$2.80	$2.39	3.9	(−11.3)
Cash flow	$1351.0	$1122.4	$1036.6	$887.8	$819.0	12.9	
Cap expenditures	$256.6	$306.0	$317.1	$316.1	$260.1		
Free cash flow	$1094.4	$816.4	$719.5	$571.7	$558.9		
Hudson United Bancorp							
Revenues	$579.5	$639.3	$732.8	$677.9	$675.0	−2.8	(11.2)
EPS	$2.01	$1.10	$1.56	$1.17	$1.40	14.3	(11.9)
Cash flow	$34.2	$185.9	$161.2	$254.6	$135.4	−20.2	
Cap expenditures	$6.7	$23.5	$31.5	$14.6	$16.8		
Free cash flow	$27.5	$172.4	$129.7	$240.0	$118.6		

TABLE 4-4   Revenues (Millions), Earnings per Share, Operating Cash Flow
(Millions), Capital Expenditures (Millions), and Free Cash Flow (Millions)
for Selected Companies (Industry Averages in Parentheses) (*Continued*)

	Fiscal Year 2001	Fiscal Year 2000	Fiscal Year 1999	Fiscal Year 1998	Fiscal Year 1997	5-Yr Annual Growth, Percent
Barra Software						
Revenues	$224.4	$186.5	$158.1	$137.4	$104.8	22.9 (30.2)
EPS	$2.19	$1.39	$0.73	$0.72	$0.77	36.8 (27.6)
Cash flow	$82.9	$62.4	$22.8	$30.2	$19.2	30.1
Cap expenditures	$4.4	$5.8	$8.7	$8.9	$3.7	
Free cash flow	$78.5	$56.6	$14.1	$21.3	$15.5	
Florida Rock						
Revenue	$715.7	$665.6	$596.6	$492.3	$456.6	11.3 (13.3)
EPS	$2.01	$1.72	$1.60	$1.36	$1.34	10.0 (8.1)
Cash flow	$122.9	$90.7	$106.8	$72.9	$69.5	15.3
Cap expenditures	$68.9	$107.3	$102.7	$95.3	$46.5	
Free cash flow	$54.0	–$16.6	$4.1	–$22.4	$23.0	
McCormick & Company						
Revenues	$2372.4	$2123.5	$2006.9	$1881.1	$1801.0	6.3 (5.7)
EPS	$2.23	$2.00	$1.59	$1.43	$1.26	15.3 (8.7)
Cash flow	$204.5	$202.0	$229.3	$144.0	$181.2	2.5
Cap expenditures	$112.1	$53.6	$49.3	$54.8	$43.9	
Free cash flow	$92.4	$145.7	$180.0	$89.2	$137.3	
Cinergy						
Revenues	$12,922.5	$8422.0	$5937.9	$5911.3	$4387.1	38.9 (20.5)
EPS	$2.78	$2.51	$2.54	$1.64	$2.30	4.1 (6.8)
Cash flow	$694.4	$620.9	$391.4	$696.9	$733.6	1.0
Cap expenditures	$843.2	$519.0	$386.3	$368.6	$328.1	
Free cash flow	–$152.2	$101.9	$5.1	$328.3	$405.5	

TABLE 4-4   Revenues (Millions), Earnings per Share, Operating Cash Flow (Millions), Capital Expenditures (Millions), and Free Cash Flow (Millions) for Selected Companies (Industry Averages in Parentheses) (*Continued*)

	Fiscal Year 2001	Fiscal Year 2000	Fiscal Year 1999	Fiscal Year 1998	Fiscal Year 1997	5-Yr Annual Growth, Percent
Enterprise Products Partners L.P.						
Revenues	$3179.7	$3073.1	$1346.5	$754.6	$1036.0	41.3 (27.4)
EPS	$2.78	$3.24	$1.78	$0.62	$0.94	39.1 (37.7)
Cash flow	$283.7	$360.7	$178.0	−$9.4	$57.8	79.2
Cap expenditures	$149.9	$243.9	$21.2	$8.4	$33.6	
Free cash flow	$133.8	$116.8	$156.8	−$17.6	$24.2	

Source: MarketGuide.com.

50 percent above industry average and twice the average for the past year. Margins are in line with ITW's competitors. Due to the recession, revenues and revenue growth fell below industry averages. However, its earnings have remained strong compared to its competitors.

Hudson United Bancorp. Although revenues declined in 2000 and 2001, management's ability to produce above-average earnings is apparent. Return on asset and return on equity in 2001 were above its 5-year average. If this trend continues, Hudson United will soon achieve better-than-average industry performance. Financial companies usually have very large debt that is collateralized by its loans, making debt-to-equity and return-on-capital ratios not meaningful.

Barra Software. Management has been doing a better job of efficiently using the capital at their disposal. Current return on capital is slightly above industry average, but it is twice their 5-year average. Gross margins are higher than industry averages. Although its revenue growth has not kept pace with the industry, its 5-year earnings growth is 40 percent higher than its competitors.

Florida Rock Industries. Current return on capital is almost twice the industry average, while 5-year average return on capital is slightly above the industry. Profit margins are in line with industry averages. Although revenue growth is slightly below its competitors, earnings growth is 23 percent higher. Management has done a better job of generating higher earnings on fewer dollars of revenue growth.

McCormick & Company. The return on capital in 2001 was substantially above its competitors, and the 5-year average is about 17 percent better than the industry average. Gross profits are in line with competitors. Revenue growth is par with the industry, but earnings growth over the past 5 years is 75 percent higher than its competitors. Compared to its competitors, management is able to squeeze more profit from its revenues.

Cinergy. Management has demonstrated an ability to generate better financial results than the average utility. Recent gross margins are below competitors, both currently and for the past 5 years. Revenue growth and return on capital are well above the competitors, but the company lags slightly in earnings growth.

Enterprise Products Partners. Management efficiency ratios indicate that Enterprise is able to better utilize its capital. Gross margins, however, are below industry averages. The 5-year average return on capital is 73 percent above its competitors.

Standard & Poor's Equity Ranking

The Standard and Poor's *Equity Ranking,* also known as the *Quality Ranking,* is an easy and effective means of categorizing management's performance. The *1999 Directory of Dividend Reinvestment Plans* states:

> Growth and stability of earnings and dividends are key elements in S&P common stock rankings. Our computerized scoring system is based on per-share earnings and dividend records of the most recent 10 years. This period is considered sufficient time to measure secular growth, to capture indications of basic changes in trends as they develop, and to encompass the full peak-to-peak range of the business cycle. Basic scores are computed for earnings and dividends, then adjusted as indicated by a set of predetermined modifiers for growth and stability within the long-term trend and cyclicality. Adjusted scores for earnings and dividends are then combined to yield a final score.

S&P Quality Rankings are as follows:

A+	Highest	B+	Average	C	Lowest
A	High	B	Below average	D	In reorganization
A–	Above average	B–	Low	NR	Not ranked

The S&P Quality Ranking focuses on the two items most valued by investors: consistency and stability in earnings growth and consistency and stability in dividend growth. This ranking can be a powerful tool in evaluating long-term performance of management in these two important attributes. Although not specifically designed to be a stock valuation tool, the S&P rankings can provide additional insight used in the stock selection process.

Many stock research companies offer estimates of future company earnings growth. When combined with a ranking for long-term consistency, these two tools can be very effective in understanding the probability that analysts' estimates will come to fruition. An A+ ranked company should have a higher probability of meeting anticipated earnings growth projections than a D ranked company. Those companies that have demonstrated an ability to generate consistent increases in their profits and dividends should have the best chance of continuing to do so in the future.

Small- and mid-cap companies may have more inconsistency in their earnings growth than their larger competitors. As companies grow in size, business usually becomes more stable and there is more consistency in earnings and dividends. Sometimes a company experiences spurts in growth as management builds the business and takes larger accounts away from competitors. Likewise, when a smaller company loses a large account, the loss may have a dramatic negative impact for a short time. Well-managed businesses will bounce back from these setbacks, by replacing the lost business. However, this may create larger swings in earnings growth and a lower ranking by S&P.

As one piece of the evaluation puzzle, the S&P Quality Rankings should not be neglected. Some companies do not have the 10-year stock trading required to qualify for the Quality Ranking and are listed as NR, or not ranked. NR is not a low rating; it simply means there has been insufficient history to develop an analysis. Table 4–5 gives S&P Equity Rankings for the previously discussed companies.

TABLE 4-5   S&P Equity Ranking for Selected Companies

Copart Industries	NR	Medicis	B–
Illinois Tool Works	A+	Hudson United	B
Barra Software	B	Florida Rock Industries	A
McCormick & Co	A–	Cinergy	B+
Enterprise Products Partners	NR		

Corporate Mission Statements, Letters to Shareholders, and Corporate Ethics Statements

Investors should be searching for companies whose management has consistently increased corporate profits. The market as a whole climbed in the 1990s due to increasing earnings and dividends, as did the stock prices of most individual companies. The bull market of the nineties can be characterized as the rising tide that lifted all boats. The extent of an individual company's capital gain, however, is directly related to management's ability to generate long-term profits. As the caretakers of investors' capital, management's primary goal should be to increase revenues and profits for the benefit of all shareholders. There are several ways to evaluate management's commitment to shareholders.

The first place to look for management's directive is the corporate mission statement. Usually adopted by the board of directors, a mission statement is a few sentences long, and it states the purpose of the corporation's existence. It is the stated corporate purpose, and management will be judged by how well they perform using the mission statement as a yardstick. Shareholders deserve a place in every public company's corporate mission statement. If increasing shareholder value is not one of the stated purposes of the company, then it can be assumed that goal is not a primary focus for management.

For example, Cinergy's Web site lists both the corporate vision statement and the corporate mission statement:

Corporate Vision

Our vision is "people making history by making a difference." It is built on creating a multiregional leadership position on a physically balanced platform that will produce sustainable above-industry-average earnings growth. We believe that our model combined with our strategic location and highly incentivized employees will allow our company to realize that vision and become one of the top investment choices in our industry over the long term.

Corporate Mission

Our mission is to transform the lives of millions of people by providing reliable, reasonably priced energy and related services in an environmentally responsible manner. We're working to make our vision a reality by successfully completing our mission in a manner that serves all of our stakeholders, including:

- shareholders
- customers
- employees
- communities and the environment

While you may not agree with this specific vision and mission statement, the interests of shareholders are prominently mentioned. Increasing shareholder value is a critical stated goal of management.

In addition to the corporate mission statement, the annual letter to shareholders from the chairman will also give astute investors insight into the priority management gives to increasing shareholder value. The letter to shareholders is written as the first few pages of the corporate annual report. It should specify not only how the company increases shareholder value during that specific year through higher revenues, EPS, and operating cash flow growth but also management strategies needed to continue growing in the future. Look for words such as "shareholder" or "company owners," and see how often the chairman refers to the corporate mission of providing investors with exceptional returns.

While there is no way to guarantee good corporate ethics, a corporate ethics statement may reveal interesting aspects about the quality of management. Jack Welch, ex-CEO of General Electric (GE), carried around in his pocket a laminated card printed with GE's corporate ethics. Breaking any of these rules is cause for immediate employment termination. If a company is strict on employee ethics, it is usually also concerned about its shareholders as well. Companies with unethical business practices are not usually very appealing investments to shareholders.

Both corporate mission statements and corporate ethics statements should be available from the company. Contact shareholder or investor relations and request a copy, or retrieve them from the company Web site. The letter to shareholders is included in every annual report, and most annual reports are now available at the company Web site. If shareholders are not mentioned in the mission statement and in the annual letter to shareholders, and if there is no corporate ethics statement, it may be time to find a company with management more focused on increasing shareholder value.

Management Stock Options

To fully comprehend stock options, investors need to understand the legal and tax considerations that affect the various plan options available to companies. The goal in this section is to provide an overview of management stock options, their effect on shareholders, and a short review of possible pitfalls for shareholders.

In many companies, management is given stock options as a part of their compensation package. A *stock option* is the right to purchase a specific number of shares at a predetermined price at some time in the future. Usually, management is offered the right to purchase stock at the current price 5 to 10 years from their contract date. In addition, management can often exercise their option, or actually purchase a specific number of shares each year. This is called *vesting*. For example, a 5-year, 1000-share option may vest 20 percent a year, which means that management can purchase 200 shares each year that they are employed by the company.

In a simplified example, Jerry is the CEO of Widgets, Inc., and he receives an option to purchase 10,000 shares over the next 5 years at today's price of $10. The options vest at a rate of 20 percent a year. In year 1, Jerry can exercise options totaling 2000 shares. If the stock price has risen from $10 to $12, Jerry receives his 2000 shares, and pays $20,000 for stock worth $24,000. In year 2, the stock rises from $12 to $14. Jerry exercises another 2000 shares and pays $20,000 for stock that is worth $28,000. In year 3, the stock price rises to $17, and Jerry pays $20,000 for his options on 2000 shares worth $34,000. In year 4, the stock climbs to $21, and Jerry again exercises his options, paying $20,000 for stock now worth $42,000. In the fifth and last year of the option package, the stock rises to $25. Jerry exercises his 2000 shares, and pays his $20,000 for stock worth $50,000. Over the 5 years, Jerry has purchased 10,000 shares at a cost of $100,000, and the stock has a value of $250,000. If in any year, the stock price had fallen below the $10 option price, Jerry would not have had to exercise his options because the value of the stock was less than the option price. Jerry could hold on to these options and purchase the shares when the stock rose above $10.

Stock options can benefit companies in many ways. Stock option programs are designed to accomplish the following objectives:

- Align the interests of management with those of shareholders
- Reward long-term success as measured by growth in company stock price
- Assist managers to focus on building profitability and efficiency
- Provide a competitive management compensation package
- Serve as a management retention incentive
- Provide a tax-effective and cost-effective means of compensation

The National Center for Employee Ownership estimates that at least 7 million employees participate in stock option programs and that the number could be substantially higher. Stock option programs are not only designed for top management. Many companies offer some form of stock option or stock purchase plan to most employees. The incentive of stock options for top management exploded in the late 1980s and into the 1990s as a means of compensation.

In 2000, the typical CEO of the major 350 corporations earned $5.2 million, half of that in the value of stock options. Many believe this represents an excessive amount of stock compensation. Given these huge rewards, managers may become obsessed with short-term stock gains and their impact on their personal wealth rather than on building shareholder value for the long term. Options may become an invitation for abuse and conflict of interest. Managers can issue overly optimistic profit projections or delay spending programs, such as research and development, to inflate short-term profits. Management can use corporate cash to buy back shares, effectively raising per share earnings and share prices. Short-term spikes in share prices provide opportunities for management to unload profitable options.

A case in point is Enron. At the end of 2000, 60 percent of its employees enjoyed a bonus of some form of annual stock options, usually equal to 5 percent or more of their salary. These totaled 47 million shares, and each share had an average purchase price of $30. At the zenith of its stock price of $90, these options represented a value of $4.2 billion and a profit of $2.8 billion.

According to an article on MSNBC, "It takes a naïve view of human nature to think than many executives won't strive to maximize their personal wealth." Given the extraordinary stock gains, it would have been difficult for Enron's managers not to be preoccupied with the stock price in relationship to their options cost. As Enron's stock soared to new heights, why would anyone complain about possible accounting problems? The immense pressure to generate huge stock option gains is not exclusive to Enron.

Stock options also increase the number of shares outstanding. As with issuing secondary offerings of stock, these extra shares dilute current shareholder holdings. According to Watson Wyatt's "1999 Stock Option Overhang Study," from 1987 to 1998, dilution from stock options at large corporations increased from 5 percent of outstanding shares to 13 percent of outstanding shares. In other words, top management had gained a 13 percent ownership of American corporations through the issuance of stock options, at a fraction of the current fair market value. Many outside directors and consultants get worried if there is more than 10 percent of new stock from options outstanding, which is a greater than 10 percent dilution. In 1997, Microsoft granted 68 million additional options, bringing its total to 446 million shares covered by stock options. This represented 18 percent of all outstanding shares. Current shareholders will eventually realize a reduction in their ownership by the same percentage, without receiving compensation.

Some believe stock options result in fake profits, inflated stock prices, and a massive, unjustified transfer of wealth from current shareholders to management.

Currently, options are not accounted for on company books as an expense. Under current accounting standards, the value of stock options, even though part of a compensation package, is not considered an employee-related operating expense to the company. Warren Buffett, chairman of Berkshire Hathaway and a strong opponent of management stock options, has said: "If options aren't a form of compensation, what are they? If compensation isn't an expense, what is it? And if expenses shouldn't go into calculations of earnings, where in the world should they go?"

According to Manitou Investment Management Ltd., a private Canadian money manager, "Issuing shares for stock options is mistakenly thought to relate to the capital of the company rather than operations, for this compensation does not appear on income statements. But it should, and the fact that it is not means that profits are overstated when there are significant options granted and outstanding."

Supporters of management stock options believe, when granted, that options have no value and thus don't need to be included in operational expenses. However, when exercised, the company has two decisions: Buy the shares on the open market using corporate cash flow for the difference between the option exercise price and the market price; or issue additional new shares, which increases the shares outstanding and dilutes current shareholders' interest. Manitou and Buffett contend the true cost to the company of a stock option is the difference between the amount received by the company when the employee exercises the option and the greater amount the company would have received if it had issued the shares at the market price at the time of exercise. Manitou believes "the value received by the employee is, not surprising, equal to the cost to the company."

The cost to companies for using stock options is not chicken feed. It is rumored that one high-tech behemoth spent 75 percent of its annual operating cash flow to repurchase shares on the open market to satisfy exercised options. Management accomplished this without reducing their reported earnings per share because cash used to buy back shares is not part of earnings-per-share accounting. Buying back shares and reissuing them to satisfy exercised options will not further dilute the current value of outstanding stock. However, most investors would agree this is not a very productive use of corporate assets and cash flow.

According to Diane Francis, reporter for the *National Post*, studies show that at the height of the market peak in technology stocks, the profits of the 145 largest U.S. companies with liberal stock option policies were overstated by as much as 50 percent on average. "In 1998, Microsoft announced a profit of $4.5 billion. But, Microsoft would have incurred a loss of $1.5 billion if the cost of exercised options would have been expensed."

Current accounting rules do not require the value of exercised options to be included when calculating company income unless the options price is lower than the market price at the time of issuance. All that is required is a footnote to the annual statement, usually in the balance sheet sections, explaining the impact of options on income. In 1993, the U.S. Financial Accounting Standards Board recommended that options be expensed. However, the CEOs, CFOs, and dot.com millionaires took to the streets in what was called "The Rally in the Valley." Under extreme pressure from companies whose stock would surely plummet as reported earnings would evaporate under the weight of their true compensation costs, the Accounting Standards Board decided to require only that a footnote appear in financial statements. According to a recent study by *The Analysts Accounting Observer,* on average the companies in the S&P 500 "overstated their year 2000 profits by an average of 9 percent, and some sectors, such as information technologies, overstated their earnings by an average of 33 percent." Their study calculated Dell Computer (DEL) would have reported a loss of $0.05 a share in earnings for 1999, 2000, and 2001 combined if option costs had been expensed. For the same 3-year period, Dell reported total earnings per share of $1.93 using the current standards of accounting for stock options.

Most damaging to current shareholders are *repriced options.* This occurs when there is a substantial drop in a company's stock price and outstanding options are revised to reflect a lower cost to management. While Joe Average Investor may take a heavy hit on his investment in the company, having their worthless higher-priced stock options replaced by new options with a lower price is unduly rewarding management. While not popular with companies due to the potential for severe shareholder discontent, repricing or replacing options is not unusual. For example, according to *Washington CEO* magazine, after the stock market declines of 2000 and early 2001, 68 companies offered management the opportunity to upgrade, replace, or reprice previous options that were underwater. These companies include Sprint, Cisco

Systems, Lucent Technologies, Amazon.com, Microsoft, Critical Path, Toys "R" Us, Novell, Network Associates, and Inktomi.

In March 2002, Warren Buffett again hammered companies with liberal stock option policies. From the 2001 Berkshire Hathaway annual report: "Though Enron has become the symbol of shareholder abuse, there is no shortage of egregious conduct elsewhere in corporate America. One story I've heard illustrates the all-too-common attitude of managers toward owners: A gorgeous woman comes up to a CEO at a party, and through moist lips purrs, 'I'll do anything you want. Just tell me what you would like.' With no hesitation, he replies, "Reprice my options.' "

Warren Buffett is speaking out about the latest abuse of shareholders by management. In 1998, accounting rules were changed to discourage the use of repriced options. While actual options repricing is not as prevalent as it was prior to 1998, many companies have taken to canceling high-priced options and replacing them with lower-priced options 6 months and a day later. They choose this waiting period to avoid having to report the options as an expense, which would reduce company profits.

Sometimes, management will issue additional stock options at interesting and opportune times. In September 2001, during the stock market collapse following the World Trade Center attacks, General Electric (GE) issued additional options based on the then distressed price. The previous July, the board approved the normal annual granting of stock options at a price of $43.75 a share until 2011. In September 2001, GE issued 50 percent additional shares at an option price of $35.48. Jeffery Immelt, CEO, received an additional 800,000 shares at the lower option price.

While stock options can be a powerful tool to reward management, cash incentives based on stock performance would be a more appropriate method of management compensation. At the very least, proper accounting for the cost to current shareholders should be required.

When reviewing company financials, be sure to analyze the diluted-earnings numbers as these take into account the impact of stock option dilution. If there is a greater than 10 percent difference between basic and diluted earnings, you should investigate further the company's stock option programs. In addition, review the annual report footnotes, as they will describe current management stock option programs. The proxy statement will also provide insight into management's current holdings along with specific stock option programs. Stock options for top management can be a great motivator and will encourage managers to build shareholders' value, but their liberal use is not in the best interest of investors.

Stock Option Investigations

Some financial Web sites will list current management stock option programs by officer of the company. For example, yahoo.marketguide.com offers stock option data concerning the most recent management stock option program. The information is grouped by *exercised options* (stock actually purchased in the past year), *exercisable options* (stock that could be purchased this year) and *unexercised options* (stock that can be purchased in the future). The data are listed per officer for both number of shares and management's profit (market value less option exercise price). Table 4–6 is a recap of stock option programs by company.

Current management holdings of company stock can be found in the annual proxy statement. The proxy statement is mailed with the

TABLE 4–6 Management Stock Option Programs for Selected Companies: Shares Outstanding, Stock Options in Shares, and Management's Profit, in Millions

	Million Shares Outstanding	Exercised Options, Millions	Exercisable Options, Millions	Unexercised Options, Millions
Medicis (MRX)	30.6	0.293 ($10.431)	0.276 ($10.753)	0.397 ($13.486)
Plum Creek (PCL)	182.6	0.000 ($0.00)	0.000 ($0.00)	0.197 ($0.072)
FL Rock (FRK)	28.2	0.113 ($2.757)	0.542 ($11.432)	0.202 ($2.541)
Copart (CPRT)	90.6	0.420 ($7.200)	1.014 ($22.656)	1.169 ($6.434)
Am Capital (ACAS)	36.5	0.021 ($0.125)	1.133 ($10.742)	0.040 ($0.500)

Source: yahoo.marketguide.com.

announcement of the annual meeting. In the proxy statement is a listing of major stockholders along with stock held by management. For example, in the April 3, 2001, proxy statement by American Capital Strategies, management and directors owned 11.3 percent of the outstanding shares. The three top executives owned 8.5 percent. Management's current stock option plan dilutes shareholder interest by 3.3 percent over the life of the option contract, usually 5 to 10 years. The stock option plans listed in Table 4–6 would seem to be acceptable motivators for management.

Focus on management's long-term ability to build shareholder value at higher-than-industry rates. The real underlying asset shareholders are buying when they purchase stock in a company is the skill of management to consistently grow profits. The S&P Equity Ranking offers an easy-to-use tool to evaluate a company's ability to generate consistent profit growth. As profits increase, share price increases usually follow. The company should have a clear focus on the importance of shareholders and of building shareholder value. Stock options have been successfully used as an effective management personnel compensation tool. However, excessive management stock options can dilute shareholders' interests and may be very self-serving.

Finding great management is only one element in determining if you should invest in a company. Stock value and the share price have as much impact on overall returns as the quality of management.

Uncovering Value in Overlooked Stocks

To buy when others are despondently
selling and to sell when others are avidly
buying requires the greatest fortitude and
pays the greatest potential reward.

—SIR JOHN TEMPLETON

xcellent management is important, but it is not a guarantee that a company's stock will prove profitable. Buying any stock, even that of the best-managed companies, when it is hugely overpriced is still a sure formula for poor stock returns. There are several tools that help in comparing the value of current stock prices: the PE ratio, the PEG ratio, cash flow per share, and share-price-to-sales ratio.

Some investors like to "go against the grain" or the current conventional wisdom, and are called *contrarians*. Sir John Templeton, founder of the very successful Templeton family of mutual funds, eloquently describes a contrarian in his quote at the top of this page. When the huge mutual funds and money managers are selling or buying, contrarians may be doing the opposite. Contrarian investing can be lucrative when it is combined with a value evaluation. Some individuals invest as if they were hitting a piñata while they were blindfolded, without giving much thought to the value of price being paid. Was that stock really worth $40 a share? If an investor can't answer that question, he or she may have a difficult time maximizing his or her investments. All investors need to understand the value of the company stock they are buying. And when a stock selection is a good choice, investors shouldn't let greed prevent them from taking profits.

Finding Value

In a rising market, studies have shown, random stock selection may be lucrative for extremely short amounts of time. However, the success stories of random investing should be viewed as entertaining and nothing more. My favorite is the story of the MonkeyDex. On January 1, 1999, Raven Thorogood III started a stock market index. In the first 6 months, it was up by 55 percent. At the end of the first year, Thorogood III's stocks were up by 213 percent. The portfolio ranked as the twenty-second best in the United States, outperforming 6000 pros and money managers.

Raven Thorogood III, however, was a 5-year-old chimpanzee and a star in the 1998 movie *Babe, Pig in the City*. Roland Perry, editor of the *Internet Stock Review*, hired Raven to throw darts at a list of publicly traded Internet companies. Raven threw between 30 and 40 darts at 133 names, and 10 stuck. This was the birth of the 10-component Internet stock index called the MonkeyDex Index. As of the writing of this book, there is no further information on the Internet concerning the multiyear performance of the MonkeyDex Index. The Web site for monkeydex.com has crashed and burned, probably much like the stocks chosen by Thorogood III's well-trained throwing arm.

The goal of stock price analysis is to determine current and potential value. Some investors use *momentum investing*, a method by which only technical charts and stock trading volumes strictly determine stock value. The value of a stock, according to momentum investors, lies in historic price movements. Other investors use a hypergrowth, subindustry style of investing. These individuals focus on, for example, growing markets of the biotechnology industry, the hand-held computer industry, or the Internet. The value of stocks to these investors is based on the hopes and dreams of the company researchers to develop new products and services that will drive up profits and stock prices.

I use a more commonsense approach. Since future earnings are the primary engines to higher stock prices, I focus on stock prices in relation to current earnings, future earnings, and cash flow.

The Price-to-Earnings Ratio

Every stock has a *price-to-earnings* (PE) *ratio*. This number is used widely by investors to compare the value of the market price to the company's current earnings. The formula for the ratio is the stock price divided by the earnings per share. In principle, the ratio is a numerical indicator of how much investors are willing to pay for each dollar of earnings. A stock that trades with a PE of 5 means that investors are willing to pay $5 for every $1 of earnings. A PE of 40 means that investors are willing to pay $40 for each $1 of earnings. High PE ratios usually mean that there are high future earnings expectations by investors. The reverse can be said for low PE stocks—that is, that low PE ratios mean that investors may have lower expectations for earnings growth.

$$\text{PE Ratio} = \frac{\text{Stock Price}}{\text{Net Earnings per Share}}$$

For example, Waddell & Reed Financial (WDR) is one of the oldest U.S. mutual fund complexes. The company was founded in 1937, and it sells investment products primarily to middle-income Americans. Waddell & Reed is a mid-cap stock with 80.027 million shares outstanding and a market cap of $2.408 billion. As of June 30, 2001, Waddell & Reed had $33.9 billion of assets under management, with $28.7 billion of mutual fund assets and $5.2 billion of managed institutional and private accounts. The company distributes funds and other financial products through a network of 2865 financial advisors operating from over 400 offices. The company believes that its financial advisor sales force was, as of year-end 2000, one of the largest in the United States. At the end of 2000, Waddell & Reed had more than 712,000 mutual fund and variable-account customers with an average investment of $45,000. Management efficiency, revenues, and earnings information are as shown in Table 5–1.

Waddell & Reed's stock trades at $30 a share. In 2001, the company posted $1.28 a share in earnings. The recession and stock market decline of 2001 negatively impacted the company's revenues and earnings. WRD's current PE ratio is 23.4 ($30 divided by $1.28). Current buyers of Waddell & Reed's stock are willing to pay $23.40 for every $1.00 the company earns. If you compare the current PE to the previous year-end ratios, WRD is trading in line with its history.

How is one to know if a PE ratio represents good value? High PE ratios usually carry higher risks because the stock has far to fall if earnings expectations are not met. A low PE ratio may mean lower risk, but

TABLE 5-1   Management Efficiency Ratio, 5-Year Revenue, EPS, Year-End Price, and PE Ratio for Waddell & Reed Financial

	Waddell & Reed	Industry Average
5-yr revenue growth	23.1	20.3
5-yr earnings growth	23.5	21.9
5-yr return on assets	22.9	4.9
5-yr return on investments	35.7	12.9
5-yr return on equity	55.4	27.5
5-yr operating profit margin	45.1	17.7
5-yr PE range	14–31	11–27

	1997	1998	1999	2000	2001
Revenues	$242 mil	$287 mil	$357 mil	$521 mil	$482 mil
EPS	$0.73	$0.85	$0.89	$1.60	$1.28
Year-end price	$15	$18	$37	$32	$30
Year-end PE ratio	20.5	21.1	41.5	20.0	23.4

Source: Marketguide.com.

the company may not have sustainable earnings growth. The current PE ratio should be at the lower end of the range. Low PE ratios may indicate subdued current investor interest and a value-priced stock.

The PEG Ratio

The *PEG ratio* compares the current stock price to the current earnings and the anticipated earnings growth rate. Many believe that each dollar of corporate earnings is worth between 1 and 1.5 times the earnings growth rate. For example, a company with $1 of earnings, growing at 15 percent a year, could have a stock price of between $15 and $22 a share. A stock that trades at one-half the earnings growth rate is considered undervalued, and a stock that trades at twice its earnings growth rate is considered expensive. Investors may examine stocks that trade below a PEG ratio of 0.5 for possible purchase and above 2.0 for possible sale.

$$\text{PEG Ratio} = \frac{\text{Current PE}}{\text{Percentage Earnings Growth Rate}}$$

Anticipated earnings growth estimates are available from Value Line and S&P Stock Guides at the local library or from financial Web sites, such as aaii.com or zacks.com. The validity of the PEG ratio is somewhat questionable due to the ratio's reliance on analysts' guesstimates of future earnings calculations. When using an online source, I recommend using consensus estimates of at least 7 to 10 brokers to establish an average earnings growth rate prediction. The chances of 10 different analysts being wrong are much less than the chances of just 1 or 2. The larger the number of analysts that cover a stock, hopefully, the more accurate is the average consensus.

The PEG ratio allows for an easy comparison between stock value and earnings growth rate. For example, as shown in Table 5–2, Company A's stock has a $30 per share price, it earns $2.25 per share, it has a PE of 13, and its earnings are expanding at 12 percent a year. Company B's stock is also trading at $30 per share, it earns $1.12 per share, it has a PE of 26, and it is growing at 25 percent a year. Which is a better value, and is a $30 share price a good value for either? The PEG ratio of Company A would be 1.08, or ($30/$2.25)/12. Company B would have a PEG ratio of 1.04, just a bit less than that of Company A. Both stocks would be trading at a PEG of around 1.0, and their stock could be considered reasonably priced.

According to Zacks.com, Waddell & Reed is expected to grow earnings at 15 percent a year over the next 5 years. With a current stock price of $30 and earnings of $1.28, the current PE is 23.4, and the current PEG ratio is 1.56. Waddell & Reed could be considered at the top end of a buy range.

Benjamin Graham, Warren Buffett's mentor, once said, "Rake the market for value." There is a danger of overpaying on the basis of antic-

TABLE 5-2   Example of PEG Ratio

	Stock Price	EPS	PE	EPS Growth Rate	PEG Ratio
Company A	$30	$2.25	13	12%	1.08
Company B	$30	$1.12	26	25%	1.04

ipated future earnings, even if all other analyses seems to be in place. The PEG ratio will assist you in evaluating value.

Using the S&P Equity Ranking along with fundamental research should help you acquire a decent understanding of management's ability to actually deliver on higher profits. Companies that have high rankings of B+ probably have an average chance of continuing to grow their earnings. A company rated A+ or A by S&P's Equity Ranking for consistency in earnings and dividend growth should have a higher probability future earnings growth. Keep in mind a company may be listed as NR, or not ranked. This is not a negative rating but rather no rating. For example, management may have exceeded 5-year industry averages in return of capital, revenue growth and gross profit margins, but lack the required 10-year trading history. S&P would rate this stock as NR.

Next Year's PEG

Investing should be a long-term proposition. As a shareholder, I am more concerned with the next 3 years' earnings than I am about the next two quarters' earnings. Short-term investors may be worried about the next 6 months, but I may highlight the outlook for the next 60 months. Because I focus on long-term earnings, I also review the PEG ratio using estimates for the next year or two. This is called the *forward PEG ratio*. Many financial Web sites offer earnings estimates for the next year along with forecasts for the current year. Like the long-term earnings growth rate, these are estimates from multiple brokers, or investment services firms. Multexinvestor.com, Zacks.com, Value Line, and S&P stock reports offer earnings estimates.

For example, Waddell & Reed is anticipated to earn $1.54 in 2002 and $1.79 in 2003. Calculating the forward PEG ratio, Waddell & Reed at $30 a share would be at a 2002 PEG of 1.39 and at a 2003 PEG of 1.22. I prefer to look forward one year to calculate the PEG ratio, and I would evaluate Waddell & Reed's stock price as having a forward PEG of 1.22. The current PEG ratio is 1.56, which indicates that the price is a bit high. Looking forward to 2003, however, Waddell & Reed's stock price is trading at about its long-term growth rate, and it could be considered as reasonably priced at a forward PEG ratio of 1.22.

PEG Ratios in Action

Table 5–3 gives the 2001, 2002, and 2003 PEG ratios for selected companies. Continue to think of the goal to "rake the market for value." Coparts, Barra, and Illinois Tool Works are the only overlooked stocks that are trading at less than the threshold of 1.50 for a 2001 PEG. Out of the 10 stocks, however, 6 have a 2003 PEG ratio of 1.50 or less. The 4 that trade higher than a forward PEG ratio of 1.50 are Hudson United, McCormick, Cinergy, and Enterprise Products. These four companies would need to come down in stock price, increase earnings growth estimates, or increase earnings estimates for the PEG ratio to drop to a value buy range. Florida Rock and Medicis could be considered overpriced based on 2001 PEG calculations, but they fall into a buy range when the 2003 PEG ratio is considered. Based on 2003 PEG ratios, the following stocks offer the best value: Barra Software, Illinois Tool Works, Copart, and Waddell & Reed.

Small- and mid-cap companies have the potential to achieve above-average earnings growth. There is usually a premium investors are willing to pay for higher profit growth. Many overlooked stocks will

TABLE 5-3   PEG Ratios for Selected Companies, as of February 2002

	Stock Price	EPS Growth, %	2001 EPS	2002 EPS, Anticipated	2003 EPS, Anticipated	2001 PEG	2002 PEG, Anticipated	2003 PEG, Anticipated
Copart	$20	26	$0.51	$0.63	$0.79	1.51	1.22	0.97
Medicis	$57	23	$1.28	$1.94	$2.26	1.94	1.26	1.10
Ill. Tool Works	$63	16	$2.62	$3.09	$3.58	1.50	1.27	1.10
Hudson United	$30	7	$2.00	$2.25	$2.40	2.14	1.90	1.79
Barra Software	$52	20	$2.04	$1.84	$2.24	1.27	1.41	1.16
Florida Rock	$40	12	$1.96	$2.22	$2.64	1.70	1.43	1.26
McCormick	$48	10	$2.20	$2.49	$2.78	2.18	1.93	1.73
Cinergy	$31	6	$2.75	$2.83	$2.96	1.88	1.83	1.75
Enterprise Products	$50	10	$2.67	$2.63	$2.65	1.87	1.90	1.89
Waddell & Reed	$30	14	$1.35	$1.54	$1.76	1.59	1.39	1.22

Source: Zacks.com.

have a higher PEG ratio than their much larger and more stable large-cap competitors. Some investors purchase larger-cap stocks at a PEG of 1.00 or less. Due to lower potential earnings growth over the long term for more mature companies, investors may consider a lower PEG ratio threshold. External business forces may cause a company to miss expectations for a quarter or two. Short-term thinkers will sell the stock, driving down the price. Long-term thinkers who are familiar with the company may realize this as a buying opportunity.

The PEG ratio is not a static number. It changes with stock price movements and actual earnings. Investors should review the PEG ratio calculations on a regular basis. A drop in stock price accompanied by a reduction in earnings may not be such a great buying opportunity. A value-astute investor can use the PEG ratio to his or her advantage.

Most important, the PEG ratio calculation gives you a benchmark you can use to judge the performance of your companies over time. To properly calculate PEG ratios, you have to research specific earnings estimates for future years and anticipated profit growth rates. If management fails to meet your expectations, you should know why. What steps is management taking to correct the situation? After answering these questions, you may consider selling the stock, or even buying more shares. Recognition of business problems and remedial strategies should be communicated through the quarterly and annual reports sent directly to every shareholder.

For example, if Florida Rock fails to meet the 2003 projected $2.64 earnings with 12 percent growth rate, you should review the reasons. Keep a record of estimates for all your stocks versus what the company actually earned. If earnings estimates are increasing, and the company is meeting these higher expectations, higher stock prices should follow. If earnings estimates are falling, and the company fails to meet these reduced expectations, you should find out why. Review how this company is performing against your expectations and evaluate if it still fits your management and value criteria.

To Pro Forma or Not to Pro Forma—
That Is the Question

According to the *American College Dictionary* given to me by my brother for Christmas 1968, the definition of *pro forma* is "according to form; as a matter of form." The term *form* implies that there are to be rules to follow. In the world of earnings accounting, *pro forma* means something very different. There is no *form* in pro forma accounting practices. *Pro forma accounting* is accounting without rules. Companies publish pro forma earnings by including or excluding whatever they feel is in their best interest.

Every quarter, companies have to report their earnings to the Securities and Exchange Commission. These reports, 10Q (quarterly) and 10K (annual), must follow *generally accepted accounting principles* (GAAP) and are subject to audit. Pro forma earnings are different from earnings calculated with GAAP.

Pro forma earnings are profits published by management that may not include some one-time expenses or may be increased by investment gains. Pro forma earnings can be used to show the profitability of the company without one-time events. As single occurrences, these usually negative financial setbacks should not be repeated and should not be of concern to investors. Sometimes pro forma earnings may exclude merger expenses, restructuring expense to close old factories and lay off workers, write-downs of obsolete inventory, or decreases in investments.

For example, Shire Pharmaceuticals (SHPGY) filed a 10K report stating $0.23 per share earnings for 2001, down from $0.78 in 2000. The 10K was completed according to GAAP. However, the GAAP earnings included $177 million in charges and expenses related to the acquisition of BioChem Pharma, a Canadian drug company. On a pro forma basis, SHPGY would have earned around $1.31 a share, excluding these one-time charges. An investor in SHPGY could think the company was still expanding profits at an acceptable rate and the acquisition of BioChem would be profitable in the long term. In this case, using a pro forma earnings report could be useful.

Some companies, however, have been known to abuse the use of pro forma earnings reporting. In the late 1990s, paper gains on stock investments were a favorite way to inflate pro forma earnings. Companies would report pro forma earnings excluding whatever management could categorize as one-time expenses. Outgoing SEC Chief Economist Lynn Turner says pro forma earnings are really "EBS earnings—Everything but the Bad Stuff." Pro forma earnings are kind of like taking a test and deleting some answers you got wrong before you determine the final score.

According to John May, editor of the online newsletter *SmartStock-Investor.com,* for the first three quarters of 2001, the 100 companies that compose the Nasdaq 100 Index reported pro forma earnings of $19.1 billion to their investors. However, these same companies reported GAAP earnings to the SEC of a loss of –$82.3 billion. That is a $101 billion difference. Microsoft, Intel, Cisco Systems, Oracle, and Dell combined reported $13.9 billion of profits to shareholders while reporting just $4.4 billion to the SEC. More than two thirds of the pro forma profits reported to investors were from adjustments made to GAAP accounting rules.

One of the oddest pro forma earnings is called *earnings before interest payments and income taxes* (EBITA). EBITA is used by many small companies or companies with heavy debt. Since interest on debt is a business expense and everyone owes taxes, I don't understand the investment value of computing profits without those costs. The EBITA figure, however, is commonly used when evaluating real estate investment trusts (REITs), and it will be discussed in a later chapter. For non-REITs, reporting earnings on an EBITA basis should be ignored.

Whenever you read about pro forma earnings, make sure you know what sleight of accounting hand the management may be offering you. Are these alterations to the profits reported to the SEC legitimate? Do they make sense to you, the shareholder? Does the company have a history of presenting annual one-time charges? Unless the SEC tightens control of pro forma reporting practices, they will be around for a while. Investors should get used to their potentially confusing nature.

Cash Flow per Share

Cash flow per share is the amount of cash per share generated by the company. Most investors should review stock value to cash flow, in addition to reported earnings. Investors who read cash flow statements on a regular basis realize their importance in stock price evaluation. It is far easier to issue favorable pro forma earnings statements than it is to issue audited year-end cash flow statements. Many times, a dramatic fall in the fortunes of a company is foretold by a severe drop in operating cash flow. For instance, Lucent Technologies (LU) reported an operating cash flow loss of $1.5 billion long before Lucent investors experienced a drop in the stock price from $50 to $5.

Cash flow information is available from financial Web sites and at your local library. Audited cash flow information is outlined in every annual report. As discussed earlier, there are several components to cash flow:

- *Cash flow from operations*: Cash generated by operating the business. Net income plus depreciation, amortization, and other non-cash adjustments.

- *Cash flow from investing*: Cash generated from investments and payment for capital improvements.

- *Cash flow from financing*: Cash generated by the sale of stock or issuance of notes and payments to repay previous notes and to buy back stock.

- *Free cash flow*: Operating cash flow minus funds used for capital expenditures.

Make sure you know which category of cash flow is being used for the calculations. Operating cash flow and free cash flow do not include funds generated by adding debt or selling stocks.

Investors should look for companies with price-to-cash-flow ratios below industry averages. This indicates that the stock is trading below the rate of its competitors and may represent good investment value. Table 5–4 lists the stock-price-to-cash-flow ratio for selected stocks, along with industry averages in parenthesis.

TABLE 5–4 Stock Price to Cash Flow for Selected Companies, Industry Averages in Parentheses, as of February 2002

	Waddell & Reed	Barra Software	Medicis
Price-to-operating-cash-flow ratio trailing 12 months	19 (14)	25 (39)	30 (41)
Price-to-free-cash-flow ratio, trailing 12 months	22 (12)	18 (24)	32 (41)

Source: marketguide.com.

Cash-flow-per-share analysis can be a powerful tool when reviewed along with cash flow growth rates. The value stocks are those whose price to cash flow is below the industry averages and whose average cash flow growth is above the industry average.

The Share-Price-to-Sales Ratio

The *share-price-to-sales ratio* is another stock value indicator. The ratio was popularized by James O'Shaughnessy in his book *What Works on Wall Street*. This ratio is the same as the market-capitalization-to-revenues ratio. Comparing share-price-to-sales ratios helps identify companies whose current market price represents good value, based on a low price-to-revenue ratio. Some investors believe this ratio is as important as the PE. Price-to-sales ratios are useful in identifying strong companies that may be experiencing temporary earnings difficulties. The PE ratios for such companies may make their stock prices look expensive. Price-to-sales ratios will vary based on the industry analyzed. Industries with low revenue growth, low earnings growth, and low profit margins typically have lower price-to-sales ratios. Industries with high earnings growth and margins will have higher ratios. The formula is the market capitalization divided by the total revenues.

$$\text{Share-Price-to-Sales Ratio} = \frac{\text{Market Cap}}{\text{Total Revenues}}$$

For example, Cascade Natural Gas (CGC), a natural gas distributing company in Washington, has a market capitalization of $219 million and revenues of $335 million. The price-to-sale ratio is 0.65. Kennametal, an industrial supplier, has a market capitalization of $1.2 billion and revenues of $1.8 billion, for a price-to-sales ratio of 0.66. As a rule of thumb, stocks that are traded at a price-to-sales ratio of 10 or greater may be considered very expensive. Small- and mid-cap stocks trading at a price-to-sales ratio of 1.5 may be considered to be fairly valued and those trading at below 1.0 undervalued. Some high revenue growth industries, such as technology, typically have a higher price-to-sales ratio than lower revenue growth industries, such as utilities. The price-to-sales ratio for a specific stock should be at or below industry averages. Listed in Table 5–5 are the share-price-to-sales ratios for selected stocks.

TABLE 5-5 Price-to-Sales Ratio for Selected
Stocks, Industry Averages in Parentheses,
as of February 2002

Company	Price-to-Sales Ratio
Illinois Tool Works	2.50 (1.59)
Florida Rock	1.59 (1.27)
McCormick	1.44 (1.57)
Plum Creek Timber	4.19 (3.98)
Seacoast Financial Services	2.13 (2.31)
Chicago Bridge & Iron	0.57 (0.73)

Contrarian Investing

Contrarian investors are the ones buying when everyone else is selling
and selling when everyone else is buying. They are the investors who
buy the most undervalued stock while selling the most overvalued
stock. Excessive media hype, reflex reaction by other investors, and a
temporary pause in earnings growth may create contrarian investment
opportunities.

No stock trades in a vacuum. There are thousands of companies
listed in various small- and mid-cap stock indexes. Some receive more
investor attention than others. Those that are consistently in the media
and are receiving lots of attention may trade at a premium. Overlooked
stock may lack media attention and investor hype. Due to a lower profile in the public, overlooked stocks may offer better value and higher
potential returns than more popular stocks. As companies consistently
increase profits and shareholder value, however, more investors may
pay attention to them. Identifying overlooked stocks takes a certain
amount of research.

In addition to seeking companies that are lesser known, many
investors will review out-of-favor sectors for value stocks. Most tech

sector stocks today could be considered very much out of favor. In the late 1990s, businesses could not spend their information technology budgets fast enough. Expenditures included Internet presence, digital video conference capabilities, broadband access, or faster and more efficient PCs. Information technology stocks were booming as a result of high information technology spending by businesses. High tech's gravy train came to an abrupt halt in 2000 and 2001. Orders dried up and projects were canceled. Information technology stocks crumbled. Many stocks lost 50 percent or more of their value. In 2002, these same stocks are still lacking investor interest as business remains sluggish. Business capital spending for information technology may not be strong until late 2003 or early 2004. Cyclical and industrial stocks will likely lead the economic recovery of 2002 and 2003. With several more quarters of weak profits ahead, many tech companies are trading at good long-term value. Knowing a turnaround is not for a while, value investors with a buy-and-hold philosophy are starting to nibble at selected tech stocks. These investors believe that the worst is over for the "tech wreck," and they are building a base for future capital gains when tech stocks once again become popular.

There are stock market situations that I call *standard reflex stock movements*. Standard reflex stock movements present potentially powerful contrarian opportunities that investors should be aware of. These stock price fluctuations can often be anticipated for companies whose stock price has been historically low. These companies may be excellent candidates for future capital gains. Many times, a low stock price is more directly related to external marketplace forces than to internal structural change in company profitability. The three most obvious standard reflex stock movement opportunities are when interest rates are close to a cyclical peak, when earnings are in a temporary decline, and when commodity market prices are abnormally low. Usually, stocks that are affected by these factors trade at unusually low prices, which means that they may offer unusually high capital gains potential. More often than not, the investor's standard reflex reaction to bad news is to sell, and this added selling pressure may create undervalued stock pricing. As the bad news subsides, the stock price should rally to a fairly valued price, creating a capital gain.

One of the most powerful reflex stock movements is in the yield-sensitive utility stocks and bonds, whose prices will move opposite to trends in interest rate changes. A stock's *yield* is the percentage return of the annual income based on the stock's price. For example, a $10 stock paying a $0.80 annual dividend yields 8 percent. As mainly income- and yield-driven investments, utility stocks are very sensitive to changes the Federal Reserve Board makes in interest rates. When the fed raises interest rates, utility stock prices usually fall. When the fed is cutting interest rates, utility stocks tend to rally. While interest rate changes don't happen often, when they do they have an impact on stock prices.

For example, in 2000, the fed aggressively raised rates to counter an overheated economy and stock market. Utility stocks faltered, and many sank to 10-year lows as interest rates peaked in the summer and fall of 2000. Investors turned away from utility investments, and their stock prices fell to undervalued levels. Accomplishing their goal, the fed gradually reduced rates, reaching a 40-year low in the winter of 2001. Many utility stocks rose with each additional rate cut announcement. After a year of cutting rates, many utilities regained all their lost ground. Some have strengthened to multiple-year highs. For astute and contrarian investors, buying utility stocks in the fall of 1999 and into the spring of 2000 would have seemed natural.

Companies like Hawaiian Electric (HE) were trading at sizable discounts. Hawaiian Electric has a 5-year average yield of 6.8 percent. Based on its $2.48 annual dividend per share, the stock has had an average price over the past 5 years of $36.50. In November 1999 and March 2000, in reaction to rising rates, Hawaiian Electric's stock price sank to $28, and its dividend yield shot up to 8.8 percent. Contrarian investors who bought HE's stock at $28 would realize $880 annual dividend income for every $10,000 invested. The stock price rallied as interest rates fell in 2001. By March 2002, Hawaiian Electric's stock was trading close to its 10-year high of $44. The contrarian investor who bought HE at $28 would have realized a capital gain of 57 percent in addition to the 8.8 percent annual dividend yield on the original investment.

Did the contrarian know Hawaiian Electric's stock price would return an average of 37.3 percent a year (28.5 percent capital gain and 8.8 percent income) for the first 2 years of ownership? Probably not. The contrarian did know that interest rate increases are always reversed. The contrarian also realized that well-managed, interest-rate-sensitive companies trading at 10-year lows are worth investigating.

The second standard reflex stock movement is the usual rebound of stock prices after a temporary battle with earnings problems. If management has proven their ability to consistently grow earnings over time, they probably have the ability to correct temporary problems. When a company is affected by negative external events and the stock price subsequently falls, management should respond decisively. If management does so, the company's stock price should rebound. These momentary lapses in profitability can affect almost any company. Contrarian investors don't flee like fickle professional money managers, but rather, they see the buying opportunity these situations create.

Omnicare (OCR) is the largest distributor of pharmaceuticals to nursing homes and assisted-living facilities. Well into the 1990s, Omnicare was growing at a rate of 20 percent or more a year, and its management was buying strategic smaller competitors to expand its business. Its stock rose from $5 in 1992 to $40 in 1998. Earnings reached a peak in 1998 at $1.30 a share. Then Medicare downwardly adjusted reimbursements to long-term-care facilities. Omnicare's profits fell to $0.72 in 1999 as a result of its lower income from Medicare business. In response, management consolidated branches, canceled contracts that were unprofitable, and realigned their business focus toward other corporate strengths. For example, OCR has a unique focus on and access to geriatric medical information, and it offers its expertise to geriatric drug manufacturers for research. Many elderly people take several medications prescribed by different doctors simultaneously. Sometimes these drugs interact with each other to cause negative side effects in the elderly patient. Omnicare publishes the most extensive annual report on drug interactions, a serious problem for the elderly. Omnicare's stock price had plummeted to under $10 a share in late 1999. Then Medicare rescinded some of its payment cuts in 1999. The result of the increased Medicare revenues, along with its success in other fields, has turned its earnings growth upward once again. In 2001, Omnicare earned $0.92 per share, and its operating cash flow hit a record $183 million. Free cash flow increased by 38 percent in 2001. The stock price rebounded to $25. While still off its all-time high of $44, Omnicare is back on track for continued growth. Investors who realized that the stock was undervalued at a price below $12 a share have been handsomely rewarded. Momentary pauses in earnings growth for well-managed companies like Omnicare may provide capital gain opportunities for contrarian investors.

The third reflex stock movement occurs when stock prices are low due to abnormally low commodity prices. Many companies depend on market forces to price their products. Examples are oil, timber, and gold. Companies in these industries have less control over their revenues and profitability. Commodity pricing in general sees trends of oversupply and low prices followed by tighter supply and higher prices. When commodity prices fall to 10-year lows, investors should look for bargains in these industries. Just by its nature, most commodities should trade somewhere around their 3- to 5-year averages. A commodity that is trading at either end of a 10-year trend may be a good candidate for review for either a purchase or a sale.

For example, in late 1998, oil prices dropped to 10-year lows, and the price was below $12 a barrel. Contrarian investors saw this as a buying opportunity. Over the long term, the price of oil had been averaging around $23 to $27 a barrel. But in late 1998 oil stocks, such as Apache Corp. (APA), a mid-size oil exploration company, were trading at multiple-year lows. For several months, investors could have bought Apache stock at under $25 a share. APA fell to a multiple-year low of $18 as earnings fell. In 1998, Apache lost $1.44 a share. Cash flow from operations was $471 million, down from $638 million the previous year. The situation changed, however. The price of oil rebounded to over $30 a barrel in 2001; Apache's earnings improved as well. In 2000, earnings reached $5.58 a share, and the stock price reached a high of $70. Cash flow rose substantially and exceeded $1.5 billion. In 2002, oil prices again backed off, to the mid-$20s, and so did APA's stock price retreating to $50 a share. Oil stocks have amply rewarded patient investors who realized the buying opportunity in 1998.

Sometimes there are several contrarian forces at work at the same time. In 2000, interest rates were rising, and prices of interest-sensitive stocks were falling. Lumber prices were also at 10-year lows. Plum Creek Timber (PCL) is a company that has historically paid a high dividend yield. Both low commodity prices and high interest rates were hammering Plum Creek Timber's revenue, earnings, and stock price. PCL's stock price fell to $24 a share, well below its average price of around $32. With a dividend of $2.28, Plum Creek Timber yielded 9.5 percent. In 2002, interest rates lowered, and lumber prices rose. Plum Creek Timber's stock price rebounded to $32, and the stock is now yielding a more normal 7.4 percent. Astute investors who were focused on overlooked stocks and contrarian opportunities could have purchased PCL stock at its low. After just 2 years, PCL investors could have realized a capital gain of 45 percent in addition to a return of 19 percent from the dividend. Investors buying PCL at the low could have realized an average annual return of 32 percent during the first 2 years that they owned the stock.

Value Investing with a Diversified Portfolio of Overlooked Stocks

One advantage of having a well-diversified portfolio is that over time an investor begins to have a thorough knowledge about the companies represented in the portfolio. When asked how her portfolio was doing, a neighbor of mine replied, "Overall, pretty well. I have some stocks whose prices have dropped since I bought them, but that is OK. For therein lies the value selection for my next investment." When evaluating a portfolio for value, some obvious choices will appear. The advantage of owning 15 stocks is that, at any given time, a few of them will offer better value than others. Table 5–6 is an example of a value calculation for diversified portfolio of overlooked small- and mid-cap stocks.

Based on the portfolio in Table 5–6, the following stocks are trading at or below their long-term earnings growth rate, and their price-to-sales ratio is less than the industry average: Scotts, Toro, Omnicare, Shire Pharmaceuticals, Chicago Bridge, and Kennametal. These could be good candidates for additional investment funds. Over time, investors will develop a better understanding of a particular company's direction, and they will usually feel more confident in its management. The longer a company is in a portfolio, the more the investor should know about its business operations. This knowledge will assist him or her in better identifying contrarian and standard reflex stock movement opportunities for that company.

For instance, I was reviewing the low stock prices of utility companies during the peak in interest rates in 1999 and 2000. As a current

TABLE 5-6 Next-Year PEG Ratio and Price-to-Sales Ratio for Selected Stocks, Industry Averages in Parentheses, as of March 2002

	Sector	Price	Next-Year PEG Ratio	Price-to-Sales Ratio
Apache (APA)	Energy	$51	1.56	2.52 (1.46)
Scotts (SMG)	Materials	$45	0.79	0.76 (1.69)
Philadelphia Suburban (PSC)	Utilities	$23	3.57	5.18 (3.31)
Progress Energy (PGN)	Utilities	$44	1.46	1.09 (3.77)
Hormel (HRL)	Consumer staples	$26	1.50	0.89 (1.57)
Clayton Homes (CMH)	Consumer discretionary	$14	0.97	1.72 (0.73)
Toro (TTC)	Consumer discretionary	$52	0.86	0.50 (1.59)
Seacoast Financial (SCFS)	Financial	$18	1.39	2.13 (2.31)
Investors Financial (IFIN)	Financial	$66	0.98	8.70 (2.26)
Pitney Bowes (PBI)	Information tech	$38	1.33	2.28 (1.35)
Omnicare (OCR)	Health care	$22	0.87	0.96 (1.23)
Shire Pharm (SHPGY)	Health care	$21	0.63	2.19 (13.18)
Chicago Bridge (CBI)	Industrials	$27	0.90	0.57 (0.73)
Kennametal (KMT)	Industrials	$37	0.88	0.69 (0.83)
CenturyTel (CTL)	Telecommunications	$32	1.26	2.19 (2.03)

shareholder in Hawaiian Electric (HE) and Progress Energy (PGN), I was very familiar with their management, and I believed their stock prices were undervalued. Thus the decision to add more of those stocks to my current holdings was fairly simple to make because I was already familiar with management's long-term performance.

"You Will Never Go Broke Taking a Profit"

Grandfather Fisher used to tell me this when we discussed investing: If you do your investing homework correctly and choose companies with excellent management whose stocks are selling at reasonable prices, your portfolio should experience periodical capital gains. This is a good thing, maybe.

We invest for only one reason: to make money. When we are successful, our greed and ego may take over and possibly cloud our better judgment. It is easy to think that a stock that has doubled in price is well on its way to quadrupling. So, rather than being prudent and selling a few shares for a profit, we, like too many investors, hang on to it.

When I am successful and a stock's price rises quickly, or even doubles, I begin to look at lightening up by selling a portion of my holdings. For example, in a portfolio worth $75,000, I might have purchased in October 2000, 300 shares of Plum Creek Timber at $22, costing $6600. The Plum Creek Timber stock price rose to $30 by February 2002, and my 300 shares were then worth $9000. Assuming the value of all other investments stayed the same, Plum Creek Timber then represented 11 percent of my portfolio. By selling 100 shares, I had $3000 in capital gains and profits that I could invest elsewhere. After paying stockbroker commissions (and 20 percent capital gains tax if I had been holding the stocks outside a tax-deferred account) I would have had about $2790 net to diversify the portfolio. My remaining 200 shares would be worth $6000. Sometimes we hit a home run.

Buyers of Apache stock at below $25 in late 1998 could have sold it at a price as high as $70 a few years later. If an investor had bought 200 shares of Apache at $25, his or her $5000 investment would have been worth over $14,000. By selling 50 shares at $50 and using the profit to further diversify his or her portfolio, the investor would own 150 shares of APA worth $10,500 and $2190 of something else. When oil prices slid in 2002, Apache's stock drifted back to $50.

There is nothing wrong with taking a profit. Although there may be tax implications, the advantages of using the profit to further diversify a portfolio outweigh the pain of paying added taxes. In fact, tax concerns are mitigated if the stock is held in an IRA account. Sometimes a portfolio becomes heavy in one sector because of outstanding performance. This happened in the information technology sector in the late 1990s.

For example, I bought $7000 of Motorola (MOT), a high-tech stock, in 1989 at a split-adjusted price of $7 a share. Over the course of the years, the stock split several more times, so that I then had 1000 shares. In April 1994, I sold one third of my position, or 300 shares, at $15 a share. The profit I made went to buy stock in other economic sectors. In September 1999, I sold another 200 shares at $30, and in January 2000, I sold another 250 shares at $50 a share. When Motorola hit a high of $55 a share, I had 250 shares remaining worth $13,500, and I had sold 750 shares at a profit of $23,000, which I reinvested. My $7000 investment in 1989 had grown to $36,500 by early 2000. Had I kept all 1000 shares, it would have had a value of $55,000.

However, Motorola stock crashed along with many other stocks in the tech wreck in 2000. The price of Motorola stock declined to $14 a share, and my original 1000 shares would have been worth $14,000. By taking profits when I did, I protected myself against the drop in Motorola's stock price. My 250 shares are currently worth $3500, and the $23,000 that I earned when I sold the other original 750 stocks I have invested elsewhere. Did I know that Motorola stock would rise to $55? No, but if I had known, I would have kept all 1000 shares and sold the entire lot at $55. Did I know the stock would tank from $55 to $14? No, but if I had, I would not have kept any shares. What I did know was that it was prudent to take periodical profits as Motorola was outperforming my expectations.

Motorola may be an extreme case, but it provides a useful lesson just the same. In 1999 and 2000, many investors found their portfolios to be heavy in high-tech stocks. As tech sector stocks became the hot area for investors, the percentage of their portfolios invested in the tech sector rose. Some portfolios were 45 percent or more invested in information technologies. These portfolios may have done well for a short time, but investors were exposed to a high risk. When the tech wreck occurred, these overweighted portfolios took the brunt of the decline. Some may have avoided these losses had they taken profits periodically.

When investors find companies with top-quality management and relatively low stock prices—that is, overlooked companies—investing in those companies can return exceptional long-term rewards. The PEG ratio and its variables are excellent tools in evaluating current stock prices and potential future earnings.

As an investor, you should focus on reported earnings, including one-time adjustments, when you evaluate stock price value. If the company occasionally offers pro forma earnings, make sure you understand the reasons for its doing so by reviewing company correspondence and news articles. Cash flow and sales-to-share-price ratios can assist you in better understanding current stock value. You should be seeking contrarian investing opportunities. While many contrarian opportunities occur infrequently, as an astute investor, you can identify them. Taking occasional profits when investments have exceeded your expectations is a prudent investment strategy. Building a portfolio of overlooked stocks, purchased when the price was right, should reward you over the long term.

Building a Portfolio

I have been burning the midday oil.
—PRESIDENT RONALD REAGAN

Geo, you are treading on thin water.
—KAREN FISHER

I t is easy to get confused. Selecting stocks and conducting research on the viability of the management in the companies the stocks represent are not necessarily fun for all investors. But they should be profitable exercises and personally rewarding over the long term.

Building a portfolio is an ongoing process. To begin, you need to feel comfortable with your stock selections. Are the stocks in line with your personal tolerance for risk? Are your selections diversified? Has management shown the ability to build shareholder value? Are your proposed purchases value priced in today's market? Remember that the price you pay for a stock will have a dramatic impact on your returns. Conducting conscientious company research is much harder than allowing yourself to be mesmerized by TV talking heads, staring at pretty graphs, or gazing at pictures in annual reports.

A lot of companies listed on the New York Stock Exchange and on the Nasdaq are poor investments. Many companies spend their corporate life in mediocrity, rewarding shareholders with below-average gains. But not all the companies. If you dig into the company businesses, research management compensation, and search for stock value, a few gems will become apparent.

Do your own research. It is your hard-earned money, and no one will look out for it with more appreciation than you will. Seek out long-term trends in your analysis, especially 5- and 10-year averages. Review the most current financial information. Current performance should show continued improvement and should be above industry averages. It is difficult to find a lot of companies that exceed every criterion, but it is important for you to include management and stock value analysis in your research. The following is a recap of management analysis and stock value criteria for overlooked stocks:

- The return on equity (ROE) and return on assets (ROA) should be 12 to 15 percent or higher, and above the industry average.
- The return on capital (ROC) should be 12 percent or higher and above the industry average.
- The debt-to-equity ratio should be less than 0.80 and less than the industry average.
- The gross margins should be above the industry averages.
- The operating cash flow should be rising, and capital expenditures should be growing steadily.
- The earnings growth should be above the industry average.
- The revenue growth should be above the industry average.
- The cash flow growth should be above the industry average.
- The dividend payout ratio should be a maximum of 65 percent.
- The S&P Equity Ranking should be B+ or higher.
- Shareholders' interests should be given attention in the corporate mission statement and other corporate communications.
- The company's management should own more than 3 percent but less than 50 percent of the outstanding stock.
- Management stock options should not exceed 10 percent of the outstanding shares.
- There should be no history of repricing management stock options.
- The next year's price-to-earnings growth (PEG) ratio should be 1.5 or less.
- The price-to-earnings (PE) ratio should be at the lower end of the five-year range.

- The price-to-cash-flow ratio should be below the industry average.

- The price-to-sales ratio should be less than 10, preferably in the low single digits and below the industry average.

In addition to looking for stocks that have the preceding characteristics, keep a lookout for contrarian opportunities. Also, take prudent profits, using the proceeds to diversify your portfolio.

A simple spreadsheet with all this information would be easy for you to develop and maintain. With the easy access to financial data on the Internet, it would take just minutes for you to make quarterly updates. Keeping this analysis in an old-fashioned three-ring binder will allow you to make fast comparisons over time. It takes time every week to keep up with your portfolio's activity. Read a financial newspaper, the business section of your local newspaper, and financial magazines. Many subscription-based investment newsletters can also expand your stock selection horizon. Surfing the Internet is another good means for keeping up to date. However, keep in mind that almost every personal finance article is written ultimately for the publisher to use in selling advertising space. When reading magazine articles about specific companies and their management, seek out factual information over subjective comments.

A note of caution: The securities analysts' business is under constant and intense scrutiny due to potential conflicts of interest between those parts of a brokerage firm offering stock recommendations and those parts that solicit financial services to businesses. Although it happens very rarely, sometimes a securities analyst may have more than strictly your potential capital gain in mind while making specific stock recommendations. For that and other reasons, you should gather your own facts and make your own subjective decisions in researching investments. Above all, you should read a lot, but remain curious as well as skeptical.

Keeping Your Eyes and Ears Open

Sometimes a good company will fall into your lap.

For example, I was researching the Donaldson Company (DCL) on the Internet. Donaldson is a manufacturer of air-purifying equipment. I accidentally typed in DON for the stock symbol, and up came information on Donnelley Corporation. DON is the world-leading manufacturer of automotive mirrors and electronics. The information stirred my interest. The more I investigated Donnelley (DON), the more interested I became. After following it in the news for a few months, I bought a few hundred shares. Donnelley complemented my portfolio as I was lacking exposure in consumer discretionary and automotive industry stocks. Even with the current automotive downturn, Donnelley has provided acceptable returns.

In 1998, my eldest daughter cashed in savings bonds given to her at birth. She was 20 years old and a junior in college. The proceeds amounted to around $4800. We discussed various ways to invest the proceeds and decided on a portfolio of seven stocks, each funded with an initial investment of $645. Together, we searched the Internet for companies that offered direct stock purchase plans. Netstockdirect .com offers a searchable database of over 1600 companies that offer direct stock purchase plans. During our research, we discovered Investors Financial Services (IFIN) listed under a search for financial services companies with investor-friendly stock purchase plans. Neither of us had heard of IFIN, but the name and company description peaked our interest. After researching IFIN in detail, we added it to the buy list, and it has been the best performer.

When oil prices were crashing in 1997, I thought it might be interesting to investigate oil infrastructure companies. These companies build oil refineries and oil terminals. Oil producing companies were getting hammered with low profits and low stock prices. They responded by cutting back on their infrastructure capital expenditure projects, and this in turn depressed revenues for oil infrastructure companies. Oil infrastructure stock prices were losing ground due to reduced revenues and comparable reductions in profits. During my investigation, I discovered Chicago Bridge & Iron (CBI). CBI is a Netherlands company whose stock is trading on the New York Stock Exchange. As expected, CBI's stock was retreating, and revenues were declining. Oil prices in late 1997 and early 1998 were trading at 10-year lows. As oil prices rebounded into 2001, increasing oil company profits were once again invested in infrastructure projects. CBI's revenues, and profitability, turned around. Oil stock prices more than doubled. CBI's stock price more than tripled.

It is important for investors to always search out new ideas. Take some time to investigate some areas you normally overlook. When researching a big name company, spend a few moments to also analyze one of its smaller competitors. The lesson of the three preceding examples is that you need to always have your eyes and ears open to identify well-managed companies with reasonable stock values that may be overlooked by the average investor.

How to Build a Diversified Portfolio of Overlooked Stocks

The first step is to examine your current holdings. Construct a list of all your stock positions and their value, including mutual funds. Within each of your mutual funds, list the top 5 or 10 stock positions and the dollar value each would represent. From this list, start to build a matrix of information on each, beginning with the industrials sector and the market capitalization. This basic information will tell you how diversified you are across industrials and market-cap categories. It should become apparent which industrial sectors are underrepresented and if you have adequate exposure to small- and mid-cap stocks.

For example, you start building a portfolio on March 1, 1996. You invest $2000 each in the S&P 500 Index Fund (SPY), Merck (MRK), Pfizer (PFE), and Intel (INTC). Every year on March 1, you add $1500 to each position. You reinvest dividends in the portfolio. After 6 years, you have invested $9500 in capital into each position ($38,000 total capital) and your portfolio is worth $63,554. The current breakdown of the portfolio is as shown in Table 6–1.

However, the S&P fund invests in some of these same stocks. The top stock positions in the SPY, along with the percent value of the fund,

TABLE 6–1 Portfolio Value of $2000 Invested on March 1, 1996, and $1500 Added Each Subsequent Year, Value as of March 1, 2002

	Value	Profit	Capital Gain
SPY	$11,567	$2,067	21.8%
MRK	$12,337	$2,837	30.9%
PFE	$22,794	$13,294	139.9%
INTC	$16,856	$7,356	77.4%

are General Electric (GE, 3.57 percent), Microsoft (MSFT, 3.32), Wal-Mart (WMT, 2.59), ExxonMobil (XOM, 2.58), Pfizer (PFE, 2.53), Intel (INTC, 2.28), and Merck (MRK 1.31). The three similar stocks and their investment value within the index are Merck ($151), Pfizer ($292), and Intel ($323). The balance of the S&P fund is listed in Table 6–2 as "Other SPY positions."

All the stocks in the portfolio are large caps. There is virtually no direct exposure to small- or mid-cap companies. The portfolio is also heavily weighted to health care and information technology. PFE and MRK represent 55.9 percent of the portfolio, and INTC and MSFT represent 27.7 percent. The value, sector, and percentage of the portfolio in each stock, would be as shown in Table 6–2.

This portfolio is in need of adjustment. It is too heavily weighted in large-cap stocks, and it does not have sufficient diversification. About half of the Pfizer and Intel positions, with a third of the Merck, could be sold to generate $27,000. These proceeds could be reallocated into six other stocks with a $4500 investment each. To further diversify the portfolio, I suggest adding stocks from other economic sectors, including energy, financials, materials, industrials, and utilities. The stock selections could be overlooked small- and mid-cap stocks, such as Apache (APA), Investors Financial Services (IFIN), Florida Rock (FRK), Progress Energy (PGN), Kennametal (KMT), and Symantec (SYMC). With these changes, the portfolio makeup could be as shown in Table 6–3.

TABLE 6–2 Value, Sector, and Percentage of the Portfolio in Each Stock

	Value	Sector	Percentage of Portfolio
Pfizer	$23,086	Health care	36.3
Intel	$17,179	Information technology	27.1
Merck	$12,488	Health care	19.6
Other SPY positions	$9,397	Various	14.7
General Electric	$412	Financials	0.6
Microsoft	$384	Information technology	0.6
Wal-Mart	$300	Consumer discretionary	0.4
ExxonMobil	$298	Energy	0.4

TABLE 6-3   Possible Adjustment to the Portfolio in Table 6–2

	Value	Sector	Percentage of Portfolio
Other SPY positions	$9397	Various	14.7
Merck	$8988	Health care	14.1
Intel	$8679	Information technology	13.6
Pfizer	$8586	Health care	13.4
Apache	$4500	Energy	7.0
Investors Financial	$4500	Financials	7.0
Florida Rock	$4500	Materials	7.0
Progress Energy	$4500	Utilities	7.0
Kennametal	$4500	Industrials	7.0
Symantec	$4500	Information technology	7.0
General Electric	$412	Financials	0.6
Microsoft	$384	Information technology	0.6
Wal-Mart	$300	Consumer discretionary	0.4
ExxonMobil	$298	Energy	0.4

Health care as a percentage of the portfolio came down from 55 to 27 percent, and information technology was reduced from 27 to 20 percent. Additional exposure was gained in five new sectors. While still a bit overweighted in health care, annual contributions could be designated to other sectors. Over time, the health care sector as a percentage of the portfolio will be reduced to decrease the risk of overexposure.

The realigned portfolio offers more exposure to small- and mid-cap stocks. The original portfolio was 100 percent invested in large caps. After adjustment, the portfolio was weighted 65 percent large cap and 35 percent small and mid-caps.

Based on how soon you will need to withdraw your funds, your portfolio could be more or less aggressive than the previous example. The longer you have to remain invested, the higher the risk you can afford. In place of Florida Rock, an investor seeking income may choose a higher-yield stock, such as Plum Creek Timber. A financial stock with a high dividend, such as American Capital Strategies, may be preferred over the growth-oriented Investors Financial Services. Water utilities are going through an industry consolidation, and the capital gains potential of Philadelphia Suburban may be a consideration. In place of an additional technology company, another economic sector could be added, reducing the information technologies sector to 13 percent. A consumer staple, such as cooking spice maker McCormick (MKC), would further diversify the portfolio.

A more drastic approach could be to sell all but $6500 each of Pfizer, Merck, and Intel, generating $32,500. The proceeds could be evenly invested with $6500 going to five new economic sectors. The largest sector investment would then be "Other SPY" (the S&P 500 fund, less positions in GE, Microsoft, Wal-Mart, and ExxonMobil) at $9400. No single stock would represent greater than 10 percent, and no industrial sector more than 20 percent of the portfolio.

Managing Volatility

Buying stocks always involves some level of risk. The actions of the overall market will greatly impact your returns. However, the method you choose to accumulate stock assets over time may allow you to mitigate market volatility.

You have two choices when you buy stock: You can buy the stocks you want all at once as a single purchase, or you can buy them over time in regular increments. The advantage of the lump-sum approach is that you have a greater amount of capital at work over a longer period of time. The disadvantage is that you may purchase near the pinnacle of a cycle, and you may have to ride out an overall decline. The risk of buying close to a market high can be avoided by investing in a routine manner.

The strategy is to invest a fixed amount on a specific date every month, every quarter, or every year. For instance, in the previous portfolio example, the investor contributed $6000 every year on March 1. The amount invested could vary from a few hundred dollars a month to several thousand per quarter. This investment pattern is called *dollar cost averaging*. When stock prices are high, fewer shares are purchased. When stock prices are low, more shares are purchased. Over time, a dollar-cost-averaging approach helps investors manage their risk against inopportune market timing.

There are several convenient methods to institute a dollar cost averaging strategy. The first is to enroll in the dividend reinvestment program (DRIP) offered by either a broker or directly from a company. According to netstockdirect.com, the leading DRIP Web site, there are over 1600 companies offering investors the option of buying company stock directly from them or their stock transfer agents. As a low-cost alternative to a broker, DRIPs and direct stock purchase (DSP) plans offer a painless way to invest in a specific company monthly, quarterly, or annually. Many full-service and online discount brokers will allow investors to reinvest dividends to purchase additional shares of stock. Sharebuilder.com caters to the dollar-cost-averaging strategist charging a $4 commission for weekly scheduled purchases.

Small-Cap Stock Volatility

According to T. Rowe Price, the large mutual fund manager, small-cap stocks are more volatile than large-cap stocks due to three factors: earnings expectations, less liquidity, and lack of information.

Companies with high earnings growth will attract attention and investor interest. Unexpected earnings gains due to excellent execution of the business plan may send a stock price soaring. However, if fast earnings growth is not realized, investors will rush to sell the stock.

With fewer shares available for trade, and therefore less liquidity, it does not take much investor interest in a small cap to push its stock price to extremes. IBM has billions of shares in circulation while a mid-cap company may have only a few hundred million. Large asset-based mutual funds sometimes have a hard time buying and selling large blocks of small- and mid-cap stocks. With fewer shares available for purchase, a lot of investor interest in a small-cap stock may push its price higher than its larger counterpart.

Smaller companies with new products, processes, and services don't usually generate the same investor enthusiasm as do older, better-known companies. Information about smaller companies may be more difficult to find. For example, when was the last time you read about Microsoft? I am sure it was recently. When was the last time you learned something new about Cascade Natural Gas (CGC) or WD-40 (WDFC)? The Internet has freed the self-directed investor from the chains of difficult research. Multiple Web sites will give you more financial information and SEC filings than you would ever need. Annual reports are available at most company Web sites. Armed with easy access to information, today's investor connected to the Internet has no excuse not to be informed.

The two time-tested strategies to mitigate small- and mid-cap stock risk are to understand stock value and to dollar cost average your purchases.

The Joys and Heartaches of Being Added to an Index

One of the interesting discussions I had with Kevin Sheehan, CEO of Investors Financial Services (IFIN), focused on the impact of successfully building shareholder value and being rewarded by being added to various stock indices. In reviewing IFIN's stock trading history, we discussed how well the company has rewarded its shareholders. The stock has risen from $10 a share to a high of $90, adjusted for stock splits. In late 2000, IFIN was added to the S&P 400 Mid-Cap Index. This created a frenzy of buying activity as the index mutual funds scurried to add the stock to their portfolios. This higher level of demand for the stock increased trading volume substantially, which, with a limited number of shares available, drove the stock price from $70 to $90. After a few months, and with more normal trading volume, the stock settled back to the high $60s range.

Copart (CPRT) and D.R. Horton (DHI), a home builder, experienced similar spikes in their stock prices in early 2002. Just prior to, and for a few months after, being added to the S&P 400 Mid-Cap Index, Copart's stock price rose from $16 to $24, and D.R. Horton's rose from $30 to $38. The stock prices for both have since fallen back to the levels they were trading at just before they were added to the indices. Seacoast Financial Services (SCFS) was added to the S&P 600 Small-Cap Index in April 2002. SCFS's stock price rose from $18 just prior to the news to $22 following the announcement.

It is not uncommon for stock prices of small- and mid-cap companies to rise when they are added to a major index and fall when they are deleted from a major index. To avoid being caught adversely in the midst of these stock price movements, investors may want to wait until the dust settles after a company has been added to an index. Being added to an index can be a verification of the potential of a specific company, but the momentary inflated interest in the stock that results may make it temporarily overpriced.

Bulls versus Bears

The only stock market prediction that can be accurately made is that there will be up markets (bull) and down markets (bear). Rising markets will always give way to declining markets, and vice versa. Between 1949 and 2002, there have been 13 rising and falling market cycles. Out of the 13 cycles, in only 2 cycles has the market decline been greater than the previous increase. Table 6–4 outlines these market cycles.

Since the bear market that started in July 2000 has not yet been officially declared to be over, the most recent market cycle may not be completed. However, assuming that the market does not retest the

TABLE 6–4 Market Cycles 1949 to 2002

	Duration of Cycle, Months		Percentage Change	
	Bull	Bear	Bull	Bear
June 1949 to October 1957	61	15	+222	−19
October 1957 to October 1960	26	10	+63	−17
October 1960 to May 1962	13	6	+29	−27
May 1962 to October 1965	43	7	+85	−25
October 1965 to May 1970	25	17	+32	−35
May 1970 to November 1971	11	7	+50	−15
November 1971 to December 1974	13	22	+31	−45
December 1974 to February 1978	21	17	+75	−25
February 1978 to April 1980	6	18	+22	−16
April 1980 to August 1984	16	7	+66	−15
August 1984 to October 1987	37	2	+150	−36
October 1987 to October 1990	32	3	+72	−21
October 1990 to July 2002(?)	119	24	+406	−46
July 2002 to ?				

lows of Summer 2002, the current market strength could be considered possibly the beginnings of the next market cycle.

Over the past 50 years, from 1949 to 2001, the average duration of a bull market was 32 months, and the market rose by an average of 100 percent. The average duration of a bear market was 11 months, and the market fell by an average of 25 percent.

Some may say that these averages are skewed due to the anomaly of two especially long and strong bull markets in the 1950s and 1990s. Removing these periods from the calculations impacts the averages. Between 1957 and 1990, the average duration of a bull market was 22 months, and the market rose by an average of 56 percent. Between 1957 and 1990, the average duration of a bear market was 9 months, and the market fell by an average of 25 percent. Either way, the average bull market lasted longer and provided a higher return than the average bear market took away.

Creating a portfolio of overlooked stocks within these market cycles may be a challenge. If you happen to begin a stock position near the start of a bear market, creating gains may be difficult and overall performance disappointing. The long-term investor, however, knows that bear markets create exceptional value for the right companies. Bear markets are not about making gains; they are about finding opportunities. If your stock selection is based on an understanding of the quality of management, then bear markets and low stock values may create better capital gain opportunities.

According to Ibbotson Associates, the S&P 500 Index has returned an average of just over 12 percent annually between 1925 and 1999. There is no other place to grow your money faster than the stock market. Careful evaluation of management and a belief in the value of the stock should help you achieve that rate of return over the long term.

The More Things Change, The More They Stay the Same

A friend of mine gave me a personal finance article from *U.S. News & World Report* dated November 11, 1974. The article is titled "Prices Always Come Back: Lessons of 50 Years in Stocks." The article centered on an interview with my friend's grandfather, Justin Barbour, a stockbroker, newspaper columnist, and investment advisor. When he wrote this article, the market was bottoming out after a decline of 45 percent. To put this into context, it would be similar to the S&P 500 Index trading at 825 today. Many of the words of wisdom of 1974 still apply.

Mr. Barbour wrote:

> As long as a bull market continues to rise and a bear market continues to go down, the trend-followers—along with most of the popularly quoted market letter writers—argue that a major trend has yet to run its course. Yet there always has to be a top to every bull market and a bottom to every bear market. And the bottoms of bear markets usually have been successively higher through the years. An investor should have enough cash reserves so he is not forced to liquidate in a bear market. An individual investor—even a person with very little cash to invest at one time—can gain financial independence if he moves gradually into growth companies with progressive managements.

Mr. Barbour's approach was to buy stocks in quality companies with good management and a proven track record:

> Invest gradually and concentrate your buying in bear markets when prices are depressed. Don't figure you can jump in at the exact low.

When asked to sum up his investment philosophy, Mr. Barbour replied:

> The intelligent, prudent investor, unencumbered by debt, does not lose by investing in well-run, established businesses with growth records—and prospects for continued growth—if he holds such securities through periods of major market declines, and adds to them when prices seem unusually attractive.

According to Ibbotson Associates, "A prominent magazine in 1926 recommended that a portfolio contain 25% sound bonds, 25% sound preferred stocks, 25% sound common stocks and 25% speculative securities." While this portfolio allocation may not be appropriate for today's investors, the importance of the statement is its date. Even though America was two-stepping its way into the Great Depression, judicious investing principles still prevailed for some.

The search for top-quality management and reasonable stock price valuations has not altered much from 1926 or 1974. Startup firms and high-tech IPOs may come and go, but the basic principles of successful investing have not changed. What were considered valid portfolio management and company research techniques 25 and 75 years ago are still valid today.

Graham and Buffett

There has been more written about Benjamin Graham and one of his students Warren Buffett than they ever wrote themselves. Warren Buffett is one of the richest people in the world, accumulating his wealth by investing in stocks and buying companies. Benjamin Graham died in 1976. He has been called the "father of value investing," and he is author of the investment classic *The Intelligent Investor* (1949).

Graham and Buffett both believe in evaluating management, company products, and share price to determine the long-term prospects for an investment. When evaluating companies as prospective investment choices, Graham and Buffett asked simple questions like, "Will the company's product or service be around in 20 years?" and "Does this company have a sustainable competitive advantage?" Graham and Buffett each have had a specific financial ratio that would signal a good stock buy. Graham evaluated *corporate net current asset value* (current assets minus all liabilities). Graham believed that a company whose stock sold for less than the net current asset value per share was worth further investigation. For example, As of June 30, 2001, Barra Software (BARZ) reported current assets of $270 million and total liabilities of $82 million, for a net current asset value of $188 million or $8.90 per share. With the current stock price of $56, Graham would have considered Barra overvalued.

Buffett has relied on the projected future cash flow of a business to determine its stock value.

What is important to remember about Warren Buffett is not his wealth but his stock-picking ability. His best-known purchases were large stock positions in Coca-Cola (KO), American Express (AXP), and

Gillette (G), but Buffett also holds investments in many small- and mid-cap companies. Buffett has built a two-pronged company, Berkshire Hathaway (BRK.A), that is involved in insurance and "other stuff." Fueled by the strong cash flow of his insurance companies, Buffett can afford to wait for the best investments and is consistently "raking the market for value."

From the 2000 Berkshire Hathaway annual report:

> Numerous business activities are conducted through noninsurance subsidiaries. *FlightSafety International* provides training of aircraft and ship operators. *Executive Jet* provides fractional ownership programs for general aviation aircraft. *Nebraska Furniture Mart, R.C. Willey Home Furnishings, Star Furniture,* and *Jordan's Furniture* are retailers of home furnishings. *Borsheim's, Helzberg Diamond Shops,* and *Ben Bridge Jeweler* are retailers of fine jewelry. *Scott Fetzer* is a diversified manufacturer and distributor of commercial and industrial products, and its principal products are sold under the *Kirby* and *Campbell Hausfeld* brand names.
>
> In addition, Berkshire's other noninsurance business activities include: *Buffalo News,* a publisher of a daily and Sunday newspaper; *See's Candies,* a manufacturer and seller of boxed chocolates and other confectionery products; *H.H. Brown, Lowell, Dexter,* and *Justin Brands,* manufacturers and distributors of footwear under a variety of brand names; *International Dairy Queen,* which licenses and services a system of nearly 6000 stores that offer prepared dairy treats, food, and other snack items; *Acme Building Brands,* a manufacturer of face brick and concrete masonry products and ceramic and marble wall tile; and *CORT,* a provider of rental furniture, accessories, and related services.
>
> In late 2000 and early 2001, Berkshire's noninsurance business activities expanded significantly through the acquisitions of *Benjamin Moore,* a leading formulator and manufacturer of architectural and industrial coatings, *Shaw Industries,* the world's largest manufacturer of tufted broadloom carpet, and *Johns Manville,* a leading manufacturer of insulation and building products.

Warren Buffett has purchased a very diversified portfolio of companies. They range from jets to jewelry to paint. Most are small- and mid-cap companies, and I bet the majority on Wall Street was overlooking them before Buffett brought them into his fold.

It is easy to say, "Buffett's large positions in large-cap stock are worth a lot of money, and if Warren is an owner of Coke, then maybe I should be too." However, I think the assembling of a portfolio of many smaller companies is the strength of Berkshire Hathaway. Individual investors have a similar opportunity to build a portfolio of stocks in small- and mid-cap companies.

Astute investors are consistently on the prowl for good investments. Many times, overlooked stocks may provide better value and capital gain opportunities. Small- and mid-cap companies usually have more volatile stock prices. Buying when the stock price dips due to momentary problems is prudent. Buying overlooked stocks from several economic sectors should reduce the overall risk associated with investing in smaller companies. The strategies of investing in smaller companies and holding stock investments for the long term are not new concepts. Warren Buffett, known for his equity positions in large companies, has quietly assembled an interesting array of smaller companies. A portion of your portfolio should be in a basket of overlooked small- and mid-cap stocks.

Individual investors have many companies to choose from. Some may offer different tax advantages to shareholders, while others may not be U.S. companies. Real estate investment trusts and companies headquartered overseas are often overlooked by investors.

CHAPTER 7

REITs and ADRs

You don't understand the Russian spirit.
People here [in Russia] don't understand
the concept of buying and selling land.
The land is like a mother. You don't sell
your mother.

—RUSSIAN PRESIDENT, BORIS YELTSIN

Many investors overlook potentially profitable investments in *real estate investment trusts* (REITs). While not known for stellar earnings growth, REITs often pay dividends larger than non-REIT stocks. Earnings growth of 6 to 8 percent is not uncommon. This growth allows for dividends to steadily increase over time.

More than 1600 foreign companies list their stocks on U.S. exchanges including the New York Stock Exchange (NYSE), the American Exchange (AMEX), or the over-the-counter exchange (Nasdaq). ADRs, also known as *American depository receipts,* offer American investors the opportunity to buy stock in these foreign companies. There are many great foreign managers running companies headquartered outside the United States, such as Nokia (NOK) and Sony (SNE). These companies are often overlooked by U.S. investors partly because it is more challenging to research foreign companies due to a lack of coverage by U.S. stock analysts.

What Are REITs?

Real estate investment trusts, also known as REITs, have been around since the 1880s. They were popular then for the same reasons they are popular today: The tax treatment of REITs is favorable, and they yield higher cash returns to their investors. According to REITnet.com, a real estate trust information Web site, there are over 300 publicly traded REITs, with combined assets of over $300 billion. Approximately 225 of these companies have actively traded stock and are often overlooked and misunderstood by investors.

Instead of investing in production capacity or services, REITs invest in real estate, and instead of generating revenues from selling products or services, most REITs derive their income from rent. As a service-oriented business, American Capital Strategies increases its revenues by adding sales and accounting staff. Florida Rock increases its revenues by buying additional rock quarries. A REIT increases its revenues by raising rents and acquiring properties. REITs usually carry higher debt levels than industrial companies, using borrowed capital to purchase additional properties. Cash flow from increasing rent should service the additional debt and cover improvements and business overhead expenses. Cash left over is the shareholders' profit and is available for distribution as dividends.

Just like any business, real estate has its cycles. Demand is directly influenced by the strength of the overall economy. When the economy is growing and business is expanding, there is a demand for new office space, retail shops, apartments, and commercial facilities. When the economy contracts, businesses close offices to cut expenses and shop owners may go out of business or move to a cheaper location. Demand can soften quickly. New supply of commercial space is increased or decreased depending on the willingness of real estate development firms to build. If interest rates are low and the economy is growing, speculative capital flows into commercial real estate. If interest rates and debt service costs are high, construction activity contracts. As do many industries, REITs go through phases. There will be periods of overbuilding and competitive rent pressures, and periods of tight supply and escalating rents. During times of oversupply, low demand, and high interest rates, real estate companies with large debt service costs may have a very difficult time.

Pass-Through Securities

Most companies are structured as corporations. Uncle Sam takes around 36 percent of reported net profits as corporate income tax. To encourage the development of real estate, the government allows REIT companies to be structured differently. If the company restricts its activities to the development of real estate or the generation of rental income, it may qualify as a *pass-through entity* by the Internal Revenue Service. If it is qualified, the company has to distribute at least 90 percent of its reported taxable income to its investors, or shareholders. A pass-through entity is a company structure most often used to pass the majority of profits and cash flow to investors.

Income tax liability for REIT profits falls on the shoulders of investors. As a pass-through, the company is not taxed, and the company income is reported as its investors' personal income. However, investors receive big dividends that more than compensate for income taxes due. With high asset depreciation, well-managed REITs will generate cash flows many times higher than the reported company net earnings. Depreciation is part of taxable earnings calculations rather than cash flow calculations. REITs will pay out to investors a large percentage of operating cash flow as dividends, and often the dividend may exceed the reported net earnings. Potential investors in REITs should note the cash flow information as it is far more indicative of performance than reported net earnings.

To qualify as a pass-through entity REIT, a company must have a minimum of 75 percent of its assets invested in real estate and generate at least 75 percent of its gross income from rents or mortgage interest. REITs are required to distribute 90 percent of their reported net earnings to shareholders.

Types of REITs

There are four major types of REITs:

- Equity
- Mortgage
- Hybrid (combination of equity and mortgage)
- Resource

Equity REITs own property, and revenues come from leasing the property. *Mortgage REITs* invest in real estate mortgages, and the interest paid to them on loans they have made creates revenues. *Resource*

REITs, a new investment concept, invests in natural resources, such as timberland. There is currently only one resource REIT: Plum Creek Timber (PCL). Plum Creek Timber, which owns over 7 million acres of timberland, recently changed to a REIT structure to take advantage of the unique tax benefits. Based on the success of PCL as a REIT structure, I anticipate other timber companies may change their corporate structure as well.

Equity REITs represent over 80 percent of all publicly traded REITs. Each REIT distinguishes itself by the selection of assets it manages. There are many different types of real estate assets from which to choose. Table 7–1 gives a breakdown of the current equity REIT industry's investment choices, by property type, as listed at reitnet.com.

Of all the equity REITs available to investors, one third manages industrial and office properties. REITs in each category specialize in these specific real estate market sections. For example, a health care REIT usually invests in medical center complexes and doctors' offices. Some health care REITs may focus on the specialized needs of the assisted-living and nursing home markets. Self-storage REITs invest in public self-storage facilities, such as Public Storage, Inc. Investors have many choices within each REIT category.

TABLE 7–1   Equity REIT Industry Property Category, as of March 1, 2001

Percentage of Total Equity REIT Industry Holdings	
Industrial, office	33.1%
Residential, apartments	21.0%
Retail	20.1%
Diversified	8.5%
Lodging, resorts	6.1%
Health care	3.8%
Self-storage	3.6%
Specialty	2.3%
Other	1.5%

Source: reitnet.com.

Historical Performance

Over the long term, REITs have historically performed just about as well as stocks. Their performance, however, includes an unusually high dividend return. Share prices for REITs are relatively flat over time compared to the capital gains potential of some non-REIT stocks. Investors like REITs for their high yield and the diversification real estate brings to a portfolio. Table 7–2 gives the long-term returns for the major classifications of REITs.

As shown in the table, equity REITs have outperformed mortgage REITs. The best performance in the real estate market is not found in financing real estate but in managing real estate assets. Mortgage REIT stock prices are very sensitive to changes in interest rates, falling when interest rates rise and rising when interest rates fall. When rates were increasing in 1999, mortgage REIT stocks were taking it on the chin. The abnormal one-year return for mortgage REITs in 2001 was caused by a dramatic interest rate decline engineered by the Federal Reserve Board.

Equity REITs could be preferred investments over mortgage REITs. Although owning mortgage assets are considered a bit safer than owning and managing real estate assets, equity REITs have the potential for better long-term returns.

According to the National Association of Real Estate Trusts, there has been impressive growth in the market capitalization of REITs over the past 30 years. In 1971, there were 34 publicly traded REITs with a total market cap of $1.4 billion. By 1981, the number of REITs had grown to 76 with a total market cap of $2.4 billion. In 1991, the number of REITs expanded to 138 worth $12.9 billion. In 2001, the largest 182

TABLE 7–2 Compounded Annual Rate of Return as of March 2002, Percent

Type	1 Year	3 Years	5 Years	10 Years	20 Years
Equity REIT	17.0	13.6	6.6	11.6	13.0
Mortgage REIT	48.8	13.7	−1.2	7.6	7.0
Hybrid REIT	30.2	9.1	−3.2	7.2	7.0

Source: National Association of Real Estate Investment Trusts.

REITs represented a total market cap of $154.8 billion. In 1971, 30 percent of all REITs were classified as equity REITs. By 2001, equity REITs made up over 80 percent of all REITs.

REITs are not always purchased for their capital gains potential. Many investors concentrate on REITs to generate income and to achieve portfolio diversification. Yet, over the past 25 years, REITs have kept up with the performance of the S&P 500 Index. According to the American Association of Individual Investors (AAII), from 1974 to 2000, annual returns from REIT investments were in line with utility performance and had almost twice the return of bonds. Table 7–3 gives the average annual returns for various major indices.

Resource REITs invest in land resources. For example, Plum Creek Timber (PCL) is the second-largest timber owner in the United States. PCL owns over 7.8 million acres of timberlands in the Northwest, South, and Northeast regions of the United States. Rather than collecting rent or mortgage interest as its source of revenues, PCL harvests and sells timber. Due to tax advantages for the company and its investors, Plum Creek Timber is structured as a REIT rather than a traditional corporation. Using the pass-through provision of a REIT structure, PCL is able to tax-efficiently distribute to its shareholders larger amounts of operating cash flow. Timber companies typically have generous cash flow, and their land value is usually understated on the corporate books. In addition, when land parcels are sold, the excessive cash proceeds are distributed to shareholders. Much like their commercial real estate investment trust counterparts, timber companies

TABLE 7–3 Average Annual Rates of Return, 1974 to 2000, Percent

	1974–2000	1974–1995	1995–1999
Equity REIT	16.2	17.7	9.7
S&P 500	17.5	15.4	28.7
S&P Utilities	16.1	15.0	15.0
Nasdaq	19.6	14.8	41.9
Russell 2000	16.1	16.4	17.2
Bonds	9.3	9.8	7.6

Source: American Association of Individual Investors.

may also have large allowances for depreciation of their land assets. PCL has been the first resource REIT to come into existence, but there will be others to follow in their footsteps. Although resource REITs are new and don't have a long trading history, investors should not be leery of them on that basis alone.

Evaluating a REIT

Like the previously discussed stock selection process, selecting a REIT involves research in the context of an understanding of the real estate marketplace. There is an abundance of information on the Internet to assist investors in researching the specific types of real estate properties owned by a REIT. Excellent information is also available concerning the market conditions in the cities in which a company owns property. The three most informative Web sites are reitnet.com, reis.com, and nareit.com.

The most important areas to research in evaluating a REIT are the following:

- Management
- Capital sources
- Location and type of properties
- Earnings and shareholder distributions

Evaluating REIT management should be carried out with the same diligence as evaluating the management of a company for any other type of investment. It is especially important to review management's experience in the real estate field. A top executive may successfully move from General Electric to Home Depot. It may be more difficult, however, for an executive to move from a semiconductor company to a company that manages leisure and resort properties. Make sure you review financial ratios, such as the debt-to-equity and return-on-equity ratios, in relationship to the overall REIT industry and the REIT subsector if available.

Access to capital is the lifeline of all corporations, but especially for REITs. In order to expand earnings at a faster rate than rent increases, REITs hunt for new properties. The ability to profitably grow the real estate asset base is critical in achieving above-average returns. Because

REITs are required to distribute 90 percent of taxable earnings to share-holders, they usually have very little retained earnings to use to add to their asset base. Therefore, debt levels and debt management are critical to a REIT's success. As the major expenses in real estate transactions, access and cost of capital are very important factors. Managers of successful REITs have figured out how to leverage the company so it has sufficient capital available to finance further expansion without taking on the burden of too much debt. Watch for credit agency changes as they may impact the cost of capital. A credit-rating downgrade by Moody's Investors Service, for example, will usually be accompanied by an increase in the cost of borrowing. Likewise, a credit-rating upgrade will usually result in a decrease in the cost of capital.

Real estate is about location, location, location. Usually, real estate in upscale locations carries a higher price and its value may appreciate faster than real estate in less desirable locations. Some parts of the United States are growing faster or have a stronger business base than others. For example, real estate in the sunbelt will probably appreciate faster than cattle grazing land in Wyoming. In addition, certain sectors of the market may be stronger than others. For example, with the growing population of seniors in the sunbelt, health care sector REITs that focus in this geographic area may be attractive.

Most REITs will list their major properties on their company Web site. Value Line and the S&P stock reports, available at the library, also will list the locations for the majority of assets. Armed with this list, you can go to reis.com and investigate the current real estate market conditions in those cities. The reports are separated by office, apartment, and commercial sectors for the top 100 markets. The information includes vacancy rates (the amount of empty space ready to rent), current average rent per square foot, and inventory growth (the amount of new construction). At reis.com, you can search the top markets by sector for those that are expected to outperform the market average over the next five years. Since a REIT's major asset base is real estate property, make sure you feel comfortable with the location of the company's investments.

For example, a search for office property locations that will outperform the market average in rent growth, and that are rated average in predicted vacancy rates and average in inventory growth over the next 5 years resulted in a list of five locations: Fort Lauderdale, Florida;

Houston and San Antonio, Texas; and Orange County and Los Angeles, California. According to reis.com estimates, these markets could provide above-average returns as rent growth will outperform vacancy rates and new construction.

The written analysis for the office sector in San Antonio includes recent market information. According to reis.com, San Antonio is not a large office market, with only approximately 24 million square feet of existing office space. The third quarter 2001 average vacancy rate was 14.4 percent, up from 8.1 percent in 2000. The large percentage rise in vacancy rates, however, reflects an increase of only 1.5 million square feet. The average asking and effective rents are $17.04 and $13.91 per square foot, down 0.5 percent and 4.1 percent, respectively. For nearby Austin, Texas, the reis.com report indicates that the market is very soft due to the area's overreliance on the high-tech sector. Vacancy rates are in excess of 17 percent and are expected to rise to over 21 percent by the end of 2002. Vacancy rates are then anticipated to decline to 16 percent by 2006. Average asking and effective rents in Austin are $24.98 and $21.29 per square foot, respectively.

Reitnet.com offers a slimmed-down version of the information, but it adds trend charts. While reis.com offers more detailed information, reitnet.com gives readers several charts depicting asking rent prices, vacancy rates, and supply and demand trends from 1997 to 2002. These charts make the presentation very user-friendly.

Research the age of the properties because older buildings usually require more maintenance. The extra costs of repair and improvements may affect profitability. Much like the old Victorian home in the 1990s movie *The Money Pit,* some REITs with a high percentage of older properties may incur higher operating expenses, which will put pressure on future cash flow and profits.

Reported Net Earnings versus Funds from Operations (FFO) and Dividends

Some new investors find it difficult to understand the concepts of reported net earnings and funds from operations (FFO). One way to understand the concepts is to remember that the FFO should be higher than the reported net earnings. Industrial companies will usually pay dividends smaller than earnings, while REITs will often pay dividends larger than earnings.

One of the tax quirks of investing in real estate is the high depreciation of assets. According to the IRS, capital investments, including real estate, can be depreciated over time. This means the company can deduct from its operating income a certain percentage of the original cost of the asset. For example, certain types of real estate may have a 30-year life span according to IRS regulations. A company can deduct from its profits a noncash charge of 1/30 of the acquisition cost every year. A company investing $30 million in real estate may be able to deduct $1 million a year from earned income. Cash flow is not decreased, but reported net profits per share are reduced by $1 million. In reality, good real estate investments will increase in value over time. This means the book value of the company, or assets less liabilities, is usually understated. When a property is sold, the difference between the depreciated cost and the proceeds is available for distribution to shareholders.

Depreciation charges on real estate are usually quite high, which skews reported earnings lower. To assist in evaluating REITs, many investors refer to the *funds from operations* (FFO). The FFO is calculated as the net earnings plus depreciation and amortization accounting charges and has been adopted as an industry-wide performance standard:

Funds from Operations (FFO) = Net Earnings + Depreciation + Amortization

Some investors will compare REITs based on FFO less capital improvements. This calculation is called *free funds from operations*. The theory of free funds from operations is that capital improvements are an essential part of operating rental properties, and therefore they should be excluded from the profit picture. If a REIT invests in older, less expensive buildings, its capital improvement expenses may be higher than those for a REIT that invests in new construction. However, due to usually lower debt service costs and lower depreciation, older properties can be as, or more, profitable than new construction.

Free Funds from Operations = Funds from Operations − Capital Expenditures

The funds from operations calculation seems to be one of the best tools for comparing REITs. It is easy to get confused between the reported net earnings and FFO. For the sake of clarity, then, keep in mind that the reported net earnings includes deductions for depreciation while the FFO does not. Also, the reported net earnings will usually be lower than the FFO. The IRS requires that 90 percent of the reported net earnings be distributed to shareholders, but it does not regulate the distribution of the funds from operations. Think of the difference between the reported earnings and the FFO as the same as the difference between the reported earnings and the cash flow.

Examples of REITs

Within the industrial and office category, there are many companies from which to choose. The following is a comparison of two very different equity REITs. The Great Lakes REIT (GL) is a small office property REIT with a focus in the Midwest. GL's market cap is $290 million. One of its competitors, Boston Properties REIT (BXP), owns some very prestigious properties and has a market cap of $3.5 billion.

Great Lakes acquires and operates suburban office properties. This company conducts searches in attractive locations for older, troubled properties that are undervalued. When it buys such properties, it increases profits through redevelopment, renovation, and tight cost controls. The properties are usually located in one of the following suburban areas: Chicago (16 properties); Milwaukee (8); Detroit (6); Columbus (4); Minneapolis (2); Denver (1); and Cincinnati (1). Great Lakes's assets consist of 32 office properties, 2 central-business-district office buildings, and 4 combination office-warehouse complexes. Tenant space totals 5.5 million square feet. As of January 2001, GL's vacancy rate was around 8 percent, below each city's average.

Even though Great Lakes has been public only 5 years, its top 10 executives have an average of 16 years' experience in the business. Rather than buy new projects in flashy neighborhoods, Great Lakes takes a unique approach to building long-term shareholder value. The company Web site states:

> In analyzing acquisition opportunities, Great Lakes REIT focuses on undervalued properties that can be acquired at attractive prices because of below-market lease rates. By refusing to overpay for acquisitions and seeking properties with embedded growth opportunities, the Company believes that it enhances its prospects for future profit growth and insulates

itself from the impact of a declining lease environment. An example of how Great Lakes REIT's acquisition strategy creates shareholder value is provided by the Centennial Center office complex. The property was acquired in 1996 for $89 per square foot with rents averaging $5 per square foot below the prevailing market rate. At the time it was acquired, Centennial Center had several large leases with 4 to 6 years remaining at very low lease rates. Great Lakes REIT was able to renew a 69,000-square-foot lease at Centennial Center in 2001 and increase the net rental rate on the space from $7.50 to $14.50 per square foot net. This lease renewal has had a significant impact on average portfolio lease rate increases to date and a favorable impact on the value of this property.

About 17 percent of Great Lakes's leases expired in 2001, 25 percent expire in 2002, 22 percent will expire in 2003, and the balance in later years. With lease renewals usually comes lease rate increases. During the first quarter of 2002, around 30 percent of leases due to expire in 2002 had been re-signed, with an average rent increase of 30 percent. Many of these were long-term, fixed-rent leases that had been priced below current market rates. For the year 2002, management believes an overall 10 percent revenue gain is achievable. The rollover of leases with higher rents will assist in increasing cash flow over the next few years. Great Lakes's property locations and features, as well as its reputation for first-class client services, enables the company to attract and retain a diverse base of over 500 tenants. No single tenant accounts for more than 3.9 percent of revenues, and the largest 21 tenants account for less than 25 percent of revenues.

Great Lakes has a track record of beating industry averages for management performance. While 2001 and 2002 have been difficult years for GL and the REIT industry, 5-year averages for return on equity (ROE), return on assets (ROA), and return on investment (ROI) are above industry averages. Great Lakes carries around 20 percent less debt than its average competitor, giving it added flexibility to snatch up additional properties when the prices are right. Current and 3-year cash flow growth has outpaced the industry, but GL lags a bit in its 5-year average growth rate. Management owns 12 percent of Great Lakes's outstanding shares.

GL's stock is currently trading at $17. At this price, Great Lakes's price-to-sales ratio is 30 percent below the industry averages, and its price-to-cash-flow ratio is at a 40 percent discount to its competitors. The annual dividend is $1.60 and offers a yield of 9.4 percent, with an annual dividend growth rate of 4.3 percent over the last 5 years. The yield is substantially higher than the industry average of 7.2 percent, but the growth rate is also about half the industry average. The earnings per share (EPS) in 2001 were $1.08, down from $1.16 in 2000. Management anticipates the EPS to be in the range of $0.98 to $1.02 for 2003, reflecting the continuing impact of the economic slowdown and a softening real estate market.

Great Lakes's funds from operations have increased 50 percent from 1997 to 2001. Its FFO increased from $1.49 in 1997 to $2.24 in 2001. The dividend followed suit, rising from $1.20 in 1997 to $1.60 in 2001. For 2002, management anticipates its FFO to be in the range of $2.16 to $2.20 and a steady dividend.

The Boston Properties REIT (BXP) is much larger than Great Lakes. Founded in 1970, Boston Properties' assets are concentrated in four core markets: Boston, Washington, D.C., Midtown Manhattan, and San Francisco. As of December 31, 2001, the company owned 147 properties, with 40.7 million net rentable square feet. The company's properties consisted of 136 office properties, including 15 properties under construction, 8 industrial properties, and 3 hotels. BXP went public in 1997 and has acquired $3.8 billion worth of properties since its IPO. Projects under construction are valued at approximately $1.1 billion. Boston Properties leases its 3 hotel properties to a partnership that manages the properties under the Marriott International name.

Boston Properties is known for owning prestigious real estate in its markets. For example, it owns the Prudential Center in Boston, the Carnegie Center in Princeton, New Jersey, and the Embarcadero Complex in San Francisco. The company recently acquired the leasehold interest and ground rent credits at the planned construction site of the Times Square Tower in Midtown Manhattan. The company was one of the final four in its unsuccessful 2001 bid for the Rockefeller Plaza in New York City.

Founded by Mortimer Zuckerman, Boston Properties has significant expertise as a developer and prefers to develop raw land or purchase prestigious established properties. Boston Properties piled on the debt as it built and acquired first-class properties. As of December 31, 2001, the debt-to-equity ratio stood at 2.56, which was substantially above the industry average of 1.46. With their management expertise, however, BXP exceeded industry return on equity by almost 50 percent. The company's FFO for 2001 was $3.57, up from $3.31 in 2000, and its FFO in 2002 is expected to climb to almost $4.00 a share.

BXP's net income per share in 2001 reached $2.40, an increase from $2.02 in 2000. Over the past 3 years, net income has grown by an average of 29 percent annually. However, the earnings per share have lagged, increasing by an average of 12 percent, due to the issuance of more shares. The added shares raised supplementary capital that was reinvested into more properties.

The annual dividend increased along with the FFO to $2.32 a share in 2001, up from $2.12 in 2000.

An investor willing to take a bit higher risk may be interested in Great Lakes. As older leases are renewed at steadily higher rates, cash flow should show equal gains. While not flashy, Great Lakes seem to have developed a winning approach to managing a commercial equity REIT. An investor seeking a bit higher profile in the REIT assets may prefer Boston Properties. While the company has taken on a substantially higher amount of debt to finance its stable of big-name real estate properties, the brains behind the company are real pros with a track record of rewarding long-term shareholders.

REITs in Transition

Publically traded REITs have been around for over 40 years. Early REITs were viewed as passive investments in a pool of properties. The sleepy world of real estate investing has dramatically changed over the past few years. The transformation of capital markets has forced REITs to reinvent themselves and to look past traditional methods of raising capital to finance acquisitions and development. As the economy began to overheat in 1997, borrowing costs increased. The influx of debt capital virtually dried up for most REITs. In addition, the equity markets were not very receptive to REIT secondary stock offerings as investors were focused on high-tech sectors. For the first time in recent history, REIT management came under extreme pressure to grow their FFO and execute a business strategy without the benefit of external capital.

The top REIT managers responded with more focused business strategies that are less dependent on outside capital and are more cost conscious. The downside to this strategy for investors is that the ratio of dividend payouts to FFO is lower now as management retains more cash flow to fund expansion.

While the dividend is mandated to be at a minimum 90 percent of the reported net earnings, it is the growth of the FFO that ultimately determines the long-term dividend growth rate. Remember that the FFO is usually higher than the net reported earnings due to the exclusion of depreciation expense. In 1994, REITs paid out 85 percent of their FFO in dividends. By 2002, the dividend-to-FFO ratio dropped to 65 percent. For example, in 1997 Great Lakes earned an FFO of $1.49 a share and paid a dividend of $1.20 a share. In 2001, Great Lakes earned an FFO of $2.24 and paid a dividend of $1.60. Great Lakes reduced the payout ratio from 80 percent (1.20 / 1.49) in 1997 to 71 percent (1.60 / 2.24) in 2001. Although investors are becoming more comfortable with lower FFO payout ratios, they should not anticipate the average REIT to return to the good old days of high FFO payout ratios. This structural change in REIT operations will improve long-term profitability and shareholder returns as more asset expansion is financed through internally generated cash flow.

Another way that REIT management has responded to a reduction of external capital is by trading assets, or selling one property to acquire another. Property sales in noncore markets, for example, generates internal capital that can be redeployed to acquire additional properties in core markets.

REITs have also turned to the private market for expansion capital. Management has been pursuing joint ventures with large money managers, such as pension funds and mutual funds. In exchange for capital to expand a REITs portfolio of real estate assets, money managers receive an equity position in the acquired asset. These large institutional investors anticipate receiving a steady return on their investment while the REIT has a new source of capital. Sometimes, large tenants may offer acquisition financing in exchange for preferential lease treatment.

The decline in external capital availability has impacted new construction. As REITs became more focused and financing became more difficult, many proposed projects were never started. Over time, this will create an environment favorable for rent increases. As supply and demand appear to be in balance for the foreseeable future, rent increases will benefit REITs with added cash flow.

Congress recently passed the REIT Modification Act of 2001 (RMA). This law changed a few of the rules for REITs. The RMA reduced the mandatory dividend payout from 95 to 90 percent of the reported net earnings. The potentially most important aspect of the RMA was the formation of a *taxable REIT subsidiary* (TRS). The provision allows REITs to own taxable subsidiaries and to offer more client services, effectively increasing client satisfaction and enhancing revenues. Previously, REITs were prohibited from providing nonlease services, and these services were therefore outsourced. *Nonlease services* may include dining services and health and fitness clubs. Proponents of the RMA argued that it will allow REITs to remain competitive with non-REIT property owners. Investors should not view the new opportunities available, however, to be a major source of revenue. The RMA is good news for investors as it tends to stabilize the REITs competitively and therefore stabilize and grow the value of their investments. The major advantage of the RMA is that it provides REITs the ability to standardize services and to gain more control over the quality of those services. Standardized services are also attractive for multiproperty clients.

Investing Risks in REITs

Unlike most industrial companies, REITs have more exposure to movements in interest rates. Most REITs carry a lot of debt; therefore, their debt service costs increase with comparable increases in the cost of money. As interest rates rise, so does the cost of capital, and as interest rates decrease, so do the costs of debt service. In addition, as many REIT stocks are purchased for their higher income features, the stock price and dividend yield will reflect the current interest rate environment. If rates are rising, most likely REIT stock prices are falling, and vice versa.

There is also the risk of overbuilding in the specific location the REIT focuses. As building cycles move from a shortage of rentable space to an oversupply and back to a shortage again, lease rates can fluctuate substantially. For example, in the late 1980s, there was a huge building boom that created oversupply in most every real estate sector.

In conjunction with an economic downturn and rising interest rates, the real estate market virtually collapsed. New construction went through a severe contraction, and many apartment and commercial partnerships could not generate sufficient lease revenues to cover their debt service. For several years, occupancy and lease rates plummeted as the oversupply of rentable space created a buyers' market. Many of these partnerships eventually went bankrupt.

As with any investment, you should be selective in your choices and understand both the industry and specific company risks to determine if REITs fit your investing style.

REITs, REITs, and More REITs

There are many different types and sizes of REITs for investors to research. You need to first consider the real estate sector that appeals to you and then find companies servicing that sector. For instance, in the health care sector, there are companies focused on owning medical centers. There are other REITs that invest in housing for the elderly. Reitnet.com offers a searchable database of REIT information. Value Line, morningstar.com, and the S&P stock reports offer company reviews of many REITs. The following is a sampling of REIT companies for you to consider, listed by market capitalization:

Equity Office Properties Trust (EOP) owns or has an interest in 669 office properties containing approximately 125 million rentable square feet of office space. No single tenant accounts for more than 2 percent of its annualized rent. EOP is the largest REIT by market capitalization. Both EOP and EQR are run by Sam Zell, a well-respected real estate developer from Chicago.

Equity Residential Properties Trust (EQR) owns 1077 multifamily residential properties containing 225,250 apartment units. Equity Residential is the largest apartment REIT and the second-largest overall REIT by market capitalization.

ProLogis Trust (PLD) owns and operates distribution facilities for manufacturers and transportation companies. Its target markets include key freight and logistics centers, such as Atlanta, Chicago, Cincinnati, Dallas, Denver, and Indianapolis. The company's portfolio contains 200 million square feet in 1700 logistics facilities.

Public Storage (PSA) owns and operates miniwarehouses. The company has total or partial ownership in 1400 storage facilities. Most properties operate using the Public Storage name and lease storage space to businesses and individuals.

AvalonBay Communities (AVB) develops apartment communities mainly in northern California. AVB's portfolio consisted of 35,650 apartment homes. The developments are usually two- and three-story buildings, and most include upscale amenities such as swimming pools and health and fitness clubs. The company's properties are also located in the Mid-Atlantic, Northeast, Midwest, and Pacific Northwest regions.

Duke Realty (DRE) invests primarily in commercial properties located in the midwestern and southeastern United States. Duke owns more than 80 million square feet of industrial space and 25 million square feet of office space. The company also has 11 retail properties and 4200 acres of undeveloped land.

Archstone Smith Communities Trust (ASN) acquires, develops, and operates apartment properties in markets the company believes have high barriers to entry. ASN operates 53,585 multifamily units; 3440 of those are in the development phase.

Kimco Realty (KIM) operates retail shopping centers. The company specializes in well-located shopping centers with strong growth potential. These smaller neighborhood shopping centers are designed to attract local customers and are typically anchored by a supermarket, discount department store, or drugstore. KIM focuses on strip malls that offer consumer essentials such as groceries, dry cleaners, and drugstores. Kimco Realty has 484 properties comprising about 64 million square feet in 41 states.

Liberty Property Trust (LRY) owns suburban industrial and office real estate. LRY leases 422 industrial and 212 office properties. The properties are located mostly in the southeastern and mid-Atlantic regions. LRY's properties are leased to about 1900 tenants. The company also owns 4 properties in the United Kingdom.

Health Care Property Investors (HCP) invests in health care–related real estate, including long-term-care facilities, acute care and rehabilitation hospitals, psychiatric hospitals, substance-abuse treatment centers, assisted-living facilities, and medical office buildings. The company has interest in 414 properties located in 43 states. The properties are leased to health care providers, such as Beverly Enterprises and Columbia/HCA Healthcare.

Hospitality Properties Trust (HPT) owns and leases hotel properties. The company owns 205 Courtyard by Marriott, Residence Inn by Marriott, Candlewood, Summer Suites, and Wyndham Garden hotels in 35 states. These hotels have 27,683 guest rooms and average 145 rooms per property.

Senior Housing Properties Trust (SNH) owns assisted-living and nursing homes. The properties are leased to companies such as Marriott, who operate the facilities. Spun off from the Marriott Corporation in 1999, SNH has expanded to include properties operated by other companies in the long-term care industry. Property management dates back to 1994 when the Marriott Corporation first began to develop seniors-oriented properties.

REITs can provide interesting investment opportunities, based on the personality and strategy of the investor. Investors seeking high yield should review the advantages of investing in REITs. Another area of overlooked stocks lies offshore. While investing directly in foreign companies is increasing in popularity, they are mostly overlooked by individual investors.

What Are ADRs?

Stocks are bought and sold all over the world, not just on Wall Street. There are stock exchanges in many foreign countries, and many foreign companies trade shares on their home stock exchanges. London, Paris, Helsinki, Tokyo, and Shanghai all have active stock exchanges.

Sometimes the U.S. exchanges allow foreign companies to trade on the U.S. stock exchanges as well. The shares that trade in the United States are called *American depository receipts* (ADRs). In some instances, one ADR represents one share of stock traded on the home exchange, while in other cases an ADR represents multiple shares. For example, one ADR of the Finnish company Nokia (NOK), the world's largest manufacturer of cellular telephones, represents three shares traded on the Helsinki exchange. ADRs are actually negotiable stock certificates that are issued by a U.S. bank and represent shares of the publicly traded foreign company. They are priced and pay dividends in U.S. dollars. The largest banks involved in ADRs are The Bank of New York and JPMorgan Chase. These banks offer information at their Web sites concerning various aspects of ADRs. One of the leading Web sites is JPMorgan's adr.com.

ADRs usually represent stock in large multinational foreign corporations. These large-cap companies are seeking additional equity capital from U.S. markets and want to enhance their image as a world-class company. ADRs are not a new concept dreamt up by some ivory tower business school grads looking to justify their jobs. ADRs have been around since the 1920s, and they were devised to address the many barriers to investing in foreign companies. These barriers include difficult access to foreign stock exchanges and the high costs of international stock trade execution.

In addition to ADRs, there are many ways to invest in overseas companies, including international mutual funds, closed-end country mutual funds, and exchange-traded funds. But most of these funds charge annual management fees, so many investors prefer to buy stock directly in the foreign company to reduce costs. There are over 1600 ADRs from 60 countries available to U.S. investors, and most of these ADRs are listed on the Nasdaq. There are almost 300 ADRs trading on the NYSE and AMEX exchanges. Conducting research on a foreign company may be more difficult than researching a domestic company. To make the chore a little easier, I suggest restricting the research list to mainly NYSE- and AMEX-listed ADRs. NYSE-listed stocks are usually larger-cap stocks than their Nasdaq counterparts. Although small is not necessarily bad, a lack of information for investors is. Due to their usually smaller size, ADRs listed on the Nasdaq may be more difficult to research. There are exceptions, such as Heineken Beer (HINKY). There is a fair amount of investor information concerning HINKY. As HINKY grows here in the United States and abroad, there should be more easily obtainable information about the company.

ADRs are growing in popularity. Individual investments in ADRs as a percentage of total U.S. foreign investments have increased from 20 percent in 1991 to 54 percent in 1999. This is a large amount of capital because total foreign investment includes things like overseas factories. Americans gain exposure to ADRs either directly or through their ownership in mutual funds. According to a study by Citibank, individual investors owned over $292 billion worth of ADRs as of December 1999. Citibank anticipates individual investor demand for ADRs to grow by 13 percent a year for the next few years.

Investing in foreign companies is much different than investing in the company right up the street. Before jumping into ADRs, you should be aware of some of the areas in which there are vast differences between foreign and domestic companies:

- Limited sector diversification
- Accounting practices
- Conversion ratios of ADRs
- Lack of investor information
- Country stability
- Currency exchange rate fluctuations
- Tax policies

While some ADRs are available in all economic sectors, most ADRs are concentrated in just a few. The largest industrial sectors offering ADRs are, in order of size, basic materials, energy, conglomerates, consumer staples, consumer discretionary, and utilities. There are few high-technology and financial ADRs. While ADRs are available from a large number of industrialized countries, the majority originate from the United Kingdom, Mexico, and Japan. These three countries are represented in more than one third of all ADRs listed on U.S. exchanges.

Canadian companies are offered special treatment when listed on U.S. stock exchanges. Canadian companies that comply with specific Securities and Exchange Commission regulations can list their shares directly on U.S. exchanges rather than going through the ADR requirements. This makes it easier for Canadian companies to trade on U.S. exchanges. There are several Canadian companies that currently are traded on the NYSE, including the Bank of Montreal (BMO).

ADRs usually report earnings based on both U.S. generally accepted accounting principles (GAAP) standards and the accounting rules of the home country. The earnings per share in the home country may be different from the EPS reported in the United States. Companies with ADRs listed in America are required to file reports with the Securities and Exchange Commission, and these reports are calculated using GAAP. Make sure you are reviewing financial results according to GAAP calculations.

The number of shares can create confusion for investors. Sometimes one ADR could represent multiple home exchange shares. British Steel, for example, has a 10-to-1 ADR ratio—that is, 1 ADR represents ownership in 10 shares traded on the London exchange. If British Steel earns $1.00 per share in the United Kingdom, 1 ADR traded on the NYSE represents $10 worth of earnings.

Many investors researching foreign companies may find what the American Association of Individual Investors calls the *information vacuum*. There are few channels available for research of foreign companies. While the stock brokerage business is becoming more global, there are still few analysts' opinions of overseas companies available to the average retail investor. For example, Suez (SZE), a French utility conglomerate with interests in the U.S. water industry, has fewer U.S. analysts following it than does Philadelphia Suburban (PSC), a small American water utility. Suez's revenues are in excess of $32 billion while Philadelphia Suburban's revenues are less than $320 million. Value Line and the S&P stock reports follow some of the larger-cap ADRs and offer their standard analyses.

Local customs and business traditions can have a huge impact on ADR investment returns. Most of us are familiar with the customs and traditions of American businesses. Few of us are as familiar with the business finesse required to be successful in Kuala Lumpur, Malaysia. In Japan, creating shareholder value is not usually a top priority for management. Expensive gifts and cash bribes are an accepted business practice in many parts of the world. Investor expectations in a foreign country may be vastly different from those in the United States. For example, most foreign companies are not as focused on paying dividends. Dividend payout ratios are usually lower for ADRs than for domestic companies.

Many companies issuing ADRs have substantial business in the United States, such as BPAmoco (BP), the British-based oil giant. Shire Pharmaceuticals (SHPGY) is based in the United Kingdom, but its North American sales represent over 50 percent of its revenues. These companies are easier to investigate as their U.S. business is followed more closely in the United States. Make sure you feel comfortable with the countries and markets the company services.

In the fall of 2001, Argentina's economy fell apart at the seams. The Argentine economy was booming in the early 1990s, but it fell into a severe recession in 1997. Currently, unemployment is 20 percent, 40 percent of the population lives in poverty, and the government has defaulted on $132 billion of foreign debt. Hyperinflation had reared its ugly head again, with the cost of some basic consumer goods, such as food and pharmaceuticals, rising 20 percent in just a few weeks. There has been rioting in the streets as Argentine citizens have protested not only rising prices but also a government austerity program instituted to regain international creditability. It may take years before the economy of Argentina regains its footing and economic stability returns. In response to the poor outlook for local businesses, Argentine stock prices have plummeted. In mid-1997, the Merval Index (comparable to the Dow Jones Industrial Average for Argentina) was at an all-time high of 850. In January 2002, the Merval Index was trading at 200. This represents a drop of 76 percent from its all-time high. As of April 2002, the Merval Index had rebounded to around 400, but there still has been a loss overall of 52 percent.

Because ADRs are stocks in foreign companies, their revenue and profit are based on their home currency. Just as U.S. companies report earnings in U.S. dollars, European companies report in the euro currency, Philippine companies report in the peso, and Japanese companies report in the yen. The foreign earnings are then converted to comparable results based on U.S. dollars. For example, a Philippine company earning 45 pesos per share, at an exchange rate of 45 pesos to 1 U.S. dollar, would show earnings as $1 per share. Over time, the exchange rate between the home currency and the United States will shift. For example, during the financial crisis of 1997, most Asian countries experienced a devaluation of their currency. This meant that it would take more of their money to equal the same amount of our money. In Thailand, the exchange rate soared from 24 baht (the Thai currency) to 1 U.S. dollar to 45 baht 1 U.S. dollar. Thus to earn the same U.S. dollar, a Thai company had to almost double its profits. Companies that were earning 25 baht per share found their earnings had fallen from $1.00 a share to $0.55 a share. The decline was due strictly to a much higher exchange rate. As earnings of Thai companies shrank in U.S. dollar terms, the value U.S. investors were willing to put on their stock also fell.

Currency exchange rates can have a great impact on how much earnings are reported in U.S. dollars. As a U.S. investor focused on financials converted to U.S. dollars, make sure you review earnings in both U.S. dollars and the foreign country's currency. You should also read the footnotes concerning exchange rates in the financial statements.

Many times, the dividends paid by foreign corporations are taxable both in the United States and in the country of origin. For instance, Chicago Bridge & Iron (CBI), a company based in the Netherlands, pays a small quarterly dividend. Every quarter, CBI withholds 15 percent of the dividend owed to U.S. investors for foreign taxes. However, at year end, shareholders can deduct this foreign tax on their U.S. income tax forms.

ADRs in Action

In 1592, a widow of a brewer set up shop in a shed behind her house in central Amsterdam, the Netherlands, and began brewing beer. She named the brew "Haystack." The widow built a reputable brewery business, and her brewery grew to be one of the top 68 regional breweries. Almost 270 years later, the Haystack Brewery caught the eye of a young businessman, Gerard Heineken. In 1864, he bought the brewery. Since then, Heineken has grown to become the second-largest brewer in the world, and its beer is sold in more countries than any of its competitors. Heineken N.V. (HINKY) is an international brewery enterprise producing and distributing leading beer brands. Heineken products are brewed in more than 100 breweries in over 50 countries. The company sells in 170 countries using the major brand names of Heineken, Amstel, Buckler, and Murphy's Irish Stout. HINKY also markets a large number of national and regional brands.

An investor may want to invest in a large beer maker and so chooses to investigate Anheuser-Busch (BUD) and Miller, which is owned by Phillip Morris (MO). There is a lot of information available about each company—management's efficiency ratios and the stock price history. However, there is very little accessible information about HINKY, which is unfortunate for the average American investor because HINKY is an excellent company to invest in. Earnings per share (in euros €, the European Community currency, the current exchange rate is approximately $1 to €1) have grown from €0.64 in 1992 to €1.58 in 2000. From 1997 to 2002, shares of Heineken on the Amsterdam exchange rose from €15 to €45. Insiders own 50 percent of the outstanding shares, and the company carries about a quarter of the industry average in debt. The stock currently trades at a PE of around 21, and its price-to-sales ratio is 2.5. HINKY's ADR began trading in the United States in January 2001 on a one-for-one conversion basis.

Heineken is a company well known throughout the world, with revenues of around $7 billion, and it has just started to trade in the United States. It is overlooked by most of Wall Street. There are only 3 brokerages offering stock recommendations of HINKY, while there are 7 covering Phillip Morris and 14 covering Anheuser-Busch.

Although Heineken has a company history spanning over 400 years, there is not a wealth of information easily available about the company. I would consider investing in Heineken only after reviewing its annual reports for the past few years, either by requesting a copy through the mail or downloading from the company Web site. In addition, investors should consistently check the business news for articles about HINKY as a means of keeping up to date with the company's growth.

Examples of ADRs

The following is a brief list of ADRs that may be of interest to investors:

P&O Princess (POC, consumer discretionary, the Netherlands) is the third-largest cruise company in the world by revenue. POC operates six of the most broadly recognized global brands in the cruise industry: Princess Cruises, P&O Cruises, Aida Cruises, P&O Cruises of Australia, Swan Hellenic, and Seetours International.

Benetton (BNG, consumer discretionary, Italy) is a unique international company offering many well-known brands. The company makes sports equipment and fashion clothes. In addition to its fashion apparel and retail stores, BNG's stable of brands include Nordica, Prince, Rollerblade, Killer Loop, Kastle, and Asolo. BGN sells over 100 million garments each year.

Fresenius Medical Care (FMS, health care, Germany) is the world's largest renal health care company. It was formed in 1996 through the merger of the Dialysis Systems Division of Fresenius AG and National Medical Care, Inc., a subsidiary of W.R. Grace. FMS is the world's largest full-service provider of dialysis care, with operations in over 100 countries.

Sony (SNE, consumer discretionary, Japan) was established in Japan in May 1946, and it manufactures various kinds of electronic equipment, instruments, and devices for consumer and industrial markets. Sony's principal manufacturing facilities are located in Japan, the United States, Europe, and Asia. Sony has a big stake in recorded music, film, and television through Sony Music Entertainment and Sony Pictures Entertainment. Sony operates an insurance and financing business mainly in Japan, and it has begun to expand into digital broadcasting and Internet-related business.

ICI (ICI, chemicals, United Kingdom) is a leading chemical company with a focus on industrial adhesives, specialty starches, fragrances, food ingredients, paints, and refrigerants. The company has a strong position in synthetic resins and polymer chemicals. ICI has more than 200 manufacturing plants and offices in over 55 countries.

Cemex S.A. de C.V. (CX, building products, Mexico) is the world's third-largest cement producer and the world's largest trader of cement. The group markets cement internationally in the United States, Europe, Asia, Africa, and the Caribbean.

Luxottica Group (LUX, consumer staples, Italy) is the world leader in prescription frames and sunglasses, focused in the higher-priced categories. Through the acquisition of Lens Crafters in 1995 and Sunglass Hut International in 2001, the company has also become the largest optical retailer in North America with over 2500 stores. Luxottica products are primarily manufactured in Italy and are marketed in approximately 115 countries worldwide under a variety of well-known brand names. The house brands include Ray-Ban, Vogue, Luxottica, and Sferoflex. Designer lines include Giorgio Armani, Emporio Armani, Chanel, Genny, Byblos,

Brooks Brothers, Sergio Tacchini, Web, Moschino, Anne Klein, Bulgari, Salvatore Ferragamo, and Emanuel Ungaro.

Kubota Corporation (KUB, industrials, Japan) was founded in 1890 and has evolved to become a leading Japanese company. KUB operates in three product groups: internal combustion engines and machinery, industrial products, and building materials and housing.

Cristalchile (CGW, industrials, Chile) manufactures glass containers sold to laboratories and to makers of wine, beer, nonalcoholic beverages, and food products. The glass container business accounts for more than 75 percent of the company's sales. CGW also produces plastic containers and materials. The company's other interests include investments in the media, communications, cable television, and wine industries.

HSBC Holdings (HBC, financials, United Kingdom and Hong Kong) is one of the world's largest banking and financial services companies. HBC's international network comprises more than 5500 offices in 79 countries and territories, operating in Asia, Europe, the Americas, the Middle East, and Africa. HBC is listed on the London and Hong Kong stock exchanges, and it has over 150,000 shareholders in more than 90 countries.

Swire Pacific Ltd. (SWRAY, conglomerates, Hong Kong) is one of the leading public companies in Hong Kong. SWRAY operates six operating divisions: property, aviation, industries, trading, marine services, and insurance. The property division owns large-scale residential and commercial properties in Hong Kong. The aviation division includes investments in Cathay Pacific Airways Ltd., Hong Kong Aircraft Engineering Company Ltd., Hong Kong Dragon Airlines Ltd., and Air Hong Kong Ltd., an all-cargo carrier. The industries division's main activity is the production of a wide range of beverages. It encompasses Coca-Cola soft drinks operations in Hong Kong, Taiwan, and parts of China, with an interest in the Carlsberg Brewery operations in Hong Kong, China, Singapore, and Taiwan. The trading division's focus includes fashion design and marketing in the United States and automobile distribution in Taiwan as well as northern and eastern China. In Hong Kong and

China, trading interests include pharmaceuticals distribution. The marine services division provides specialized vessels to the offshore oil industry. Substantial investments in Hong Kong include ship repair, tugboat operations, and container terminal services in both Hong Kong and China. The insurance division comprises underwriting, brokering and agency operations in Hong Kong and London.

Suez SA (SZE, utilities, France) is a global utility company that is active in energy, water, and waste services. The company's energy business is focused on the sale of electricity, gas, and associated energy services. Suez provides water management and wastewater treatment and water treatment process engineering. Waste services include waste collection, sorting, recycling, processing, biorecycling, waste-to-energy conversion, and storage of residential and industrial waste.

Real estate investment trusts offer interesting tax and income advantages. However, REITs need to be evaluated based on a slightly different analysis. Funds from operations, in addition to reported earnings per share, should be reviewed. Building stock positions in two or three different REITs could easily diversify a portfolio. The advantages of adding real estate exposure to a portfolio is often overlooked by many investors. Investing in foreign companies is also getting easier. Investor interest in American depository receipts (ADRs) is growing. While it is more difficult to research many ADRs, discovering the unnoticed foreign company can be profitable for investors and well worth the extra research efforts.

CHAPTER 8

Overlooked Trends

The trend is your friend.

—An Old Wall Street Adage

The strategy that underlies trend investing is relatively simple, and it has been in use for many years. This is an example of the way it works: A demographic trend in the United States shows that Americans are getting older and that the population over age 65 will double in the next 30 years. The overall aging of the population will create higher demand for new medicines. In addition, the pace of medical breakthroughs is accelerating, and many of the discoveries rely on drug therapy as the core treatment, which will create higher demand for drugs. So the future of the drug industry should be bright for the foreseeable future. Many investors would see this trend as a signal to buy stocks in the pharmaceutical industry, preferably in one of the big companies such as Pfizer (PFE) or Merck (MRK). Other well-publicized trends include brand-name superiority and the globalization of business.

There are several other potentially powerful but largely overlooked trends that may also develop into excellent investment opportunities:

- The transformation and continuing consolidation of the water business

- The outsourcing of corporate functions

- The global accumulation and the intergenerational transfer of personal wealth

- Global resources

Each of these trends may offer investment opportunities overlooked by many on Wall Street.

Water

"Water, water, everywhere,/Nor any drop to drink," Samuel Taylor Coleridge wrote in *The Rhyme of the Ancient Mariner*, part ii, in the early 1800s. Smart investors are realizing the wisdom in this statement as drinking water supplies become short. The current consolidation and transformation of the water business should offer interesting opportunities for investors.

Entire books have been written about the economics and technology of water supply. Simply put, humans, plants, and animals need water to survive. Life on this planet is sustained only with an abundance of clean air and water. These resources are becoming scarcer and scarcer in some areas of the world. At least a third of the planet's 6 billion people do not have access to regular rations of potable water, and steady population growth suggests more thirsty people are in our future. Global warming may threaten the existing distribution of water supplies by altering precipitation patterns and potentially speeding evaporation. From the Yellow Rivers Project in China to the restriction of water runoff from hog farms in Kansas, our water supply and protection efforts are shifting. At $8 a gallon, "designer" bottled water is already seven times more valuable than gasoline. The overall annual demand for bottled water in the United States is growing at an estimated 11 percent.

The issue of who owns the rights to particular bodies of water has often created heated debate. For example, the water from the Colorado River runs through Colorado, Arizona, and California. Can the state of Arizona construct a dam and reduce water availability to those downstream? Who owns the water in the Great Lakes, collectively the largest body of fresh water in North America?

Since the 1820s, there have been written agreements between the United States and Canada concerning the fate of the fresh water in the

Great Lakes. In the late 1990s, an Ontario-based company proposed a novel business venture: Ladle 156 million gallons of fresh water out of Lake Superior every year and deliver it by tanker to parts of water-parched Asia. Its application was denied. A joint commission from the states surrounding Lake Superior agreed that massive commercial draining of the lake could deplete overall water levels. This water loss could threaten the livelihood of communities and commercial businesses that depend on water from Lake Superior.

The Perrier Group of America is the leader in the bottled-water industry. The company, a subsidiary of the Swiss-based Nestlē Company, has proposed to drill into an underground water reservoir in Mecosta County, Michigan. The reservoir is fed by Lake Michigan. Perrier has requested permission to sell up to 262 million gallons of Great Lakes' water each year. Perrier's proposal is substantially larger than the venture proposed and denied to ship water to Asia, and Perrier's application is pending.

Investors can research water investments from several angles: pollution control and remediation, water collection and delivery, wastewater treatment, and transfer pump infrastructure.

Many ongoing pollution problems are affecting our water supply. A good example exists where I live in Sagamore Beach, Massachusetts. Our local town water supply comes from community wells that tap an underground reservoir, called the *Sagamore Lens aquifer*. The Massachusetts Military Reservation (MMR), comprising the Otis Air Force Base and Army Camp Edwards, sits right on top of the Sagamore Lens. The aquifer is the sole water source for over 38,000 people. From the 1940s to the 1970s, the MMR was a very active site as an Army training facility and an Air Force Northern Atlantic patrol base. In the MMR test firing range areas, thousands of unexploded shells from rockets and mortars were buried underground. These shells leach potentially harmful chemicals into the ground, and traces of lead from the small-arms ranges are prevalent as deep as 6 to 20 feet under the topsoil. It was also common between 1940 and 1972 for military installations to dispose of hazardous waste, such as jet engine oil and jet fuel, in landfills and drywells. These factors have combined to create a truly hazardous situation because the MMR is just a scant 300 feet above the Sagamore Lens, and the soil separating the two is mainly very porous sand.

Researchers have identified 78 pollution source areas and 10 major *toxic plumes,* or areas of concentrations of toxic waste, in the aquifer. Some are spreading at a rate of nearly 1 foot per day. One plume is within 1000 feet of a major town well. The government has established 12 groundwater remedial systems sites, and it is presently working on 8 plumes originating from the MMR. These sites pump out 12 million gallons per day, which is then decontaminated and returned to the aquifer via the groundwater that feeds it. This project is expected to expand increasingly in scope until 2004, and it will be in operation for 20 to 30 years. Hundreds of sites across the country have situations similar to the Sagamore Lens.

Growing Scarcities of Water.   U.S. Filter, a Vivendi Environmental company, has analyzed the future of worldwide supplies of potable water. The company has projected that during the next 20 years, many geographic areas will face a severe reduction in the availability of water. Geographic areas are categorized by U.S. Filter—in declining levels of water availability—as *water abundant, water concern, water stressed, water scarce,* and *water crisis.* For example, in the United States, U.S. Filter predicts that much of the Northeast and Midwest will be downgraded from water abundant to water concern. Most of the Southwest and Florida will be downgraded from water concern to water stressed. Much of Asia and North Africa will be downgraded from water stressed to water scarce.

According to U.S. Filter, there is no large geographic area that will be upgraded in availability of water. The only areas worldwide that are anticipated to maintain their category rating are parts of the southern Midwest and northern southeast of the United States, the Amazon region and the southern Pacific coast of South America, Finland and Sweden, and the northeast tip of Australia.

Water Monopolies.   A $76 billion industry, the U.S. water market is getting more complicated and global every year. As the last bastion of regulated monopolies in this country, usually consumers and businesses have only one supplier for water service, and that supplier is either their local municipality or an investor-owned company. The investor-owned company might be headquartered in the United States or Europe. However, as was true for telephone service in the pre-AT&T breakup era and electricity before deregulation, consumers and businesses usually have no choices for their supplier of water services. As an industry that is highly regulated at the state and federal levels, the water business offers investors stability of revenues and profits. However, the water industry is also faced with increasing pressures for costly upgrades to facilities to meet more stringent federal and state water regulations. Some U.S. distribution systems are in such disrepair that they face water distribution leakage rates of greater than 50 percent.

I don't anticipate water assets to be deregulated any time soon. Unlike the electric, gas, or telephone utility networks, the water industry is not interconnected. As a mainly municipal responsibility, there is very little physical connection between even neighboring systems. The basis of deregulation is the ability to substitute one supplier's product with another. However, that is not structurally possible today for the water business. In addition, most water districts serve small numbers of people. Plus, water has historically been a low-cost item for most Americans, and there has been no political pressure to deregulate. However, as water bills increase and as more municipal water districts sell out to private companies, some day down the road deregulation may come to the water business.

Privatization and Outsourcing of Water Services.   There are over 60,000 water service districts in the United States. Of those, 85 percent serve fewer than 3500 households, and 25,000 are municipal water districts. Many are having a difficult time complying with federal clean-water regulations. Many smaller districts don't have the cash flow or the expertise to continually upgrade their facilities. A few water districts serve large cities and have millions of customers. The cost to upgrade these large municipal districts is a cause of great concern among city budget directors. Of the existing wastewater treatment facilities, 97 percent are owned by municipalities, and fewer than 10 percent are operated under third-party service contracts.

Water and wastewater management are one of the costliest portions of a city's annual budget. The issue can affect a city's economic health and competitiveness. Atlanta Mayor Bill Campbell has said, "Infrastructure repairs will be second only to crime as the major defining issue for cities." Mayor Campbell knows what he is talking about, as Atlanta needs to spend over $1 billion to bring the city's water system up to current EPA standards. The EPA estimates that 20 percent of our nation's wastewater treatment facilities don't meet current standards and that $190 billion will be needed over the next 20 years to upgrade the water supply infrastructure. Under the weight of these financial burdens, municipal water districts are forming long-term relationships with investor-owned companies, or they are selling out to such companies completely. The role of the local water commissioner and the town-operated water district is silently, but dramatically, changing. According to former New York Governor Mario Cuomo, "Government's role is not necessarily to provide services anymore but to see that they are provided."

Public concern has also been growing about the quality of our tap water. According to Erik Calonius, author of "The Privatization of Water," *ITT Industries' Guidebook to Global Water Issues* (February 2001), EPA records show that "more than 50 million Americans were exposed to contaminated municipal water in 1995. Nearly 900 communities, including New York City and Washington, D.C., have issued boil orders (to purify the tap water) since 1991 to protect citizens."

Why would a municipal water district sell to an investor-owned company? According to Etown, a private water utility, the benefits to a municipality may include better and more efficient water quality compliance, a transfer of future capital investment requirements from the municipality to the investor-owned company, improved operations and customer service, better control of rate increases, and municipal budget and local tax relief.

The federal government has encouraged this fundamental change in the water business. The federal government funds many municipal infrastructure projects, such as wastewater treatment facilities or water main pipeline upgrades. In 1992, the feds abolished the requirement that municipalities repay funds granted to build water infrastructure if it is sold. Prior to 1992, a municipality selling a wastewater treatment facility that had received money from the feds for construction would have to repay the funds. Municipalities can now retain these funds, so local governments are encouraged to review their water system assets.

Case Studies of Water Privatization.   The following case studies in water services privatization initiatives are excerpted from Robin Johnson and Adrian Moore's article, "Opening the Floodgates, Why Water

Privatization Will Continue," Policy Brief 17, Reason Public Policy Institute, rppi.org, Los Angeles, August 2001.

A late-1999 report by the city of Indianapolis examined the success of the White River Environmental Partnership (WREP) in running the city's sewer collection system and wastewater treatment plants since 1994. The report measured performance in three crucial areas: (1) *Employee treatment:* Employee wages and benefits have risen between 9 and 28 percent, accident rates have dropped 91 percent, and grievances are down 99 percent. (2) *Environmental compliance:* White River Environmental Partnership has improved on the city's record of environmental compliance in exceeded permits and effluent discharges. (3) *Cost savings:* Over five years, privatization saved the city $78 million, surpassing the expected savings of $65 million. In 1997, after three years of contract performance that exceeded expectations, the city decided to replace the existing five-year contract with a new 10-year contract extending through 2007. Total savings from the contracts from 1994 to 2007 are expected to total $250 million. To date, the city has used most of the savings for capital improvements in the sewer system and treatment facilities and for rate reductions.

More recently, Atlanta released the results of an audit of the first 18 months of its 20-year contract with United Water to run the city's water utility: All payments and fees charged so far are warranted, with no evidence that the firm is using change orders or budget manipulation to increase revenues; the firm is using state-of-the-art technology and environmentally sound practices; and costs to the city have been minimized wherever possible.

Privatization has succeeded not just in large cities but in smaller communities as well. A public-private partnership in Mount Vernon, Illinois, not only saved money and improved performance; it also led to expanded economic growth for the city of 17,000.

In the mid-1980s, Mount Vernon was under a sewer connection ban because of compliance problems at its wastewater treatment plant, meaning the city could not accept any more sewer customers and was unable to attract or expand industry. The city entered into a 20-year service partnership with Environmental Management Corporation (EMC) to design, build, and operate (DBO) an upgraded and expanded wastewater treatment facility. Sewer restrictions were lifted after the first phase of construction was completed.

The agreement is guaranteed to meet EPA effluent standards and, in fact, led to the wastewater system operating significantly better than all EPA permit limitations. In addition, the agreement saved the city approximately $3 million in tax dollars and was completed in substantially less time than alternate proposals. The impact on economic development was impressive. Within 18 months of the first phase of construction, the city attracted approximately $300 million in private investment.

Monmouth, Illinois, a city of 10,000, privatized its water and wastewater services as part of a contract with a firm to operate all public works services. The agreement saved the city approximately $300,000 (nearly 20 percent), improved the quality of services, and was a key factor in the city's recovery from severe financial problems.

The privatization of water assets is not just an American phenomenon. The Asian Development Bank (ADB), the International Monetary Fund (IMF), and the World Bank all support the role of investor and privately owned companies as the primary supplier of water and wastewater treatment services. These organizations believe that developing countries cannot afford to subsidize water and wastewater services. The Asian Development Bank reports that in 1992, the government of Thailand decided to expand the country's water supply system and to manage the resources with a private company. The government repossessed the water supply facilities and leased them to East Water Company for 30 years. "East Water is making profits annually, the quality of service has improved, nonrevenue water is less than 5 percent, the company is listed on the Thai stock exchange, and the government is not burdened with expenditures for water supplies—a win-win situation for all." In 1997, the Philippines government followed suit and awarded 25-year water supply and sewerage services concession contracts for the Metro Manila area. According to the ADB, service quality has improved markedly with regular hours of supply, fewer interruptions, an improvement in water quality, and significantly reduced water bills. In Chennai, India, the local government has contracted out operation and maintenance services for the sewage pumping stations along with water truck delivery services. The city realized pumping station cost savings of 40 percent. Water delivery costs declined by half and volume of water delivered increased by 100 percent.

Investor-Owned Water Utility Services. Moody's Investors Services, in a report issued July 2000, states that "within the next decade, the water utility business in the United States will likely be transformed into a few large water companies or systems on the national level. The larger, investor-owned utilities will mitigate rate hikes by applying significant capital costs over a broader customer base." Acquisitions and geographic diversity reduce the effect of adverse weather conditions in one part of the country on a water company's cash flow. Municipal water districts are sometimes subject to political pressures not to raise local water rates, whereas an independent company may have an easier time generating higher revenues through systematic rate increases.

Investor-owned water utilities usually offer three basic services: outright purchase of water assets or contract operation of water assets, purchasing or operating wastewater services, and metering services. The United States is lagging behind Europe in their privatization efforts, and many water utility companies in the United States are European owned. The U.S. water utility companies are aggressively expanding their service areas, and the European companies are actively buying U.S. water businesses.

For instance, American Water Works is the largest investor-owned U.S. water utility. The company's utility subsidiaries and affiliates serve approximately 10 million people in 23 states. Their focus has been to acquire the water assets of municipalities and to gain economies of scale by integrating neighboring municipality services. In January 2001, American Water Works agreed to be acquired by RWE, a large German water and electric utility.

Philadelphia Suburban (PSC) is the second-largest investor-owned U.S. water utility. It has built an impressive list of water assets in the Northeast and Midwest, and it is expanding into the Southeast. PSC serves nearly 2 million residents. Its aggressive growth-through-acquisition strategy has resulted in approximately 70 acquisitions in the last 5 years, at a cost of $124 million.

Southwest Water (SWWC) is an interesting mix of water collection and distribution assets, and metering services. The business of meter reading has moved past the days of Lovely Rita from the lyrics of an old Beatles song. Water meters that are interconnected and that electronically report to the company individual water usage have replaced the "meter maid." SWWC is expanding its market reach with high-tech meter services in 23 states. Approximately 75 percent of revenue comes from water-metering services to municipalities.

Pennichuck (PNNW) is a small water utility serving central New Hampshire and western Massachusetts. As one of the few independent small water utilities, PNNW is ripe to be acquired by a larger company seeking a foothold in New Hampshire and Massachusetts. A utility seeking to expand in the Northeast could begin by purchasing Pennichuck. Neighboring municipal water districts could be acquired and merged with Pennichuck's operations.

U.S. companies, however, are quite small compared to their European counterparts. The world's two largest water companies are Vivendi Environmental (VE) and Suez SA (SZE). Both are French companies and have ADRs that trade on the NYSE.

Vivendi Environmental comprises Vivendi Water (worldwide water products and services); Onyx (solid waste and industrial services); Dalkia (energy services); Connex (transportation); and FCC (Spanish company engaged in environmental- and construction-related industries). VE is the largest environmental services company in the world with annual revenues of more than $24 billion. U.S. Filter, a Vivendi Water company, is North America's largest integrated water services company providing comprehensive management of water and wastewater systems. Vivendi Water generated $13 billion in revenues in 2001. The United States accounts for 30 percent of its revenues.

Suez SA is a global utility services company that is active in energy, water, and waste services. SZE provides electricity, public works, and construction, as well as financial services and insurance products. The energy business is focused on the sale of electricity, gas, and associated energy services. Suez provides water management and wastewater treatment engineering. Waste services include waste collection, sorting, recycling, processing, biorecycling, waste-to-energy conversion, and storage of residential and industrial waste. SZE also provides a range of communications services to complement its core activities. SZE supplies water services in over 120 countries and provides potable water to 77 million residents worldwide. Table 8–1 compares these companies.

As the transformation of the water business in the United States evolves, two groups are emerging: the large players and the small players. The larger cities usually prefer to contract services with the larger companies. For instance, U.S. Filter was just awarded a multiyear contract to provide wastewater treatment services for the city of Indianapolis, Indiana. The city of Atlanta has awarded a 20-year contract to United Water Services, a subsidiary of Suez. Beginning January 1999, United Water Services began operating and maintaining Atlanta's 2 water treatment plants, 12 water system storage tanks, 7 zone-transfer pumping stations, 25,000 fire hydrants, and a 2400-mile network of water distribution mains. United Water Services will install a premier computerized maintenance management system to track and record all maintenance and repairs performed for the city, which will have online access to the system at all times. The company will also manage billing, collections, and customer service functions. The smaller municipalities often favor the smaller, investor-owned companies. Analysts anticipate Philadelphia Suburban will acquire around 20

TABLE 8–1 Company Comparisons: Suez (SZE), Vivendi Environmental (VE), American Water Works (AWK), Philadelphia Suburban (PSC), Southwest Water (SWWC), and Pennichuck (PNNW), as of December 2001

	Revenue	Market Capitalization	Latest EPS
Suez	$32.6 billion	$15.9 billion	$1.82
Vivendi Environmental	$24.8 billion	$10.9 billion	$2.07
American Water Works	$1.6 billion	$4.3 billion	$1.61
Philadelphia Suburban	$307 million	$1.6 billion	$0.87
Southwest Water	$115 million	$134 million	$0.65
Pennichuck	$23 million	$60 million	$1.55

Source: Quicken.com.

municipal water districts in 2002, growing its total customer count by 80,000.

Investors should find water investments an interesting opportunity as the business continues to change, especially in the United States. While the consolidation trend is beginning to attract media attention, this economic sector is largely overlooked by the average investor.

Outsourcing

Management guru Tom Peters once said, "Do what you do best, out-source the rest." Businesses are finding increased value in outsourcing portions of their business operations to third parties. Just as municipal water districts have realized the competitive advantages of contracting for their services, there are several powerful trends going on within other industries as well. The worldwide market for outsourced services exceeds approximately $3 trillion a year, with the largest section being information technologies (IT). The IT outsourcing market is about $554 billion. IT outsourcing comprises many vastly different services and market segments that are growing at different rates. Some IT services markets are growing at an annual rate of 7 percent, while others are expanding at 27 percent.

Outsourcing is not a new phenomenon. According to the *Harvard Business Review,* outsourcing has been identified as one of the most important management ideas and business practices of the past 75 years.

Popular Outsourced Tasks.   Outsourcing is the process of contracting with third parties outside a company to perform tasks previously performed by the company's own in-house personnel. The most popular functions a business is likely to outsource are the following:

- Accounting
- Marketing
- Technology services
- Contract manufacturing
- Payroll
- Personnel
- Warehouse and delivery

- Management information services

- Tax compliance

- Engineering

- Procurement

Why are companies rushing to hire outsiders to do what had been company work? Because it is usually cheaper, faster, and more efficient. According to James Fitzgerald, manager for Electronic Data Systems, Africa Region, a large technology outsource services company, "It is enough of a challenge for most businessmen to protect their established customer base from global competition. To aggressively expand their operations into new markets requires something extraordinary. We have seen the end of the monolithic organizational structure and the emergence of operations that separate the customer-facing activities from the back office." The most common justifications and benefits of corporate outsourcing are the following:

- Corporate time and assets are better used.

- Company can better focus on its core competencies.

- The quality of an outside contractors' services is often higher than the in-house staff's because the outside contractor has more extensive and varied experience.

- The company can reduce or redeploy its existing staff.

- Outsourcing can enable a company to respond quickly to changing market conditions related to its own core competency.

- Outsourcing can enable a company to respond quickly to changing technology related to its own core competency.

- There may be cost savings achieved by outsourcing.

- Outsourcing costs can be expensed as variable costs rather than fixed costs.

- Lines of accountability may be easier to manage.

- Outsourcing may give a company access to world-class capabilities and expertise in the functions being outsourced.

- Outside contractors may have greater access to valuable resources and skilled labor that in-house personnel do not have.

Large and small corporations are moving quickly to outsource vast parts of their business as they cut costs and restructure their organizations. Labor is getting more expensive in terms of payroll expense and employee benefits. Managerial tasks are getting more complicated as businesses rely more heavily on technology to increase worker productivity. Increased productivity and reduced costs will add profit to the bottom line. Outsourcing is all about doing things faster, cheaper, and better.

Logistics Operations.   What has historically been an issue of corporate control is now an issue of cost. For example, many companies like to be in total control of their distribution. They want to own the warehouse and the delivery trucks to gain control over inventory management and delivery service. However, costs are escalating, and many companies are seeking lower-cost outsourced service from *logistics companies.*

With a market capitalization of $68 billion, United Parcel Service (UPS) is still overlooked by many investors. UPS provides an excellent example of the benefits of outsourcing logistics responsibility. UPS has a relatively new subsidiary, UPS Logistics. One of their clients is the Wrigley's Gum company. For its 110-year history, Wrigley's had internally controlled its distribution in 140 countries. In 2000, they created a new division, Wrigley's Health Care, with the introduction of antacid gums. Management at Wrigley understood that the new product would be distributed through marketing and distribution channels different from their historic channels. Wrigley's preference was to create a separate distribution system to handle the new clients, and the company reviewed its options. After a thorough evaluation, UPS Logistics was selected to provide a package of services. UPS Logistics manages the entire sales fulfillment transaction, from the time the order is placed by the client until Wrigley's is paid. UPS Logistics provides order processing, inventory management, transportation, and billing to and collections from the client. Wrigley's ships from its factory to a central UPS Logistics warehouse, and orders are phoned in directly to the warehouse. Accuracy in order processing has been 99.4 percent, and on-time delivery has been 99.9 percent.

Payroll and Human Resources.   Payroll and human resources outsourcing services are growing mainly in small- and mid-sized businesses. The liability for personnel mistakes, along with the growing employee administration costs, are driving many business managers to seek alternatives to in-house human resources departments.

Paychex (PAYX) provides a full range of payroll services. PAYX focuses on smaller businesses and assumes the responsibility for the entire payroll department. Clients merely phone in employee hours, and Paychex delivers unsigned company checks along with the necessary IRS and Social Security paperwork. Paychex offers payroll tax filing services as well. In 1986, I managed a 30-employee company. For years, there had been an in-house bookkeeper who was responsible for collecting invoice payments, paying bills, processing payroll, and providing our accountant with monthly profit-and-loss information. The bookkeeper would spend almost a half a day every week doing payroll and payroll-related tax forms manually, as we had no computers. By outsourcing this responsibility immediately to PAYX (even before we computerized the operations), we were able to free up an additional 4 hours a week the bookkeeper could use calling clients for money they owed our company. Payroll accuracy increased, and employees were happier because there were fewer mistakes.

As the engine for our economy, small- and mid-sized businesses will continue to grow in numbers and in employees. This should continue to expand the opportunities for the payroll outsourcing industry.

Administer, Inc. (ASF), is a leading personnel management company serving as a full-service, human resources department for small- and medium-sized businesses. Revenues in 2001 were $4.4 billion. The company's Personnel Management System provides clients with a broad range of services. These include benefits and payroll administration, personnel records management, health and workers' compensation insurance programs, employee recruiting, and liability management. ASF offers Internet-based services, such as its *Best Practices Human Resources Handbook.* The handbook provides clients comprehensive information, including tips on avoiding common human resource mistakes.

With the responsibility for personnel and human resources getting more complicated, many companies are looking to outsource these functions. Employee benefits management and recruiting responsibilities are very time-consuming and costly. These factors will lead to a continued growing market, especially with small- and medium-sized businesses.

Information Technology. The largest and most complex segment of the global outsourcing industry is information technology services (ITS). ITS range from company desktop PC management to Internet services to mainframe networking services. ITS companies come in all sizes, from IBM (IBM) and Electronic Data Systems (EDS) to small privately held firms. According to Accenture Consulting, the average ITS contract is between $200 million and $700 million, and it lasts for about 7 years.

In the 1990s, due to the need to increase corporate profit margins, companies began to focus on employee and business productivity. The need to increase productivity has been a driving force in ITS outsourcing growth. For many companies, as product pricing power evaporated with increased global competition, the need to generate more efficient operations became paramount. The productivity enhancement tool of choice is computerization. However, developing in-house software becomes more intricate and expensive over time. Companies are increasingly turning to outsource specialists for their information technology needs.

The areas of greatest ITS potential are computer software maintenance, Internet-related systems, broadband and wireless systems, and customer call centers. Most interest in ITS comes from the manufacturing, telecommunications, retail, insurance, and financial services industries.

For example, Computer Sciences (CSC) is one of the largest U.S. computer services companies, and it maintains offices in nine countries. CSC offers a wide range of information technology consulting and computer systems integration services to commercial and government clients. CSC provides systems analysis, applications development, network operations, and desktop management. The company also provides consulting and technical assistance in the enhancement and integration of multilocation computer systems. CSC has served the U.S. federal government market for over 40 years. The company focuses on the development of software for mission-critical systems for U.S. Department of Defense applications. It also provides the government with assistance in network management, intelligence, satellite communications, and aerospace. The IRS recently selected CSC as part of a consortium of ITS companies to help modernize their systems.

Perot Systems Corporation (PER) is a worldwide provider of business strategy information technology services. PER has reported revenue of over $1 billion, and it employs more than 7500 specialists in the United States, Europe, and Asia. PER offers technology-based solutions that focus on all aspects of customer development strategies and customer-related computer systems. Perot Systems' goal is to make clients more effective in servicing their customers. PER market concentration is on four industries: financial services, energy, health care, and travel and transportation. These industries are targeted for their rapidly changing business environment, potential future growth, and the increasing importance of information technology.

Investors have many companies from which to choose in the ITS industry. As with all technology-related businesses, ITS is consistently becoming more complex. It is important for investors to review the specific business model for the computer services company and the length of time the company has been in business. More experienced and larger ITS companies should generate the cash flow required to consistently develop and upgrade their management systems services. Established companies should have proven their ability to profit from rapid technological changes.

Business-to-Business Procurement.   The days of a large corporate purchasing staff are numbered. One of the advantages of the Internet is the opportunity for more competitive bidding for procurement. With the crash of the Internet stock market in 2000 and 2001, the term "B2B" may bring back unpleasant memories. Specialty and commodity product purchasing, however, is changing dramatically. More companies are requesting bids from Internet buying groups. Many of these procurement sites are operated by the larger companies in their specific industry. Known as *e-procurement,* the Internet is fast becoming the most productive tool in the procurement process. For example, several of the large chemical manufacturers banded together and formed a buying group Web site. Cost savings to buyers are anticipated to be substantial as more suppliers are able to bid on new business.

The vendors of the software used in e-procurement are relatively small companies, such as Ariba, Commerce One, and Intellisys. Because it is a relatively new service, I would suggest researching the group very carefully. While the prospects appear bright, it is too early to tell who the major players will be. However, keep your eye on this segment of outsourcing, as it has great potential.

Contract Manufacturing.   There is a constant tug-of-war inside every manager's corner office between in-house and outside product production. Most every manufacturing company relies on a certain level of contract manufacturing, from the raw die casting of aluminum parts to the purchase of completed subassemblies, or components. With the accelerating speed of product changes in the technology field, outsourcing high-tech manufacturing responsibilities is becoming economically viable.

For instance, some believe Nortel Networks is becoming just a marketer of products, as the vast majority of its manufacturing is increasingly being outsourced. In early 2002, Nortel announced it was selling 17 of its 25 factories, and it will be having its products manufactured entirely by outside vendors. Ericsson, the large Swedish cell phone company, has awarded a $3 billion contract to have its phones manufactured for them. Hewlett-Packard's printer manufacturing business is 100 percent outsourced. Microsoft's new electronic game called *Xbox* is manufactured under a contract with Flextronics (FLEX), one of the leading U.S. contract manufacturers. In May 2001, Motorola (MOT) signed away 15 percent of all manufacturing of its communications enterprise equipment division to Flextronics, and it committed to a $30 billion 5-year procurement contract. In December 2001, Motorola announced it was selling two cell phone factories to Celestica (CLS), a contract manufacturer, and it signed a $1 billion, 3-year procurement contract to outsource the production to CLS.

More companies are turning their manufacturing responsibilities over to outside firms and focusing on product design and marketing. The most likely electronic products to be outsourced are computers, telecommunication and networking equipment, consumer electronics, and subassemblies, such as printed circuit boards. Outsourcing is an effective means of reducing the amount of capital needed to operate a business and giving a boost to the company's return on capital. By selling off manufacturing assets with long-term contracts for production time, companies are able to redeploy their resources to develop newer technology and market their products. Product costs change as the fixed expenses of manufacturing overhead are dramatically reduced.

Product costs become variable based on production volumes. The expense to operate the manufacturing facility, including items like capital improvements required for retooling new products, is now borne by the contract manufacturer. The asset base and capital requirements to profitably operate a product development and marketing company are far less than operating a fully integrated manufacturer.

The advantages of contract manufacturing are not just limited to the United States. Sony, the Japanese consumer electronics giant, recently sold two factories, one in Japan and one in Taiwan, to a contract manufacturer: The reason Sony gave for the move was the declining profitability of its manufacturing divisions.

The twentieth century was a time for vertical integration. Direct control over the manufacturing and distribution functions was a key element in the push by companies to own all aspects of their business. The twenty-first century is starting out as a time for organizations to slim down and focus on their core businesses. As industrial giants continue to move out of the manufacturing business, contract manufacturers are stepping in. This new breed of manufacturer is buying abandoned brick-and-mortar assets and turning them into new hubs of manufacturing. Not encumbered by research and development needs, or the task of successfully marketing their products, contract manufacturers can focus on just one thing—making products faster, more efficiently, and cheaper. Contract manufacturers usually rearrange the original factory layout in order to design the facility for quick product changes. In addition, as contract manufacturers grow in size, their buying power increases and their production costs are reduced. Contract manufacturers are emerging as substantial businesses, with great future prospects.

There are two basic types of contract manufacturers. One group specializes in large-volume, low-cost orders while the other focuses on short-run production. The high-volume manufacturer will usually have a low mix of products and seek out additional low-cost contracts to ensure production efficiencies. The largest companies in the contract manufacturing business are usually focused on low-cost, long production runs. Contracts can be substantial, such as a $3 billion deal between Ericsson and Flextronics or a $4 billion deal between Avaya (formerly part of Lucent Technologies) and Celestica. According to Deutsche Banc Alex. Brown analyst C. Whitmore, the percentage of outsourced handset cell phones grew from 10 percent in 2001 to 18 percent in 2002. Almost one in five cell phones sold worldwide is made by a contract manufacturer.

The largest contract manufacturers are Solectron (SLR) with revenues of $16.8 billion, Flextronics (FLEX) with revenues of $10.4 billion, and Celestica (CLS) with revenues of $9.7 billion.

There are many smaller contract manufacturers focusing on the high-mix, short-production-run market. These companies are usually smaller and offer the flexibility of low-volume, complex products. While the major trend is the outsourcing of large-volume production, the small manufacturer has the opportunity to make a higher profit margin. For example, in 1999, the average operating profit margin for large, or low-mix, manufacturers was 4.2 percent. The average operating profit margin for high-mix manufacturers was 9.2 percent. The more flexible, smaller production runs are more profitable. Jabil Circuits (JBL), with revenues of $4 billion, is one of the leaders in the high-mix contract manufacturing business.

The advantage many larger contract manufacturers have is the ability to build a network of factories where labor is lower cost. For example, Flextronics has a series of factories in China, Malaysia, and northern Mexico. From this base, Flextronics manufactures items like cell phones for Nokia, Alcatel, and Motorola. Within the network, similar parts manufacturing can be grouped to specific facilities, increasing efficiencies. Flextronics' China and U.S. facilities may make components for final assembly in the factories in northern Mexico.

Technology stocks experienced a huge run-up in stock price 1999 to 2000, and high-tech contract manufacturers participated in the overvaluation problem. The downturn in 2001 and 2002 has hurt sales and revenues for the industry. Lower profits and a lack of investor interest have crushed the stock prices of most contract manufacturers. With bright prospects and low stock prices, some contract manufacturers offer interesting investment opportunities. This economic sector seems ripe for investor research as there may be a few long-term bargains. Although I don't think it is likely that we will see stock prices climb to their lofty heights of a few years ago, an economic rebound, coupled with improving business, should be very positive for this group.

The Global Accumulation and the Intergenerational Transfer of Personal Wealth

Another powerful trend often overlooked by investors is the growth in financial assets worldwide and the pending transfer of wealth from parents and grandparents to the current baby-boom generation. These two trends will shape financial services companies for the foreseeable future.

According to Kevin Sheehan, Investors Financial Services, the market for managed financial assets is growing between 12 and 27 percent annually, varying country to country. As the economies of the world expand, new wealth is generated, and some of that wealth ends up in the hands of professional money managers. Retirement accounts have been converted from fixed-cash-payment pension plans to defined contribution and investment plans. Much of America's retirement account asset base is invested either in employer stock or mutual funds. Mutual funds are popular among many of the discount stockbrokers as they are easier to sell to individual investors.

According to the Securities Industry Association, securities firms raised a record $3.2 trillion of new capital in 2001 for U.S. businesses. Since 1990, securities firms have raised an astonishing $20 trillion in capital for U.S. businesses. This amount includes public offerings, private sales of stock, and medium-term notes. The numbers do not include the added billions raised by federal, state, and municipal governments. Even with a declining stock market, share trading volumes continue to grow. Annual trading volume in 2001 was 840 billion shares, three times the annual volume of just 5 years ago.

Individual ownership of stocks in the United States is on the increase. In 1999, 78 million Americans owned stock or mutual funds. That was almost three times the number of investors in 1979. Almost half of U.S. households currently own financial assets. Over the past 25 years, Americans have been getting smarter about their money and have reaped the rewards of the longest and strongest bull market in history. The value of Americans' liquid assets rose from $1.7 trillion in 1975 to $15.6 trillion in 2001. There has also been a dramatic shift in where these households have been investing. Table 8–2 outlines where Americans have their money invested.

TABLE 8-2   U.S. Households' Liquid Financial Assets

	1975	2001
Total value	$1.7 trillion	$15.6 trillion
Equities	29 percent	40 percent
Bank deposits	55 percent	23 percent
Mutual funds	2 percent	19 percent
Bonds	14 percent	11 percent
Money market funds	NA	7 percent

Source: Federal Reserve Flow of Funds Accounts.

Over three quarters of liquid financial assets is invested in securities-related products, including stocks, bonds, mutual funds, and money market funds. Not only did the value of Americans' assets grow nine-fold, individual investors were putting more of their assets into the stock markets. Over the past 20 years, individual U.S. investors have increased their ownership of foreign equities. In 1980, U.S. investor purchases and sales of foreign equities were valued at $250 billion. In 2001, trading in foreign securities exceeded $25.8 trillion.

From 1990 to 2000, companies in the securities industry generated record profits. Industry-wide pretax profits grew from $200 million in 1990 to a record $21 billion in 2000. The recession of 2001, along with declining stock values, reduced revenues by 20 percent and profits by 50 percent. Even with this temporary dip, the industry generated $11 billion in profits. The growth in profitability of the financial services firms is impressive, with industry-wide profits up 50 fold in 10 years.

From 1933 to 1999, the U.S. government prevented the cross-ownership of banks and securities firms. In 1999, the government lifted its objections, and the industry rushed to consolidate. From 1999 to 2001, there were over 300 mergers involving U.S. securities firms. One third of the security firm mergers involved banks while another third were acquired by foreign financial services companies. Today, 18 percent of securities firms are owned by banks.

I had a meeting recently with Robert Boon, vice president of private banking at the Cape Cod Bank and Trust Company (CCBT). CCBT is a small community bank that offers a full array of financial services. CCBT has a network of 29 full-service branches, it offers trust and portfolio management services, and it operates an insurance agency and stock brokerage company. We discussed how a community bank can compete against the financial strength of the large regional and national banks.

According to Mr. Boon, offering diverse services and having the ability to cross-market these services is crucial for the survival of smaller banks. The Norwest Bank merger with Wells Fargo in 1999 focused on the strength of Norwest to cross-market new financial products to existing clients. Commercial and retail customers are becoming more sophisticated and are demanding one-stop financial shopping. Banks have to provide these services, which will lead to further consolidation within the financial services industry.

As may be expected, the bull market of the 1990s did wonders for the financial services industry. Money was free flowing to new IPOs, and the average brokerage account balance grew by about 20 percent a year. Financial services firms were getting substantial fees for arranging financing either though stock or bond offerings. Established companies were merging with competitors and paying huge investment banking fees. With the U.S. economic recession and stock market declines in 2000, 2001, and 2002, fee-based revenues for financial services companies has declined. A large percentage of fee-based revenue is profit, and in 2001, industry profit declined faster than the decline in revenues.

I anticipate that Americans will continue to earn higher real wages and individual investors will continue to prefer the securities-based assets of stocks, bonds, and mutual funds. Retirement programs will remain focused on market-driven securities as the primary investment vehicles. The size of international funds under management will continue to grow as mutual funds are introduced as investment choices to more people worldwide. All recessions eventually end and turn into periods of economic prosperity. The current weakness in financial services profitability will also improve over the next few years. There will be continued consolidation within the financial services business as banks and insurance companies meld with the opportunities of stockbrokers.

As individual investors' portfolios got hammered in 2000 through 2002, many novice and seminovice investors have given up trying to pick their own stocks. Internet trading, most often used by individual investors, has declined dramatically. As the bull market ended in early 2000, individual trading using Internet brokers weakened from 27 percent of all executed trades in the second quarter of 2000 to 17 percent by the second quarter of 2001. Individual investors shied away from buying and selling individual stocks and began to move into mutual funds. There is a belief that professional money managers can provide better portfolio management than individuals. Stock picking in the bull market of the nineties may have been considered "easy" due to the strong financial tide that lifted almost all stocks. In the market declines of 2000 and 2001, many of the "easy" stock selections proved to be anything but long-term winners. After seeing as much as 30 percent or more of their portfolio value evaporate, many individuals threw in the towel and moved to professionally managed accounts. Brokerage houses are accommodating investors by reducing the amount needed to qualify for a managed account. Whereas previously many active money managers were not interested in an account valued less than $250,000 to $500,000, today's money managers may consider account balances of $50,000 to $100,000.

Within the financial services sectors, money managers and firms that supply services to the money management industry should continue to do well. Money managers charge an annual fee based on the value of the assets managed. Assets and management fees grow by attracting additional capital and new investors or through an increase in the market value of the portfolio. Over the next few years, both new capital and overall market value are expected to continue their growth of the 1990s.

Companies such as Franklin Resources (BEN) and State Street Bank (STT) will be successful in the better times ahead. BEN has a market cap of $11.1 billion, and it is known for its Franklin and Templeton mutual fund families. BEN has grown its managed assets even as the economy and overall stock market has declined. In March 2002, BEN reported assets under management of $274.5 billion, up from $215 billion in 2001. State Street offers money management through its State Street Advisors Mutual Fund family, and it offers institutional custodial services similar to those available from Investors Financial Services. Over time, STT's assets under management and management fees will continue to strengthen. As the stock market improves over the next few years, professional money managers should offer growing returns for patient long-term investors.

As previously mentioned, Investors Financial Services (IFIN) is one of my favorite companies in the money management services sector. IFIN will benefit in the long term from the continued worldwide growth of financial assets and the strong trend of client outsourcing more back-office responsibilities. Barra Software (BARZ) offers highly complex financial analysis tools to improve the productivity of money managers, and it should continue to benefit from these trends. Raymond James (RJF) is a small, full-service brokerage house that focuses on the individual, retail investor. Located mainly in the Southeast and Midwest, RJF's business strategy is based on improving its fee-based business, such as investment advisory fees and asset-based fees. In 2000, fee-based revenues composed 46 percent of total revenues, up from 36 percent in 1995. RJF is projected to increase earnings by 15 percent a year over the next few years. As baby-boomers begin to retire and move out from the umbrella of city living, financial services companies that focus on personal service to individual investors in more rural and small-town settings should experience improved business. Raymond James fills that market niche.

Baby-boomers are entering their fifties and sixties. Life expectancy rates are getting older. Even though the average life expectancy of a 65-year-old is now 82, we all will pass away one day. When we do, the assets we build over our lifetime will be inherited by our heirs, will go to charity, or will be used to pay taxes. As a country, our assets have been growing nicely over the decades.

John Havens and Paul Schervish authored a report on this topic titled "Millionaires and the Millennium: New Estimates of the Forthcoming Wealth Transfer." According to this report, wealth owned by individuals in the United States, net after debt, stood at $33 trillion. Of this total, $22 trillion is held in nonliquid financial assets, such as a home, land, and privately held businesses. Liquid assets, such as stocks and bonds, represent about $15 trillion of value. Consumer debt for mortgages and credit cards is estimated at $4 trillion.

Over the next 55 years, value of this wealth will increase as it has over the past 50 years. The most used studies conducted in 1990 estimated that the transfer would be around $10 trillion. However, Havens and Schervish projects a substantially higher level of wealth transfer.

Between 1998 and 2052, they estimate that there will be an intergenerational transfer of between $41 trillion and $136 trillion in assets. Havens and Schervish's low estimates take into consideration meager additional saving and investing rates by individuals along with a 2 percent annual real growth in asset value. Our parents and grandparents will leave us with inheritances that sometimes are valued at $1 million or more just from the value of their home. As the illiquid assets are sold to generate cash for the estate's disbursal, the percentage of an individual's net worth in real estate may decline, with the added cash going into liquid assets of stocks and bonds.

There is much talk in Washington, D.C., concerning the partial privatization of the Social Security system. Proposals usually include the option for every American to invest a portion of their Social Security taxes directly in the stock market. Currently, any "surplus" in the Social Security system is invested in government bonds. The option to invest even a small percentage of an individual's Social Security account into mutual funds should add substantial amounts of fresh capital to the financial services industry.

The current inheritance tax laws are confusing, at best. Inheritance taxes are due to be temporarily phased out. However, there is also growing interest in Washington to permanently eliminate inheritance taxes altogether. If inheritance taxes are abolished, the amount of wealth to be transferred should increase substantially because presently taxes can be as much as 50 percent of an estate.

Both the worldwide growth in financial assets and the pending intergenerational transfer of wealth provide an interesting backdrop for the future of financial services companies. Combined, these two trends should reward financial services investors over the long term.

Global Resources

As the population grows, some basic resource needs will grow also. These include oil to power our economies and our automobiles, fertilizers to increase crop and food production, timber to build our houses and to make paper, and electric and natural gas energy to light and heat our homes. Previously in this chapter, we discussed the growing stress on global water resources. The same can be said for other resources as well. Astute investors can locate small- and mid-cap companies poised for growth in these sectors that are overlooked by most on Wall Street.

Everyone knows the importance of oil to the global economy. Over time, as countries develop industrialized economies, the importance of oil and oil byproducts increases. Growth in aviation creates higher demand for jet fuel. More delivery trucks demand more supplies of diesel fuel. Even the ownership of a family car is multiplying at a rapid rate in many parts of the world. Higher use of plastics in manufacturing increases the consumption of petroleum-based chemicals.

While the U.S. and European countries reduced the rate of oil consumption following the 1973 to 1974 oil price shocks and embargo, third world countries significantly increased their consumption. In the 10 years after 1973, oil consumption fell in Western Europe and Japan by 2 percent and in the United States by 14 percent, but the countries of the old Soviet Empire increased consumption by over 40 percent during the same time frame. As manufacturing has moved from developed to underdeveloped countries, so has the consumption of oil. Factories in developing countries are not as fuel efficient as those in developed countries. The U.S. Department of Energy estimates that developing countries use more than twice as much oil as the developed countries to produce one unit of economic output. Not only does the added, and less efficient, manufacturing capacity in developing countries drive oil consumption higher, an increase in the general standard of living creates higher consumer consumption as well. Developing countries accounted for 26 percent of the world's consumption of oil in the early 1970s. Now their share is close to 40 percent, and growing.

From 1990 to 2000, worldwide oil consumption grew by 1.2 percent a year. Current worldwide consumption is around 76 million barrels a day, and growing annually by around 1 million barrels a day.

A survey conducted at the Annual Energy Symposium in Houston in December 2001 offers some enlightening findings. Over the next 3 years, industry experts expect more volatile oil pricing, increased consolidation and restructuring, higher spending to explore for new reserves, and a significant impact from new technologies. Of those who attended the conference, 80 percent believed new oil exploration and development technology will have a positive impact on both the discovery of new oil reserves and the recovering of more oil from each well. New seismic devises to aid in locating oil deposits and more sophisticated drilling techniques will assist companies in meeting the increasing demand for oil.

As a cyclical commodity business, it is important for investors to buy oil stocks when the price of oil is low. Oil stocks move in direct relationship to the trend in oil prices. When the price of oil is low, some oil companies may have a difficult time making a profit. When prices are high, however, oil companies have the potential to be very profitable.

The consensus is that "normal" oil prices should be between $23 and $27 a barrel. Buying oil stocks when the price of oil is over $30 a barrel may not be prudent, but loading up for the long term when the price of oil drops below $15 to $18 could be beneficial. Like other commodity industries, it is sensible to be a contrarian when it comes to investing in oil stocks. Those opportunities may not come very often, but the astute investor knows to take advantage of them. For instance, anyone who bought oil stocks in 1998 when oil was at $12 a barrel should have doubled or tripled his or her investment by 2000. Apache (APA), for example, rose from $18 a share to $70 as oil prices climbed from $12 a barrel to $32. In late 2001, oil prices dropped to $18 a barrel, and Apache stock dropped to $43. By early 2002, oil prices rebounded, and APA's stock rose to $55.

Within the oil business, there are other interesting opportunities. As the worldwide demand for oil increases, so will the need for oil infrastructure. Oil terminals and refineries need to increase capacity to keep up with a steadily rising demand. Chicago Bridge & Iron (CBI) is one of the leading oil infrastructure-producing companies in the world. Much as Apache's stock price is tied to the price of oil, CBI's future is directly impacted by the capital expenditure budgets of the oil companies. In 2000, the large oil companies announced 10-year increases in their infrastructure budgets. As the long-term demand for infrastructure projects grows to meet a rising demand for oil and petrochemicals, oil infrastructure companies, like Chicago Bridge & Iron, should positively benefit.

Natural gas is another global resource that is going through a transition. The electrical power needs of the United States continue to grow. The four largest sources of fuel for electrical generation are oil, coal, natural gas, and nuclear reaction. Coal and natural gas are the preferred fuels due to their availability and stability in price. In 1997, natural gas accounted for 14 percent of electricity generation. The newest power plants are fueled by natural gas, and by 2030, it is estimated that 33 percent of electricity generation will be fueled by natural gas. The economics of transporting natural gas by ship are becoming more favorable. The technology is called *liquefied natural gas* (LNG). The ability to import LNG will create competition to the current gas pipelines from Mexico and Canada. Driven by greater use of natural gas by utilities and industrial customers, the demand for natural gas could increase by 2 to 3 percent a year. That doesn't seem like much, but the steadily increasing demand will create higher profits over time for natural gas companies.

Residential and commercial use of natural gas is also increasing. Natural gas is less expensive than fuel oil or electricity to heat homes. Heavy industries, such as aluminum smelting in the Northwest, are switching from oil fuel to natural gas due to its lower cost.

Small natural gas distribution companies should continue to offer long-term shareholder returns. Cascade Natural Gas (CGC) is a good example of a regional natural gas distributor. CGC distributes natural gas to over 185,000 customers in the states of Washington and Oregon. Over the past several years the company has maintained one of the highest customer growth rates in the United States. Cascade has experienced growth rates in excess of 5 percent while the industry has a customer growth rate of approximately 2 percent. CGC has a market cap of $236 million.

National Fuel Gas (NFG) explores, transports, and sells natural gas. Its distribution subsidiary sells or transports natural gas to more than 700,000 users in western New York and northwestern Pennsylvania. National Fuel Gas Supply, a subsidiary, stores and transports natural gas for outside companies through more than 3000 miles of pipeline and about 30 underground storage fields. Natural gas exploration arm Seneca Resources explores for and buys oil and gas reserves in Appalachia, California, and coastal Texas and Louisiana. National Fuel Gas also invests in foreign energy projects in Eastern Europe, markets energy to utilities and retail customers, and processes timber. NFG has a market cap of $1.9 billion.

Timber is another global resource often overlooked by investors. As a renewable resource, timber has become big business. Investors can buy stock in companies that own timberland and sell either finished wood products, such as lumber, or provide the harvested timber to the sawmill industry. Timberland is a unique combination of factory and warehouse. If demand for its timber wanes, a timber company merely reduces the amount it harvests. The balance of the timber can wait for another time. As trees age, they become more valuable. When demand slackens, those trees that were not harvested will continue to grow and increase in value. When demand is robust, most timber companies have the ability to easily increase their harvest rate.

Although timber as an investment has been overlooked by most investors, long-term returns have been outstanding. Over the past 75 years, timber assets have appreciated an average of 14 percent a year. Net after inflation, the real rate of return has fluctuated between 6 percent and 10 percent annually. During the 1990s, according to the Hancock Timber Group, a private institutional timber investment fund, U.S. timberland returned an average of 17 percent a year.

Who owns timberlands? Nearly one third of the United States is forested, or approximately 737 million acres, of which 490 million acres are considered viable for commercial purposes. Private citizens own 59 percent of commercially viable forests, but only about 3 percent of that is actively used for timber harvest. The government owns over 27 percent of those commercially viable forests. Timber and forest product companies own about 14 percent, or a bit more than 68 million acres. However, the amount of timber harvested from government land is small and growing smaller. In 1988, the amount of timber harvested from federal lands was 49 million cubic meters. By 1996, timber sales from federal lands were just 9 million cubic meters. In Oregon, the amount of timber harvested from government-owned lands (57 percent of total forests) decreased from 4430 million board feet in 1989 to 650 million board feet in 1995. Harvest from industry and private lands (21 percent of the total forests) in Oregon was relatively stable at 3720 million board feet and 3430 million board feet, respectively. Stricter federal land regulations and more "roadless" areas set aside (a current federal land-use proposal) may reduce timber harvest from federal lands by an additional 6 percent. With long-term reductions in timber availability from federal lands, timber companies and their timber assets could become more important, and more valuable.

Plum Creek Timber (PCL) is a good example of a well-managed timber company. PCL started over 50 years ago, and it has grown to become a large owner of western and northeastern timber. PCL currently owns 7.8 million acres of timber and 11 wood products plants producing lumber, plywood, and medium-density fiberboard. Manufactured products (68 percent of revenues) are sold to large retail building materials companies such as Home Depot (HD) and Lowe's (LOW), in addition to servicing smaller retailers through a network of 45 independent wholesalers. PCL also exports logs harvested from its land.

Plum Creek Timber had been a publicly traded *master limited partnership* (MLP) until its conversion to a REIT in July 1999. As a REIT, PCL is able to utilize special tax breaks given to owners of real estate investments. To qualify as a REIT, PCL must invest 75 percent of its total assets in real estate (timberlands), generate at least 75 percent of its profits from harvesting and selling timber, and must distribute 90 percent of its taxable income to its shareholders. With a slowdown in new-home building in 1999 and 2000 due to higher mortgage rates, the overall economic slowdown in 2001, and in view of the fact there was excess production of lumber industry-wide, PCL experienced a decline of revenues and profits. However, this decline should be viewed as temporary, and PCL will return to its winning ways as the general economy improves. PCL has a very high $2.28 per share annual dividend, yielding 7.6 percent at its current price of around $29.

Rayonier (RYN) is another timber company worth investigating. Rayonier is a leading international forest products company with operations around the world. RYN trades, merchandises, and manufactures logs, timber, and wood products, and it is a major producer of high-value-added specialty pulps. RYN has expanded its chemical cellulose segment, used to make noncommodity-grade pulp products. With business in 60 countries, the company derived 43 percent of its 2000 sales from customers outside the United States and Canada.

Rayonier's performance fibers division (46 percent of 2000 total sales) is a leading manufacturer of high-performance cellulose fibers. Cellulose specialty products have a wide variety of end uses, including rigid packaging, photographic film, pharmaceuticals, cosmetics, detergents, sausage casings, food products, thickeners for oil-well-drilling muds, and cigarette filters. RYN also supplies performance fibers for absorbent hygiene products. These fibers, typically referred to as *fluff fibers,* are used as an absorbent medium in products such as disposable baby diapers, sanitary napkins, convalescent bed pads, industrial towels and wipes, and nonwoven fabrics.

Rayonier's timberland management segment (22 percent) manages timberlands, sells standing timber to third parties, and sells timberlands for both future harvesting and real estate development. At the end of 2000, RYN owned, leased, or controlled about 2.3 million acres of timberland in the United States and New Zealand. RYN has a very active land management program that includes selling general timberland for others to manage and harvest and selling higher-value real estate properties for commercial and residential development purposes. The Wood Products and Trading business segment (32 percent) manufactures and sells dimension and specialty lumber and medium-density fiberboard, it purchases and harvests timber (primarily from third parties), and it sells logs and wood panel products.

Some investors like timber investments to diversify their portfolio. Timber company stock prices tend to move counter to general stock market movements. Timber companies are not as flamboyant as many high-tech businesses, and they usually gets pushed to the background as investors focus on the flashy and new-tech gadgets. When the stock market is hot, timber companies tend to lag in price. When the economy slows down, investors tend to flee the more speculative high-tech field and focus on more mundane but steadily growing companies. Interest in timber assets tend to increase during times of economic weakness.

Timber is a basic commodity and moves in cycles. Between 1990 and 2000, lumber pricing experienced three major bottoms: in 1990 at $180 per thousand board feet, in 1995 at $208, and in 1998 at $265. Major market tops occurred twice in 1993 at $480, in 1996 at $480, and in 1999 at $440. In the winter of 2000, lumber prices again hit a 10-year low of $180. Interest rates were climbing, and there was a general fear among investors that the housing and paper markets would be in for a spill. Plum Creek Timber was trading at around $22, with an almost 10 percent dividend yield. As with most commodities trading at 10-year lows, shrewd investors began to investigate the reasons, and astute individuals bought PCL in the low $20s. Since then, PCL and the price of lumber have retraced from their decline. PCL is now trading around $30.

According to Robert Gibb, personal finance columnist for *The Canadian MoneySaver* magazine, "All is not right with Paul Bunyan." There is an ongoing trade dispute between the governments of the United States and Canada concerning the pricing of trees for logging, also known as *raw stumpage fees.* In the United States, public timber cutting rights are sold at auction, and the price for raw stumpage fees is based on what loggers and timber companies are willing to pay at that time. As 95 percent of U.S. timber comes from private land, rather than state and national forests, the issue of the U.S. government's direct involvement in setting market prices is insignificant. In Canada, however, the government owns 95 percent of the productive timberland. Forests are under the control and supervision of the Canadian provincial (like our states) governments, and not the Canadian federal government. Part of the provincial government's responsibility is to set the amount of stumpage to be cut and the price. According to Mr. Gibb, "The right to log, and at what price, on public land is set provincially by stumpage fees. The U.S. contention is that state-set stumpage fees are predetermined and artificially low, and therefore they amount to a subsidy. We believe that in any Canadian auction system, there would be few local companies with the resources to bid. This would likely translate to even lower stumpage fees."

This is not an irrelevant problem. According to Mr. Gibb, annual revenues for the timber industry in Canada are about $60 billion. As a much smaller economy than the United States, the timber industry in Canada is a significant portion of the economy, especially in the province of British Columbia. Mr. Gibb estimates that on a percentage basis, an equivalent industry in the United States would generate around $600 billion.

The United States and Canada have in the past negotiated various import restrictions and duties on Canadian lumber coming to the United States. The most recent lumber treaty expired, and the two sides could not come to a new agreement. The United States has now imposed a 30 percent import duty on all Canadian lumber imports.

Mr. Gibb characterized the timber disagreement as follows: "Because of our historic and trading relationships, disputes between our nations are more like a family quarrel at a festive dinner. We don't talk for a while, but eventually we will get over it. The timber dispute is typical." Investors in timber resources should be aware of this dispute. However, over the long term it should have modest impact on the performance of U.S. timber companies.

Investors should thoroughly investigate the water industry, the outsourcing services industry, the financial services industry, and the natural resources industries. Scouring these fields for the best-managed companies offering acceptable current stock valuations should result in several investment candidates.

Some investors may prefer to bypass the task of conducting individual stock research. These investors could buy mutual funds and rely on the investment decision process of the professional money manager. However, investing in mutual funds may not be the best use of your savings.

Author's Note.   During the writing of this book, Pennichuck (PNNW) accepted an acquisition offer from Philadelphia Suburban Corporation (PSC) valued at $106 million. The consolidation of the U.S. water industry marches on.

Mutual Funds

Too many investors overlook the costs of owning mutual funds. This oversight can have a dramatic impact on overall net annual returns. Most fund investors mistakenly focus on the annual gross returns as publicized by the fund. Instead, they should focus on net returns after fees and taxes. While choosing an individual stock may be a bit more complex, buying stock in overlooked companies can be more rewarding than buying shares in a small-cap mutual fund.

Some investors may want to take a shortcut to researching and following small- and mid-cap stocks. These individuals may be drawn to buy an actively managed small- or mid-cap equity fund. However, actively managed mutual funds may be bad for your financial health. There are tax issues and fees that may substantially erode the overall fund performance. Some investors may prefer to invest in small- and mid-cap index funds or exchange-traded funds that are lower cost. These funds also have fees, although they are substantially less. Individual investors who develop a diversified portfolio of individual overlooked stocks will have essentially implemented their own mutual fund strategy without the annual costs.

Mutual funds have been around for a long time. The concept is simple and very popular. Mutual funds are an easy way to diversify a portfolio without spending the time to select individual stocks. There is a common belief that the pros running the mutual funds are able to achieve a better return than an average individual investor. However, many fund investors have not thought much about the annual management fees or increased tax exposure associated with most funds. Sometimes 401(k) retirement plans only offer a choice of mutual funds. Fund selection becomes critical if it is the only choice. In that case, diligent research and understanding of the fund is paramount.

As an alternative to actively managed mutual funds, a well-researched portfolio of individual overlooked stocks, purchased at value prices, should amply reward long-term investors.

What Is a Mutual Fund?

Investors can pool money and hire a professional to make their investment decisions for them. Collectively, the pool, commonly known as a *mutual fund,* reaps the benefits of the pro's insight and stock-picking ability. Money managers, however, charge investors fees for their services, and any capital gains tax liability is passed on to investors of the fund. The value of the fund per share is known as the *net asset value* (NAV). Over time, the NAV is expected to rise and with it the investment value for the fund investors. Sometimes, a fund may trade at a discount to its NAV. When this occurs, fund buyers are paying less than the assets of the fund.

With investors pooling their capital, a mutual fund will purchase a portfolio of different stocks. The fund may have a specific focus that is of interest to some investors. For instance, I may want to invest in gold. Rather than researching all the gold companies, I could just buy a mutual fund that invests in many different gold stocks.

Some funds specialize strictly in specific overseas markets, whereas others will try to replicate the S&P 500 Index. Some funds may be very aggressive, such as Internet or IPO funds, while others are very conservative, investing in tax-free municipal bonds. Mutual funds come in just about every investing style imaginable.

Mutual funds are popular because they are easy to invest in and the hard part of finding profitable investments (finding overlooked companies with top-quality management whose stock is selling at reasonable prices) is left to someone else. Mutual funds are available to investors from the funds themselves or from stockbrokers. Some mutual funds restrict distribution only to brokers. Charles Schwab built his brokerage business by selling mutual funds to the investing public for a lower commission than the traditional stockbroker charged.

U.S. equity funds are categorized by their capitalization focus and the fund manager's investment style. The most common categories are the following:

- Large cap
- Mid cap
- Small cap
- Income
- Value
- Growth

Large-cap funds focus on large capitalization stocks, mid-cap funds on mid-cap stocks, and small-cap funds on small-cap stocks. Value funds usually seek stocks that are considered undervalued. Growth funds usually search for companies that have outstanding growth prospects. Income funds usually focus on generating a high dividend.

Mutual fund investors should make sure their fund selections have a 5-year and 10-year history for comparisons. Funds should be compared using the same type of trend analysis used when researching stocks.

Mutual Fund Fees

It would seem that mutual funds would be the perfect solution to successful investing and easy portfolio diversification. However, buying mutual funds may not be as simple or easy as investors believe. One reason there are over 6500 mutual funds from which to choose is that the money management business is very profitable. The worldwide profit potential for fund managers is expected to grow by between 12 and 20 percent a year. Where do the fund managers get their revenues? The answer is that they charge their clients fees, usually based on the value of the assets. As clients' account balances increase due to additional capital contributions, reinvestment of dividends and capital gains, the money manager realizes greater revenues.

According to *Mutual Fund* magazine, the "average" mutual fund charges an annual fee of 1.5 percent of the account balance. All funds maintain a cash balance. Depending on the fund's structure, fees are deducted from the cash balance of the fund on a quarterly basis. Cash is generated by the fund in one of four ways: sales commissions to buy or sell (called *loads*), a portion of dividends or interest on current investments, a portion of realized capital gains, and a portion of new investment capital. The NAV of the fund is calculated, and the manager's fee is deducted, which then lowers the NAV. Over time, as the assets in the fund increase, so does the real-dollar amount paid to the fund managers. Based on total industry-wide mutual fund assets of over $3 trillion, it could be safe to say that professional money managers as an industry reap over $45 billion in annual fees, regardless of any funds' performances. That is $45 billion annually that could, and should, have been saved for the fund investors' future.

Some mutual funds charge a commission to buy or sell their fund shares, and this is known as a *load*. If there are no commissions, the fund is known as a *no-load fund*. Some funds impose a sales commission if the shares are not held for a specific amount of time, such as 3 years. Loads cannot exceed 8.5 percent, but many funds charge 3.5 to 5.0 percent commission. Like a stockbroker's commission, loads reduce the investor's net dollar amount invested. Just because a fund may be no-load, where buying and selling shares are free, investors should not think their fund is fee free. A no-load fund may have higher annual management fees to compensate.

Mutual fund fees can be separated into several categories and may be substantially above or below the 1.5 percent average. Fees are not only used to pay for investment advice. Money management revenues also pay for the telephone bill, postage, rental of office space, and salaries for telephone solicitors. Operating expenses usually range from 0.2 to 2.0 percent of the fund's assets. Some funds charge a very controversial *12(b)-1 fee*, which is charged for advertising expenses, annual reports, prospectuses, and sales literature. If a fund charges a 12(b)-1 fee, current investors are being asked to pay the cost of finding new fund investors. Someone has to pay for those expensive TV ads, and it is usually current fund holders. The SEC has capped 12(b)-1 fees at 1 percent annually of the fund's assets.

Morningstar, Inc., is a leading mutual fund advisory service. Their publications are available by subscription, at your local library, or on the Internet at morningstar.com. Morningstar offers a historic profile of a fund's return and investment risk, along with a rating system of 1 to 5 stars (1 star is low, 3 is average, and 5 is high). Prior to purchasing any mutual fund, investors should research the fees, fund performance, and the specific stocks owned by the fund.

Building your own mini-mutual fund focused on overlooked stocks should be much less expensive. There should be no "management fees" because you are in charge of decision making. Capital gains taxes are due only when you choose to sell a position in the portfolio.

The funds listed below focus on investing in small- and mid-cap company stocks, and all of them have a history of at least 10 years. These randomly chosen funds will demonstrate differences among funds, as well as problems inherent with mutual fund investing in general. The fund name, ticker symbol, principal investment focus, assets as of March 2002, Morningstar's star ranking, and Morningstar's fund description and comments as of March 2002 follow:

Fidelity Value Fund (FDVLX) is a mid-cap value fund with the goal of long-term capital appreciation. Its assets total $16.61 billion, and its Morningstar rating is 4 stars. "Economic growth is more important to this fund than it is to most of its peers. That's because its portfolio is typically chock-full of industrials stocks. This approach hasn't led to consistent returns, and investors can find better value options elsewhere."

Fifth Third Multi-Cap Value Fund (MXSEX) invests in a wide variety of mostly mid-cap value assets, with at least 65 percent in equities, and $62 million in assets. Its Morningstar rating is 4 stars. "Run by a deep-value investor, this fund often has big stakes in beaten-down sectors. Management has been wary of high valuations for years, keeping a large portion of the fund's assets in cash. This offering will typically excel in a value-led market though."

T. Rowe Price Small Cap Value Fund (PRSVX) is a small-cap value fund with the goal of long-term capital appreciation and $1.797 billion in assets. Its Morningstar rating is 5 stars. "This fund embraces more micro-caps than many of its peers. Though these stocks can cause heartache in jittery markets, broad sector diversification and low-priced issues have held the fund steady. When smaller is better, it scores returns that could steal any heart."

Prudential Small Company Fund (*CHNDX*) is a small-cap value fund with the goal of long-term capital appreciation and $606 million in assets. Its Morningstar rating is 4 stars. "This offering has shed its deep-value skin, opting for a mix of both growth- and value-oriented names. That makeover has produced mediocre results thus far, but it's too early to tell how the fund will fare over the long haul."

Table 9–1 reviews the fees charged by each fund.

The SEC mandates that each new investor be provided with a prospectus. In the prospectus, the fund supplies information concerning the fees it charges. The fund projects expenses for 3-, 5-, and 10-year time frames, based on a $10,000 investment, 5 percent annual NAV growth, and redemption at the end of the period. If the fund performs better than 5 percent annually, the real dollars paid in fees could be much higher. Make sure you read this carefully and understand what you are paying to have your money managed for you.

The Securities and Exchange Commission has a mutual fund cost calculator at its Web site, sec.gov/investor/tools/mfcc/holding-period.

TABLE 9–1   Fund Fees for Fidelity Value Fund, Fifth Third Multi-Cap Value Fund, T. Rowe Price Small Cap Value Fund, Prudential Small Company Fund

	Sales Load, %		Expense Fees, %	Expense Projections, 10–Yr, $10,000
Fidelity Value Fund	None		0.48	$701 (low)
Fifth Third Multi-Cap Value Fund	0.25		1.83	$2148 (average)
T. Rowe Price Small Cap Value Fund	1.00	(if sold 1 yr)	0.90	$1131 (low)
Prudential Small Company Fund	5.00		2.06	$2190 (average)

Source: Morningstar.

htm. This calculator allows investors to estimate the total cost of owning a specific fund based on its past performance and its specific fee structure. The calculator estimates both the fees and the value of the potential earnings lost by paying the fees, also known as the *forgone earnings*. If you have access to the Internet, visit the SEC Web site and review your projected costs before buying any mutual funds. Table 9–2 outlines the estimated cost and performance for the four mutual funds, based on the most current expense ratio and their respective 10-year annual return from 1991 to 2001.

If an investor were to buy $10,000 of each of these funds, for a total investment of $40,000, in 10 years the funds may be worth $125,700. However, the investor would have paid a total of $10,400 in fees and would have forgone potential earnings of $7,600, for a total cost of holding these funds of $18,000. The investor could have had a portfolio worth $143,000 by not paying mutual fund fees and achieving the same annual returns. It may not be difficult to match the real investment returns of these funds. Over the past 10 years, the S&P 500 Index average annual return was about 14 percent.

The difference between cost estimates as reported in the fund's prospectus and the SEC cost calculator is simple, but dramatic. The fund estimates are based on a 5 percent compounded rate of return, while the calculations from the SEC Web site were based on much higher actual performance. In addition, the SEC Web site calculated the foregone earnings, giving the investor a clearer picture of the actual costs of owning a mutual fund. For example, Prudential Small Com-

TABLE 9–2 Estimated Future Fees and Fund Performance, 10-Year Average, $10,000, Fidelity Value Fund, Fifth Third Multi-Cap Value Fund, T. Rowe Price Small Cap Value Fund, Prudential Small Company Fund

	Return, %	Fees	Foregone Earnings	Projected Value
Fidelity Value Fund	14.59	$1065	$768	$37,202
Fifth Third Multi-Cap Value Fund	14.00	$3686	$2667	$30,718
T. Rowe Price Small Cap Value Fund	14.64	$1956	$1429	$35,786
Prudential Small Company Fund	11.06	$3791	$2757	$21,999

Source: Securities and Exchange Commission.

pany Fund will list their 10-year fee structure at $2190 in their prospectus, but the actual fee cost to investors may be as high as $3791 (in addition to foregone potential future earnings of $2757) for a total holding cost of $6548, if the fund continues to return 11.06 percent annually.

In order to match the return of the market on a net investment basis, mutual funds have to outperform the market equal to its fees. For example, Prudential Small Company Fund charges a 2.09 percent fee. If the market goes up by 10 percent, to match the market performance, the Prudential fund has to go up by 12.09 percent. Management will deduct their 2.09 percent fee from the fund, leaving investors with a 10 percent return. It is possible for Prudential to outperform the market by less than its fees. For example, the fund may return 11 percent, 1 percent better than the market. In this case, the fund can brag that it beat the market by 1 percent when in reality, after deducting fees, investors realized a net underperformance.

Each and every year, mutual funds charge each and every investor management fees. It is a fact of life for mutual fund investors. Whether the fund is held in a tax-deferred account or in a taxable account, the fund managers always get their cut. Over time, mutual fund fees and the foregone potential earnings can add up to a substantial amount of money.

Mutual Fund "Phantom" Capital Gains Taxes

As mutual fund managers trade stocks and bonds for a profit, each capital gain triggers a tax event. Federal tax code requires all mutual fund investors to report their share of the fund's capital gains on their individual income tax return. Mutual funds send annual tax statements both to the IRS and to fund investors indicating dividends paid and the amount of *undistributed capital gains*—that is, the gains made by the fund that have not been distributed to investors. The fund generally uses the proceeds of the sale to buy other equities, to pay fees, or to pay investors seeking to redeem their shares. However, the fund holders are responsible for the tax liability from the capital gain. Although fund holders have not sold the shares of the fund or generated any capital gains firsthand, they are responsible for the tax due.

The phrase *phantom capital gains tax liability* refers to the increased federal and state income taxes paid by mutual fund investors under those circumstances in which the investors did not create the capital gains themselves by selling their fund shares at a profit. Over time, this tax liability can add up. It is likely that some fund investors pay more in added income tax than they receive in dividends. Table 9–3 outlines the dividends paid, undistributed capital gains, and capital gains tax liability calculated at 20 percent, for the same four funds from 1991 to 2000.

In other words, investors in three out of four funds we are reviewing, except the Fifth Third, paid more in additional income taxes than they received in dividends. Make sure you review the dividend and undistributed capital gains history of your mutual fund selections. Ten-year mutual fund capital gains distribution history is available from the printed version of the Morningstar reports, usually found at your library. It is worth your time to manually calculate the potential tax liability to get a clearer picture of the costs to own a specific fund.

With the current long-term capital gains tax around 20 percent, funds with undistributed capital gains greater than five times the dividend will create a tax liability greater than the dividend. Because most funds reinvest both the capital gains and dividends paid back into the fund, fund investors don't realize any cash flow to offset the tax liability. In addition, as with ownership of individual stocks, mutual fund divi-

TABLE 9–3   Fund Dividends per Share, Undistributed Capital Gains per Share, Estimated Capital Gains Tax Paid per Share, and the Difference between Dividends Received and Taxes Paid, 1991–2000

	Dividends	Undistributed Capital Gains	Estimated Taxes Paid	Difference between Dividends and Taxes Paid
Fidelity Value Fund	$5.31	$33.60	$6.72	–$1.41
Fifth Third Multi-Cap Value Fund	$2.19	$10.34	$2.06	$0.13
T. Rowe Price Small Cap Value Fund	$1.69	$8.79	$1.75	–$0.06
Prudential Small Company Fund	$0.00	$9.89	$1.98	–$1.98

dends are also taxable as a part of individual earned-income calculations. Table 9–4 outlines both earned-income taxes due from the dividend (in the 35 percent tax bracket for combined federal and state income tax) and the capital gains tax.

For every Fidelity Value Fund share held, the estimated cost in additional income taxes paid is $8.57. As most investors reinvest mutual fund dividends, we usually pay the taxes we owe the government out of our earned income. Investors owning 100 shares of Fidelity Value Fund from 1991 to 2000 would have paid $857 in taxes over that 10-year period.

The latest buzzword in the mutual fund industry is *tax-advantaged funds.* Simply put, tax-advantaged funds don't have a high turnover of assets, which creates a lower phantom capital gains tax liability. For example, suppose an index fund sells only when a stock is dropped from the index and buys only when a stock is added to the index. Index funds are considered tax advantaged as they do not trade stocks based on the fickle opinion of a mutual fund manager.

Morningstar lists after-tax returns over time for all the funds it follows. In addition, it offers the potential future capital gains exposure as a percentage of assets and the portfolio turnover ratio. The turnover ratio indicates, on a percentage basis, the amount of assets the fund buys and sells in any given year. A high turnover ratio and potential future capital gains exposure indicates a higher potential phantom capital gains tax that fund investors may have to pay in the future. Table 9–5 outlines the average turnover percentage over the past 10 years, along with the current potential capital gains exposure as a percentage of fund assets.

TABLE 9–4   Estimated Earned Income Taxes Due on the Dividend per Share, Estimated Capital Gains Tax Due per Share, and Total Estimated Taxes Due per Share, 1991–2000

	Dividends	Earned Income Tax	Capital Gains Tax	Estimated Tax Due per Share
Fidelity Value Fund	$5.31	$1.85	$6.72	$8.57
Fifth Third Multi-Cap Value Fund	$2.19	$0.76	$2.06	$2.82
T. Rowe Price Small Cap Value Fund	$1.69	$0.59	$1.75	$2.34
Prudential Small Company Fund	$0.00	$0.00	$1.98	$1.98

TABLE 9-5 Average Annual Turnover Rate, Potential Capital Gains
Exposure, Pretax 10-Year Average Return and 10-Year Average after
Phantom Capital Gains Tax Return, 1991–2000

	Average Annual Turnover, %	Potential Capital Gains Exposure, %	Pretax Annual Return, %	After-Tax Annual Return, %
Fidelity Value Fund	87.4	−1	14.59	11.93
Fifth Third Multi-Cap Value Fund	142.5	23	14.00	11.53
T. Rowe Price Small Cap Value Fund	16.2	30	14.64	12.90
Prudential Small Company Fund	61.2	13	11.06	8.89

Source: Morningstar.

As shown in Table 9–6, deducting fund management fees from the
10-year average annual after-tax return should be enough to make any
fund investor weep. Keep in mind that the S&P 500 Index generated
about a 12 percent average annual return over the past 75 years. Developing your own portfolio of individual overlooked stocks may provide
better returns than many actively managed mutual funds.

These funds have served their investors poorly when phantom capital gains taxes and annual management fees are deducted from their
reported performance. These funds illustrate the problems of relying
on the most actively managed mutual funds as investment vehicles.

TABLE 9-6 Before-Tax 10-Year Average Return, After-Tax 10-Year Average
Return, 2000 Expense Ratio, After-Tax, After-Fee Estimated Annual Return,
1991–2000

	Before-Tax Annual Return, %	After-Tax Annual Return, %	Expense Ratio, %	After-Tax, After-Fee Return, %
Fidelity Value Fund	14.59	11.93	0.48	11.45
Fifth Third Multi-Cap Value Fund	14.00	11.53	1.83	9.70
T. Rowe Price Small Cap Value	14.64	12.90	0.90	12.00
Prudential Small Company Fund	11.06	8.89	2.06	6.83

While funds may seem to be an attractive alternative to investing in individual companies, it is important for investors to understand the true cost and net returns of mutual funds.

Mutual Funds and Tax-Deferred Accounts

One way to minimize the effect of taxes on ownership of mutual funds is to purchase them in a tax-deferred account, such as an IRA or a 401(k). Capital gains in tax-deferred accounts are not taxed, and the phantom capital gains tax liability is not an issue. However, the annual management fee should be. Keep in mind that reported annual returns do not include their fees, and investors must deduct the expense ratio manually to understand their net investment return.

Many times there are no other choices but mutual funds for tax-deferred accounts. Many employer-sponsored plans offer enrollees the options to select from a basket of funds but no individual stocks. If held in a tax-deferred account, capital gains taxes are not an issue. Investors should, however, determine the net return after fees and compare it to the underlying average. Make sure you review a minimum of 5-year returns, with an eye on the 10-year analysis. For example, the Prudential Small Company Fund reported a 10-year average annual return of 11.06 percent. The small-cap index, The Russell 2000, returned 15.11 percent, for an underperformance by Prudential of 4.05 percent annually. Pile on an expense ratio of 2.09 percent, and Prudential's underperformance grows to a whopping 6.14 percent, even if held in a tax-deferred account.

You should invest in funds that have systematically outperformed the underlying market average by at least their expense ratio.

Fund Portfolio Analysis

Make sure you review what the fund owns. This information is also found in the Morningstar publication, or in the fund's quarterly and annual reports. For example, the top 10 holdings of the Fidelity Value Fund are American Standard, Republic Services, Waste Management, Harsco, Freddie Mac, John H Harland, Fannie May, CNF, Consolidated Stores, and Snap-On Tools. I am sure most investors don't know half the companies listed, but if they own shares of Fidelity Value Fund, they probably should. Research at least a short profile of each company, available either at your local library or on the Internet. As a minimum, investors who own multiple funds should review the top 10 holdings for duplication. If you currently own four funds, each with a position in Microsoft, do you need another fund that also owns Microsoft? Probably not.

"The Grand Infatuation"

According to William Bernstein, author of the article "The Grand Infatuation," superior fund performance is a fleeting phenomenon. Mr. Bernstein reviewed the work of Micropal, a fund performance analysis company. Micropal's worldwide database of fund performance dates back 3 decades. Starting in 1970, Micropal looked at the top 30 performing funds for a 5-year period and followed their performance to 1998. The results, shown in Table 9–7, are very revealing. Funds that

TABLE 9–7 Average Annual Returns, Top Fund Performance for 5 Years versus Fund Performance to 1998

	Top 30 Funds Returns, %	All Funds Returns, %	S&P 500 Return, %
Top funds 1970–1974	0.78	−6.12	−2.35
Returns 1975–1998	16.05	16.38	17.04
Top funds 1975–1979	35.70	20.44	14.76
Returns 1980–1998	15.78	15.28	17.67
Top funds 1980–1984	22.51	14.83	14.76
Returns 1985–1998	16.01	15.59	18.76
Top funds 1985–1989	22.08	16.40	20.41
Returns 1990–1998	16.24	15.28	17.81
Top funds 1990–1994	18.94	9.39	8.69
Returns 1995–1998	21.28	24.60	32.18

Source: fundsinteractive.com.

outperformed the underlying market averages for 5 years underperformed the market after that.

In each period, the top 30 performing funds for a 5-year period underperformed the S&P 500 for the balance of the time frame. Investors clamor to buy the hot money managers, without realizing their stellar performance is most likely to be fleeting. It is human nature to want to invest in the best-performing funds, with the reasonable expectation that the performance will continue. However, analysis doesn't bear that out. The best funds of today historically lag in performance going forward.

Exchange-Traded and Index Funds

Some investors prefer low-cost exchange-traded funds (ETFs) or index funds. ETFs are funds with very low turnover and low fees that invest in specific securities. They are not usually actively managed, which keeps the fees low. The portfolio is very stable, and the phantom capital gains tax is a minor issue. ETFs trade mainly on the American Exchange and are available in a wide variety of investment themes. For example, there are ETFs that invest in computer software makers, semiconductor manufacturers, or retail companies. There are ETFs for every S&P economic sector, including energy, technology, and consumer staples. Investors may choose a fund that tracks an overall index, such as the Dow Jones Industrial Average ETF or the S&P 500 ETF, or specialty ETFs, such as the Dow Jones Small Cap Index ETF. There are over 100 ETFs to choose from. A host of financial companies offer ETFs, such as Barclays Bank, Vanguard, and Merrill Lynch. ETFs are unmanaged portfolios of stocks that usually replicate a specific index or economic sector.

Once an ETF is established, the investment portfolios within the ETF don't change much over time. Investors buying an ETF know what is in their portfolio and can make an intelligent decision about the long-term desirability of owning those particular stocks. On the other hand, actively managed mutual funds buy and sell on a consistent basis. The portfolio of a mutual fund changes based on the manager's belief in the future potential of each position. Fund managers are not required to immediately disclose stock trades, and they report their holdings only twice a year. Investors don't usually find out about portfolio changes until several months after the mutual fund buys or sells.

This makes it difficult to accurately determine what is in the mutual fund prior to investing.

Currently, no ETF charges more than 1.0 percent annually. ETFs are usually purchased through a broker, however, so there are purchase and sales commissions. There are online and discount brokers, with very low commissions. For example, sharebuilder.com charges commissions of $4 per regularly scheduled purchase and offers a wide variety of ETFs from which to choose. There are a few ETFs, such as Vanguard's S&P 500 Index Fund, which can be purchased directly without the expense of paying a broker.

Based on recent trading volume, these are the most popular ETFs:

iShares Goldman Sachs Software Index (IGV), specialty technology

iShares Dow Jones Industrial Index (IYJ), large blend

iShares Dow Jones Internet Index (IYV), specialty technology

streetTracks Morgan Stanley High Tech Index (MTK), specialty technology

iShares Dow Jones Technology Index (IWZ), large growth

iShares Dow Jones Real Estate Index (IYR), specialty real estate

iShares Dow Jones Financial Index (IYG), specialty financials

streetTracks Dow Jones Global Titans Index (DGT), large blend

iShares Russell 1000 Value Index (IWD), large value

streetTracks Dow Jones Small Cap Value Index (DSV), small value

I interviewed John Wasik, author of *Bear Proof Your Investments*, concerning ETFs and mutual funds. Mr. Wasik has an interesting opinion on ETFs and index funds. He believes actively managed mutual funds can create severe problems for their investors: "Actively managed mutual funds have high portfolio turnover, are tax punishing, and perform poorly over the long term. Fees and taxes are due even if the fund loses value. Most people could benefit from a studied strategy of buying and holding equities and index ETFs." "Get into an index fund and stay there," is Mr. Wasik's advice.

Investors can easily build a core portfolio of ETFs that focus on specific investing styles. For instance, an investor could choose a portfolio of low-cost ETFs:

Vipers Total Market Fund (VTI), 0.15 percent expense ratio

iShares S&P Small-Cap 600 Index (IJS), 0.25 percent expense ratio

iShares S&P Mid-Cap 400 Index (IJJ), 0.25 percent expense ratio

iShares S&P Europe 350 Index Fund (IEV), 0.60 percent expense ratio

The investor gains a diversified core portfolio, with the added exposure to both small- and mid-cap stocks. The S&P Europe 350 Index ETF adds international exposure and diversification. From this core of low-cost, tax-efficient index funds, an investor can begin to expand into various individual equities.

Profitable investing takes time and a bit of effort. Passing the responsibility of money management to others is costly and may result in market underperformance. When mutual funds are your only choice, make sure you understand the fund you are buying. ETFs may be preferable due to their lower cost. However, investing in individual overlooked stocks and building a mini-mutual fund of your own can be much more rewarding.

CHAPTER **10**

Putting It All Together

Money is better than poverty,
if only for financial reasons
—WOODY ALLEN

Too many individuals prefer not to think about their futures. Living for today is easy. Scrimping and saving for tomorrow is much more difficult. However, if you don't focus on your future and your future financial needs, when the future becomes today, you will be ill prepared. Developing an investment checklist and understanding the steps to finding value-priced, overlooked stocks should help you beat the overall market returns. Following the advice and stock-picking techniques outlined in this book should improve your chances of getting ahead financially.

Chapter 1 Key Points

You need to be systematically saving and investing a portion of your earned income.

Pay off consumer debt, especially credit card debt.

Start early in your life and invest smartly.

The longer your money is invested, the lower the investment risks.

Stocks have historically outperformed bonds and money market accounts.

Chapter 2 Key Points

Diversify your portfolio with stocks and bonds.

Increasing corporate earnings is the major factor in the search for higher share prices.

Be an investor, not a speculator.

Diversify across economic sectors and market capitalizations.

Chapter 3 Key Points

Companies go through life cycles with defined stages.

Overlooked companies have specific and identifiable characteristics and attributes.

Chapter 4 Key Points

The importance of the quality of management cannot be overstated.

There are several important management efficiency ratios that can be used to evaluate performance.

Review both current management efficiency ratios and their long-term trends.

S&P rankings may provide insight into the probability of continued corporate success.

Mission statements, letters to shareholders, and ethics statements give added insight.

Management stock option programs warrant careful investor review.

Chapter 5 Key Points

Find investments with great long-term value.

Review a few stock value tools before investing in a specific company.

Be aware of contrarian investing opportunities.

Take systematic profits in an investment that outperforms.

Chapter 6 Key Points

Build a portfolio of overlooked stocks to complement other investments.

Manage stock market volatility.

Bull markets usually last longer and offer higher returns than bear markets take away.

Intelligent investment criteria are timeless.

Chapter 7 Key Points

Diversify your portfolio with REITs and ADRs.

REIT and ADR investing criteria differ from the criteria that apply to other types of equities.

Chapter 8 Key Points

There are powerful trends within overlooked industries.

These trends offer exceptional long-term opportunities for companies and investors.

Chapter 9 Key Points

Actively managed mutual funds are popular because they are easy to invest in.

Mutual funds may be more expensive than investors realize.

Know the companies your fund invests in.

The best-performing funds over a 5-year time frame don't continue to outperform.

ETFs and index funds are acceptable alternatives to actively managed mutual funds.

Develop your own mini-mutual fund of overlooked stocks.

Profitable investing requires continuous learning. New investment opportunities, overlooked companies, and new ways of analysis make profitable investing a continuous challenge. While not every investment decision will prove to be a winner, being selective and focusing on your personal investment criteria will greatly improve the likelihood of achieving your financial goals. Staying the course and raking the market for investment bargains are proven methods of increasing personal wealth over the long term.

The potential investment opportunities of overlooked stocks are available to all who take the time to adequately research them. Small- and mid-cap companies with proven managers and reasonable stock prices are not difficult to find when you know where to look. Utilizing the tools you learned in this book will put you head and shoulders above the average investor, especially those investors who purchase only actively managed mutual funds.

Maximizing personal wealth should be the ultimate financial goal of everyone.

Standard & Poor's Global Industry Classification Standard

A s an investor builds a portfolio, it is important to hold many different stocks in different industries. Review the industry classification of each stock you own. As you watch your portfolio grow in value, it is easy to lose track of diversification. The listing below should help you in assessing your own current level of diversification.

Standard & Poor's developed a widely accepted categorization of economic sectors. In 2000, S&P updated and refined their categorization, and it is presented below. Investors should review the subindustry categories in detail as new investing ideas may arise. For example, Harley-Davidson (HDI), the manufacturer of heavyweight motorcycles, and Home Depot (HD), the building materials retailer, are categorized in the consumer discretionary sector.

Standard & Poor's Global Industry Classification Standard (GICS)

Economic Sector
    Industry Group
        Industry
            Subindustry

Energy
    A. Energy
        1. Energy Equipment and Services
        2. Oil and Gas

Materials
    A. Materials
        1. Chemicals
            Commodity Chemicals
            Diversified Chemicals
            Fertilizers and Agricultural Chemicals
            Industrial Gases
        2. Specialty Chemicals
        3. Construction Materials
        4. Containers and Packaging
            Metal and Glass Containers
            Paper Packaging
        5. Metals and Mining
            Aluminum
            Diversified Metals and Mining
            Gold
            Precious Metals and Minerals
            Steel
        6. Paper and Forest Products

Industrials
    A. Capital Goods
        1. Aerospace and Defense
        2. Building Products
        3. Construction and Engineering
        4. Electrical Equipment
            Electrical Components and Equipment
            Heavy Electrical Equipment
        5. Industrial Conglomerates
        6. Machinery
            Construction and Farm Machinery
            Industrial Machinery
        7. Trading Companies and Distributors
    B. Commercial Services and Supplies

1. Commercial Services and Supplies
    Commercial Printing
    Data Processing Services
    Diversified Commercial Services
    Employment Services
    Environmental Services
    Office Services and Supplies
C. Transportation
    1. Air Freight and Couriers
    2. Airlines
    3. Marine
    4. Trucking and Railroads
    5. Transportation Infrastructure
        Airport Services
        Highways and Railtracks
        Marine Ports and Services
Consumer Discretionary
A. Automobiles and Components
    1. Auto Components
        Auto Parts and Equipment
        Tires and Rubber
    2. Automobiles
        Automobile Manufacturers
        Motorcycle Manufacturers
B. Consumer Durables and Apparel
    1. Household Durables
        Consumer Electronics
        Home Furnishings
        Homebuilding
        Household Appliances
        Housewares and Specialties
    2. Leisure Equipment and Products
        Leisure Products
        Photographic Products
    3. Textiles and Apparel
        Apparel and Accessories
        Footwear
        Textiles

C. Hotels, Restaurants and Leisure
    1. Hotels, Restaurants and Leisure
        Casinos and Gaming
        Hotels
        Leisure Facilities
        Restaurants
D. Media
    1. Media
        Advertising
        Broadcasting and Cable TV
        Movies and Entertainment
        Publishing and Printing
E. Retailing
    1. Distributors
    2. Internet and Catalog Retail
        Catalog Retail
        Internet Retail
    3. Multiline Retail
        Department Stores
        General Merchandise Stores
    4. Specialty Retail
        Apparel Retail
        Computer and Electronics Retail
        Home Improvement Retail
        Specialty Stores

Consumer Staples
    A. Food and Drug Retailing
        1. Food and Drug Retailing
            Drug Retail
            Food Distributors
            Food Retail
    B. Food, Beverage and Tobacco
        1. Beverages
            Brewers
            Distillers and Vintners
            Soft Drinks

2. Food Products
  Agricultural Products
  Meat, Poultry and Fish
  Packaged Foods
3. Tobacco
C. Household and Personal Products
  1. Household Products
  2. Personal Products
Health Care
  A. Health Care Equipment and Services
    1. Health Care Equipment and Supplies
      Health Care Equipment
      Health Care Supplies
    2. Health Care Providers and Services
      Health Care Distributors and Services
      Health Care Facilities
      Managed Health Care
  B. Pharmaceuticals and Biotechnology
    1. Biotechnology
    2. Pharmaceuticals
Financials
  A. Banks
  B. Diversified Financials
    1. Diversified Financials
      Consumer Finance
      Diversified Financial Services
      Multisector Holdings
  C. Insurance
    1. Insurance
      Insurance Brokers
      Life and Health Insurance
      Multiline Insurance
      Property and Casualty Insurance
      Reinsurance
  D. Real Estate
    1. Real Estate
      Real Estate Investment Trusts
      Real Estate Management and Development

Information Technology
- A. Software and Services
    1. Internet Software and Services
    2. IT Consulting and Services
    3. Software
        Application Software
        Systems Software
- B. Technology Hardware and Equipment
    1. Communications Equipment
        Networking Equipment
        Telecommunications Equipment
    2. Computers and Peripherals
        Computer Hardware
        Computer Storage and Peripherals
    3. Electronic Equipment and Instruments
    4. Office Electronics
    5. Semiconductor Equipment and Products
        Semiconductor Equipment
        Semiconductors

Telecommunication Services
- A. Telecommunication Services
    1. Diversified Telecommunication Services
        Alternative Carriers
        Integrated Telecommunication Services
    2. Wireless Telecommunication Services

Utilities
- A. Utilities
    1. Electric Utilities
    2. Gas Utilities
    3. Multiutilities
    4. Water Utilities

Source: standardpoors.com.

Overlooked Company Reviews, Energy Sector

Many investors seek a place to start their research on overlooked stocks. The following appendixes offer in-depth company reviews of a few often overlooked small- and mid-cap companies that may be of interest. In these reviews, an investor should look for long-term reasons to continue his or her research to determine if a particular company fits the investor's specific diversification and risk tolerance. This is only a partial list of overlooked companies, but it provides some good examples of the types of companies investors may uncover in their search.

The company reviews are presented by sector in Appendixes 2 through 11. The following is an alphabetical list of the companies reviewed:

American Capital Strategies	Apache Corporation	Barra, Inc.
CenturyTel	Chicago Bridge & Iron Company N.V.	Cinergy Corp.
Copart, Inc.	Donnelly Corporation	Enterprise Products Partners L.P.
Federal Signal Corporation	Flextronics Corporation	Florida Rock Industries, Inc.

Franklin Resources, Inc.	Heineken N.V.	Hormel Foods Corporation
Hudson United Bancorp	Illinois Tool Works, Inc.	Jabil Circuit, Inc.
Kennametal, Inc.	McCormick & Company, Inc.	Medicis Pharmaceutical Corporation
Omnicare, Inc.	Paychex, Inc.	Philadelphia Suburban Corporation
Pitney Bowes, Inc.	Plum Creek Timber Company, Inc.	Progress Energy Ltd.
Raymond James Financial, Inc.	The Scotts Company	Seacoast Financial Services Corporation
Shire Pharmaceutical	Southwest Water	Symantec Corporation
TDS	The Toro Company	Waddell & Reed, Inc.
WD-40 Company		

Apache Corporation (APA), an independent energy company that explores for, develops, and produces natural gas, crude oil, and natural gas liquids, has grown recently through acquisitions. In North America, the company's exploration and production (E&P) operations focused on the Gulf of Mexico and Gulf Coast, and on the Anadarko, Permian, and Western Canadian Sedimentary Basins. Internationally, APA has E&P efforts off the shore of western Australia and in Egypt. In addition, the company conducts exploration in Poland, and offshore The People's Republic of China. Oil and gas accounted for 48 and 52 percent of total reserves, respectively. Production in 2000 totaled 95.2 MMBOE and consisted of 53 percent gas and 47 percent oil and natural gas liquids.

The company believes it is often more attractive to buy particular assets, rather than entire companies, due to cultural differences between boards of directors. In May 1999, it bought from Shell Offshore its interest in 22 producing fields and 16 undeveloped blocks located in the Gulf of Mexico. The purchase price was $687.6 million in cash, plus 1 million common shares. In December, APA purchased from Shell Canada (a separate entity) properties in western Canada. The acquisition also included 300,000 net acres of undeveloped lease holdings, a gas processing plant, and a substantial seismic database.

In January 2000, APA bought from Repsol properties located in western Oklahoma and the Texas Panhandle, with proven reserves. In June, it acquired from Collins & Ware properties located in the Permian Basin and South Texas. In August, the company bought from Occidental Petroleum 32 producing fields located in the Gulf of Mexico. The purchase price of $385 million was financed through a public equity offering of 9.2 million common.

Chicago Bridge & Iron Company N.V. (CBI), incorporated in 1996, is a global engineering and construction company specializing in the design and engineering, fabrication, field erection, and repair of bulk liquid terminals, storage tanks, process vessels, low-temperature and cryogenic storage facilities, and other steel-plate structures and their associated systems. The company has been engaged in the engineering and construction industry since being founded in 1889.

In February 2002, the company, through its subsidiary, Howe-Baker International, L.L.C., acquired the assets of TPA, Inc. The acquired business is a full-service company specializing in sulfur removal and recovery technologies for the refining, gas processing, and chemical manufacturing industries.

Flat-bottom tanks—that is, aboveground storage tanks—are sold primarily to customers operating in the petroleum, petrochemical, and chemical industries around the world. This industrial customer group includes many of the world's major oil and chemical companies. Depending on the industry and application, flat-bottom tanks can be used for storage of crude oil-refined products, such as gasoline, raw water, potable water, chemicals, petrochemicals, and a large variety of feedstocks for the manufacturing industry.

Low-temperature/cryogenic tanks and systems are used primarily for the storage and handling of liquefied gases. Applications extend from low-temperature (over 30°F to −100°F) to cryogenic (−100°F to −423°F). Customers in the petroleum, chemical, petrochemical, specialty gas, natural gas, power generation, and agricultural industries use these tanks and systems to store and handle liquefied gases such as LNG, methane, ethane, ethylene, LPG, propane, propylene, butane, butadiene, anhydrous ammonia, oxygen, nitrogen, argon, and hydrogen.

Repair, maintenance, and modification services are performed primarily on flat-bottom tanks and pressure vessels. While the company has focused on providing these services primarily in the United States, efforts are underway to expand these services throughout the world. Customers in the petroleum, chemical, petrochemical, and water industries generally require these types of services.

Turnaround services are offered to a wide variety of customers. A *turnaround* is a planned shutdown of a refinery or other process unit for repair and maintenance of equipment and associated systems. The work is usually scheduled on a multishift, 7-day-per-week basis to minimize downtime of the facility. Personnel, materials, and equipment must come together at precisely the right time to accomplish this labor-intensive operation. The company offers this service to its customers in the petroleum, petrochemical, and chemical industries throughout the world.

The company provides engineering, procurement, and construction services for customers in the hydrocarbon industry, specializing in natural gas processing plants, refinery and petrochemical process units, and hydrogen and synthesis gas plants. Natural gas processing plants treat natural gas to meet pipeline requirements and to recover valuable liquids and other enhanced products through better technologies. Refinery and petrochemical process units enable customers to extract products from the top and middle streams of the crude oil barrel. Synthesis gas plants generate industrial gases for use in a variety of industries through technologies. (Commentary not provided by the *S&P Stock Guide.*)

Enterprise Products Partners L.P. (EPD) is an integrated North American provider of natural gas processing and natural gas liquids (NGL) processing transportation and storage services. The company is a limited partnership that conducts substantially all of its business through Enterprise Products Operating L.P. (the operating partnership), the operating partnership's subsidiaries, and a number of joint ventures with industry partners. The company was formed in April 1998.

The company's NGL operations are concentrated in the Texas, Louisiana, and the Mississippi Gulf Coast area. A large portion is concentrated in Mont Belvieu, Texas, which is the hub of the domestic NGL industry and is adjacent to a large concentration of refineries and petrochemical plants. The company's operations are segregated into five business segments. These segments are fractionation, pipeline, processing, octane enhancement, and other.

Fractionation. NGL fractionation facilities separate mixed NGL streams into discrete NGL products: ethane, propane, isobutane, normal butane, and natural gasoline. The company's NGL fractionation operations include seven NGL fractionators. The company's propylene fractionation business consists of two polymer-grade propylene facilities.

Pipeline. The company's pipeline segment includes its ownership interests in a 2942-mile network of transportation and distribution pipeline systems and related hydrocarbon storage facilities and import-export assets. Among the major pipeline systems owned by the company are the Dixie Pipeline, the Louisiana Pipeline System, and the Lou-Tex Propylene Pipeline System. The segment also includes the company's pipeline systems, storage facilities, and the Houston Ship Channel Import/Export terminal.

Processing. The processing segment consists of the company's natural gas processing business and related merchant activities. At the core of the company's natural gas processing business are 12 natural gas processing plants located on the Louisiana and Mississippi Gulf Coast. The NGL production from these facilities, along with that from the Mont Belvieu isomerization facilities, supports the merchant activities included in this operating segment. The company's natural gas processing facilities are primarily straddle plants, which are situated on mainline natural gas pipelines, which bring unprocessed natural gas production onshore from the Gulf of Mexico. Straddle plants allow plant owners to extract NGLs from a natural gas stream when the market value of the NGLs is higher than the market value of the same unprocessed natural gas.

Other.   This operating segment is primarily composed of fee-based marketing services. The company performs NGL marketing services, for which it charges a commission. The company utilizes the resources of its gas processing merchant business group to perform these services. This segment also includes other engineering services, construction equipment rentals, and computer network services that support various plant operations.

Overlooked Company Reviews, Materials Sector

Florida Rock Industries, Inc. (FRK), incorporated in 1945, is principally engaged in the production and sale of ready-mixed concrete, the mining, processing, and sale of sand, gravel, and crushed stone (construction aggregates), and the production and sale of portland and masonry cement. The company also produces and sells concrete block, prestressed concrete, and calcium products, and it sells other building materials. All of its operations are conducted within the southeastern United States, primarily in Florida, Georgia, Tennessee, Virginia, Maryland, Washington, D.C., and North Carolina. The company also has an investment in a stone quarry and a sand and gravel plant in Charlotte County, New Brunswick, Canada.

The company manufactures and markets ready-mixed concrete, concrete block, and precast and prestressed concrete. It also markets other building materials. Its concrete operations serve most of Florida, with the principal exception of the panhandle; southern and southwest Georgia; central Maryland; the Richmond-Petersburg-Hopewell, Williamsburg, Hampton, Newport News, and Norfolk/Virginia Beach areas of Virginia, along with northeastern Virginia and Washington, D.C.

At most of the company's Florida and Georgia concrete facilities, it purchases and resells building material items related to the use of ready-mixed concrete and concrete block. Prestressed concrete products for commercial developments and bridge and highway construction are produced in Wilmington, North Carolina. Precast concrete lintels and other building products are produced in Kissimmee, Florida.

The company produces portland and masonry cement in Newberry, Florida, which is sold in both bulk and bags to the ready-mix concrete industry and the retail home improvement markets. Calcium products for the animal feed industry are produced in Brooksville, Florida, and for the roofing industry in Fredrick, Maryland.

By pursuing an aggressive acquisition strategy, **Plum Creek Timber Company, Inc. (PCL)** has increased its timber holdings over the past decade from 1.4 million acres to more than 7.8 million acres, becoming the second-largest private timberland owner in the United States. Located in three distinct regions (the Northwest, the Northeast, and the South), PCL's geographically diverse timberland holdings help the company reduce its exposure to regional economic fluctuations. PCL, which qualifies as a REIT for tax purposes, produces lumber, plywood, and other wood products at its nine mills located near the company's timberlands in Montana and Idaho. PCL's October 2001 merger with The Timber Company, a separate operating group of Georgia-Pacific Corp., more than doubled its timber holdings for a purchase price of $3.4 billion. The company has about 2.0 million acres of timberlands in the Northwest, 1.4 million acres in the Northeast, and some 4.4 million acres in the Southern region. Logs are sold to unaffiliated domestic wood product manufacturers, pulp and paper mills, and into the export market; logs harvested in the Northwest region also supply PCL's own lumber and plywood facilities.

Manufacturing operations include four lumber mills, two plywood plants, one medium-density fiberboard facility, and two lumber remanufacturing facilities. Lumber products include common and select boards, studs, edge-glued boards, and finger-jointed studs. Products are targeted to domestic lumber retailers, such as retail home centers, for use in repair and remodeling projects; they are also sold to stocking distributors for use in home construction. Value-added products and services such as consumer appearance boards, pull-to-length boards, premium furring strips, premium studs, and pattern boards are targeted to specialty markets and have made PCL less dependent on the more volatile home construction market. The company produces high-grade plywood sold mainly in specialized industrial markets, including boat, recreational vehicle, and fiberglass-reinforced panel manufacturing. It supplies medium-density fiberboard (MDF) to customers in North America and Asia; some of the more common uses of MDF include furniture and cabinet components, architectural moldings, doors, and store fixtures.

The Scotts Company (SMG) and its subsidiaries are among the oldest and most recognized marketers and manufacturers of products used to grow and maintain lawns, gardens, and golf courses. The company is composed of three segments: the North American Consumer Business Group (75 percent of FY 01, (September, sales), the Global Professional Group (10 percent), and the International Consumer Group (15 percent).

The company continues to drive its category growth and increase its market share through an aggressive consumer pull marketing campaign, launched in 1996. SMG holds the leading market position in North America (52 percent) and Europe (21 percent). Long-term initiatives include lawn services and plant biotechnology. The company's sales are seasonal and susceptible to global weather conditions, primarily in North America and Europe. Periods of wet weather can slow fertilizer sales but create a demand for pesticides, and vice versa. SMG believes its recent acquisitions have diversified its product line and reduced its risk exposure to weather conditions.

The North American Consumer Business Group is composed of the Consumer Lawns, Consumer Gardens, Consumer Growing Media, and Consumer Ortho Products groups. In FY 01, SMG created a single sales force aligned around its key customers, and reduced the number of distributors and agents servicing customers. *Consumer lawn products* include fertilizers, fertilizer combination products, and weed control products. *Consumer garden products* is a line of water-soluble fertilizers sold under the Miracle-Gro brand. *Consumer growing media products* is a line of growing media products for indoor and outdoor uses sold under Miracle-Gro, Scotts, Hyponex, Earthgro, and other labels. *Consumer Ortho Products* markets weed control, insect control, and plant disease control products under the Ortho brand name. The company purchased the Ortho product line from Monsanto in January 1999.

The Professional Business Group's core business is horticulture, primarily in the nursery and greenhouse markets. SMG sells its products to commercial nurseries, greenhouses, landscape services, and specialty crop growers.

SMG's International Consumer Group provides a broad range of fertilizers in more than 40 countries. In FY 01, 37 percent of North American Consumer segment sales went to Home Depot, 20 percent to Wal-Mart, 11 percent to Lowe's, and 12 percent to Kmart.

Overlooked Company Reviews, Industrials Sector

Federal Signal Corporation (FSS) is a diversified manufacturer that focuses on niche markets that it can dominate through superior technology. Its products and services are divided into four operating groups: Safety Products, Tool Products, Environmental Products, and Fire Rescue. The Sign operating group is currently being offered for sale, and it has been classified under discontinued operations.

In 2001, Environmental Products contributed 26 percent to sales and 19 percent to operating income; Fire Rescue 35 and 26 percent; Safety Products 24 and 36 percent; and Tool Products 15 and 18 percent. The Fire Rescue group manufactures chassis; fire trucks, including Class A pumpers, minipumpers, and tankers; airport and other rescue vehicles; aerial access platforms; and aerial ladder trucks. This group primarily sells to municipal customers, volunteer fire departments, and government customers. The Fire Rescue group backlog at year-end 2000 totaled $255.6 million, up from $246.5 million at December 31, 1999.

The Environmental Products group manufactures street sweeping, industrial vacuuming, and municipal catch basin/sewer cleaning vehicles, hydroexcavation equipment, glycol recovery vehicles, and high-pressure water blasting equipment. The products are sold primarily to municipal customers, private contractors, and government customers. At December 31, 2000, the Environmental Products group backlog was $72.3 million, up from $57.2 million a year earlier.

The Tool Products group makes die components for the metal stamping industry; precision metal products for nonstamping needs; and carbide, polycrystalline diamond, and cubic boron nitride precision cutting and grooving tools. The products are sold mostly to industrial markets. The backlog at year-end 2000 totaled $14.7 million, up from $13.1 million a year earlier.

The Safety Products group produces visual and audible warning, signaling, and communications devices; hazardous area lighting and communications products; safety containment products for handling and storing hazardous materials; and parking, revenue, and access control equipment and systems. The backlog at year-end 2000 was $18.5 million, down from $27.3 million a year earlier.

In March 2001, FSS acquired Athey Products Corp., for about $12 million in cash. Athey, which makes mechanical sweeping products, had 2000 sales totaling $25 million. In March 2000, the company acquired P.C.S. Co., which manufactures precision tooling, ejector pins, core pins, sleeves, and accessories for the plastic injection mold industry. Also in March, FSS obtained a new product line for its Environmental Products group by acquiring the Vaxjet patented closed-loop, waterblast surface cleaner.

Illinois Tool Works, Inc. (ITW), incorporated in 1915, manufactures and markets a variety of products and systems that provide specific, problem-solving solutions for a diverse customer base worldwide.

As a whole, Illinois Tool Works can be categorized as a producer of highly engineered nuts and bolts, components, assemblies, and systems, but the categorization stops right there. The company operates more than 500 small industrial businesses in a highly decentralized structure that places responsibility on managers at the lowest level possible, in order to focus each of these business units on the needs of its particular customers. Each business unit manager is responsible, and is held strictly accountable, for the results of his or her individual business. The company grows by developing new products and makes numerous acquisitions of small- to mid-sized businesses. ITW is diversified not only by customer and industry but also by geographic region, with about 30 percent of revenues and 20 percent of operating profits derived overseas.

The Specialty Systems segment (49 percent of revenues and 46 percent of operating profits in 2000) produces longer-lead-time systems and related consumables for consumer and industrial packaging; marking, labeling, and identification systems; industrial spray coating equipment and systems; and quality assurance equipment and systems. Important markets are food retail and service, general industrial, food and beverage, construction, and industrial capital goods. International sales accounted for 17 and 11 percent of 2000 Specialty Systems revenues and earnings, respectively. Segment operating profit margins in 2000 were 14 percent.

The Engineered Products segment (45 percent of revenues and 49 percent of operating profits in 2000) produces short-lead-time plastic and metal components, fasteners, and assemblies, industrial fluids and adhesives, fastening tools, and welding products. The largest markets served are construction, automotive, general industrial, consumer durables, and electronics. International sales accounted for 14 and 10 percent of 2000 Engineered Products revenues and earnings, respectively. Segment operating profit margins in 2000 were 16 percent.

ITW's Consumer Products division (4 percent of revenues and a $14 million loss in 2000) primarily makes small electric appliances, physical fitness equipment, and ceramic tile, primarily for the construction and consumer durables markets. This segment was derived from the late 1999 acquisition of Premark International, Inc. It's expected the company will eventually sell this unit, which is not surprising since historical 3-year average segment operating profit margins have been less than 3 percent.

The company also has a leasing and investment segment, which accounted for 2 percent of revenues and 5 percent of operating profits in 2000. The segment holds about $1.2 billion of investments in commercial mortgage loans and real estate, equipment leasing, affordable housing, and property development. Segment operating profit margins in 2000 were 54 percent.

Kennametal, Inc. (KMT), is a vertically integrated manufacturer and marketer of consumable tools and related supplies for the metalworking, mining, and highway construction industries, as well as specially engineered products for a variety of other industries. KMT believes it is the largest North American and second-largest global provider of consumable metalworking tools and supplies and the largest worldwide provider of mining and construction tooling. EPS in FY 01, June, totaled $2.17, versus $2.13 in FY 00, excluding special items in each period.

The company is one of the world's leading producers of cemented carbide tools and high-speed steel tools, and it maintains a strong competitive position, especially in the United States and Europe. Some 30 percent of FY 01 sales were outside the United States.

The Metalworking segment (55 percent of FY 01 net sales) makes and markets a full line of metalworking products and services for a wide variety of industries that shape and cut metal parts including manufacturers of automobiles, trucks, aerospace components, farm equipment, oil and gas drilling equipment, railroad, marine, power generation equipment, machinery, appliances, factory equipment, and metal components, as well as the job shops and maintenance operations. Metalcutting operations include turning, boring, thread-ing, grooving, milling, and drilling. The company's tooling systems consists of a steel toolholder and an indexable cutting tool such as an insert or drill made from cemented tungsten carbides, ceramics, cer-mets, high-speed steel, and other hard materials.

The Advanced Material Solutions Group (20 percent) produces and markets tungsten carbide products used in engineered applica-tions, coal mining and highway construction, including circuit board drills, compacts, and metallurgical powders used in the oil industry. The company is a leading maker of carbide products used in engi-neered product applications. J&L Industrial Supply (16 percent) pro-vides metalworking consumables and related products to small- and medium-sized manufacturers in the United States and the United Kingdom.

Full Service Supply (9 percent) sells metalworking consumables and related products to manufacturers in the United States and Canada. The unit also offers integrated supply programs that provide inventory management, just in time availability, and programs that focus on total cost savings.

In FY 01, May, **Paychex, Inc. (PAYX)**, which provides payroll processing and human resources and benefits services for small- to medium-size businesses, recorded its eleventh consecutive year of record revenues and net income, and its tenth consecutive year of net income growth exceeding 30 percent.

PAYX was founded in 1971 to serve the payroll accounting services of businesses with fewer than 200 employees. The company currently has more than 100 locations, serves more than 375,000 clients throughout the United States, and ranks as the second-largest U.S. payroll accounting service company. PAYX operates exclusively in the United States, where there are about 6 million full-time employers. About 98 percent of these have fewer than 100 employees, and they represent the company's primary customers.

The company's payroll segment prepares payroll checks, earnings statements, internal accounting records, and all federal, state, and local payroll tax returns, and it provides collection and remittance of payroll obligations. PAYX's Taxpay Services, used by 83 percent of clients, provides automatic tax filing and payment, preparation and submission of tax returns, plus deposit of funds with tax authorities. Employee Pay Services (used by 53 percent of clients) provides a variety of ways for businesses to pay employees, including the traditional paper check, direct bank deposit, a debit and purchase card option, and a special type of check called *Readychex*. PAYX also provides digital check signing and inserting, and it licenses payroll and human resource software (*Rapid Payroll*).

PAYX's ability to continually expand its client base and increase the use of ancillary services has led to the consistent growth of this segment. Client retention rates are typically about 80 percent, as many customers go out of business, reflecting the failure rate for small companies in general.

The company's Human Resources/Professional Employer Organization (HRS/PEO) segment provides employee benefits and management and human resources services. The Paychex Administrative Services Product (PAS) offers businesses a bundled package that includes payroll, employer compliance, human resources, and employee benefit administration and employee risk management. As of May 31, 2001, the PAS and PEO products combined serviced over 60,000 client employees.

PAYX offers 401(k) plan recordkeeping services, group benefit and workers' compensation insurance services, Section 125 Plans, and management services directly to clients. The company's outsourcing services provide regulatory compliance, health care benefits, 401(k) administration, and other services. As of May 31, 2001, this segment had over 19,000 401(k) clients.

APPENDIX 5

Overlooked Company Reviews, Consumer Discretionary Sector

Copart, Inc. (CPRT), is a provider of salvage vehicle auction services in the United States. The company provides vehicle suppliers, primarily insurance companies, with a full range of services to process and sell salvage vehicles through auctions, principally to licensed vehicle dismantlers, rebuilders, repair licensees, and used-vehicle dealers. Salvage vehicles are either damaged vehicles deemed a total loss for insurance or business purposes or are recovered stolen vehicles for which an insurance settlement with the vehicle owner has already been made. The company offers vehicle suppliers a full range of services that expedite each stage of the salvage vehicle auction process and minimize administrative and processing costs. It generates revenues primarily from auction fees paid by vehicle suppliers and vehicle buyers, as well as related fees for services such as towing and storage.

The company has grown from 12 auction facilities in northern California in 1994 to 84 auction facilities located in 37 states in 2001. During the fiscal year ending July 31, 2001, the company acquired 3 additional salvage vehicle auction facilities and opened 5 new facilities.

Copart offers online supplier access, salvage estimation services, transportation services, vehicle inspection stations, and DMV processing. CoPartfinder is the company's Internet search engine, designed to enable users to locate specific vehicle parts quickly and efficiently.

If you drive a car today, there is a good chance it has one or more **Donnelly Corporation (DON)** products built into it. DON supplies automotive customers with rearview mirror systems, modular window systems, and handle products. Management believes the company is one of the largest makers of exterior rearview mirrors in the world and that it has the largest market share in the United States for interior rearview prismatic mirrors and modular window systems. Net sales to Ford and DaimlerChrysler contributed 27 and 19 percent, respectively, of the total in 2000.

The continued introduction of new advanced technologies is a key element of the company's strategy. Over the past 5 years, the company has introduced many new mirror technologies including various lighting, electronic, and mechanical features that improve the overall safety and functionality of a vehicle's mirror system. The company received a major order for business integrating advanced electronic features into interior rearview mirrors to support General Motors' OnStar system. A recent product offering is the company's SmartRelease trunk release system, which uses electronic sensors to detect heat and motion and automatically opens the trunk if it senses a person trapped inside. In November 1999, the company introduced the SPM technology to produce EC automatic-dimming rearview mirrors that the company believes are more durable than competing products available on the market.

DON makes modular windows that are produced by molding glass, hardware, weather stripping, and other components into one unit that can be used for windows and sunroofs. It also produces a wide variety of interior and exterior door and liftgate handle products for Ford, Honda, Mazda, Nissan, and Porsche. The company's nonautomotive business, Information Products, Inc., represented less than 5 percent of sales in each of the past 3 years.

The company announced significant restructuring plans in 1997 and in 1999 to improve the overall profitability of its European automotive operations. The remaining reserve balance for these plans was $3.2 million as of December 31, 2000. DON anticipated that all actions associated with the plan would be substantially completed by the end of 2001. In 1999, the company changed its fiscal year end from the Saturday nearest June 30 to December 31.

In February 2001, DON acquired the remaining interest in the Don-nelly Electronics joint venture it did not already own. Donnelly Elec-tronics produces circuit board assemblies used in the company's rearview mirrors and other automotive products.

Founded in 1914 to build engines for farm tractors, **The Toro Com-pany (TTC)** turned away from its agricultural roots when a golf course superintendent suggested that the company design a tractor-towed mower for golf course fairways. By 1925, TTC's turf maintenance machines were in service on many major U.S. golf courses. Through internal development, acquisitions, and alliances, the company has become a leading designer, manufacturer, and marketer of outdoor maintenance equipment in the consumer, commercial, and irrigation market.

The company's brands include Toro, Toro Wheel Horse, Lawn-Boy, Exmark, Toro Sitework Systems, Drip In, Lawn Genie, Irritrol Systems, and Pope. Its three key segments, professional, residential, and distrib-ution, generated 57 percent, 32 percent, and 11 percent of FY 01, Octo-ber, total sales, respectively. A fourth reportable segment, "other," is used for corporate activities and intersegment eliminations. In FY 01, 81 percent of sales were generated in the United States. Order backlog at the end of FY 01 was $88.5 million, 29 percent lower than the prior year.

TTC's professional segment consists of golf course products, land-scape contractor products, grounds maintenance and other profes-sional products, residential and commercial irrigation products, and agricultural irrigation products. These products are sold mainly through distributors and dealers to professional users engaged in maintaining golf courses, sports fields, municipal properties, and resi-dential and commercial landscapes.

The residential segment consists of walk power mowers, riding mowers and lawn and garden tractors, home solutions products, snow removal products, and retail irrigation products. These are sold to homeowners through distributors, dealers, home centers, and retailers (hardware, mass, and Internet).

The distribution segment sells Toro and non-Toro professional and residential products directly to retail dealers and customers. TTC aimed to use its company-owned distribution facilities to develop a best-practices model that could be replicated by its independent distributors.

Consistent with its "5 by Five" long-term profit improvement strategy initiated in May 2000 and aimed to yield a 5 percent after-tax return on sales by FY 03, TTC planned to close its Evansville, Indiana, and Riverside, California, manufacturing facilities in FY 02. Those restructuring actions aimed to optimally manage manufacturing capacity utilization, reduce product cost, and yield about $10 million in annual savings starting in FY 03. With about $61 million in capital spending planned for FY 02, TTC expected to continue to expand its existing manufacturing facilities, including an additional facility that was under construction in Mexico.

APPENDIX

Overlooked Company Reviews, Consumer Staples Sector

Heineken N.V. (HINKY) is an international brewing group, with operations in more than 170 countries. In 2000, the total volume of beer brewed by the Heineken Group was 97.9 million hectoliters. The group comprises a large number of operating companies and holds various minority interests. Heineken is also active through export and licensing partners. Production is based at more than 110 breweries in over 50 countries. The main thrust of Heineken's activities is in Europe. Heineken N.V. has its roots in Amsterdam, where, in 1864, Gerard Adriaan Heineken acquired the Hooiberg (Haystack) brewery. This brewery itself dated from 1592. The group's leading international brands are Heineken and Amstel. These brands are supplemented and supported by a large number of national and regional brands, as well as by a number of specialty beers.

The beers brewed by Heineken are positioned in the premium, mainstream, or specialties segment of the market. *Premium beer* is the umbrella term for lagers that, on the basis of their quality and brand image, can realize a selling price that is significantly higher than that of mainstream beers. The *mainstream segment* represents the largest and mid-priced section of the market. *Specialties* are beers that differ from lager in taste, color, and brewing process or in some other way. Light beers and lagers containing fewer calories, and nonalcoholic beers also form separate segments. The Heineken Group has only a very limited presence in the low-priced segment.

In parts of Europe, the group owns beverage wholesalers, through which, in addition to beer, it supplies a supporting range of soft drinks, wines, and spirits to the on-premise sector. Some of the soft drinks are produced in the company's own facilities. Research and development (R&D) are coordinated from the company's R&D center in the Netherlands. Group companies and associated breweries worldwide receive technical and technological support services from the Netherlands. (Commentary not provided by *The S&P Stock Guide.*)

Probably best known for its ubiquitous Spam, **Hormel Foods Corporation (HRL)** is a diversified producer of consumer foods. Founded in 1891 as George A. Hormel & Company, the company got its start as a processor of meat products, principally pork. Over the years, it has expanded its business both internally and through acquisitions. Although pork remains the major raw material for Hormel products, the company has emphasized for several years the manufacture and distribution of branded, consumer packaged items over the commodity fresh meat business closely associated with its business of the past.

New product introductions in the past few years have emphasized a variety of branded turkey products, produced under the Jennie-O label; and the fast-growing ethnic food market, with the Chi-Chi's line of Mexican foods, House of Tsang oriental sauces and food products, and Mediterranean food products under the Peloponnese and Marrakesh Express labels. In FY 00, October, meat products accounted for 52 percent of sales; prepared foods 27 percent; and poultry, fish, and other 21 percent.

Meat products include fresh meats, sausages, hams, wieners, and bacon. Prepared foods include canned luncheon meats, shelf-stable microwaveable entrees, stews, chilis, hash, meat spreads, and frozen processed products. Jennie-O turkey and Farm Fresh catfish products are included in the poultry, fish, and other business segment. Important brand names are Hormel, Black Label, By George, Cure 81, Curemaster, Di Lusso, Dinty Moore, Homeland, Layout Pack, Light & Lean, Little Sizzlers, Mary Kitchen, Range Brand, Rosa Grande, Sandwich Maker, Spam, Wranglers, Jennie-O, Kid's Kitchen, Fast 'N Easy, Dubuque, Quick Meal, Old Smokehouse, and House of Tsang. Hormel holds 5 foreign and 32 U.S. patents.

In recent years, Hormel has been focusing on processed, consumer branded products that have year-round demand to help the company minimize the seasonal variation experienced with commodity prices. Pork continues to be the primary raw material for most of the company's products, and although live pork producers are moving toward larger, more efficient year-round confinement operations, the industry still experiences some seasonal variation in supply. Thus, although the expansion into selling of processed items has reduced the company's exposure to commodity prices, it has not eliminated it.

Hormel markets its products internationally through Hormel Foods International Corporation (HFIC). Hormel Foods International has been increasing its presence in the international marketplace through joint ventures and placement of personnel in strategic foreign locations. Significant joint ventures have been established in Mexico, China, and Australia. Hormel expects to continue the investment of personnel and capital in foreign operations for the foreseeable future.

For more than 4 decades, **WD-40 Company (WDFC)** sold only one petroleum-based product, known as WD-40. However, with the acquisitions of the 3-IN-ONE Oil brand in 1995, the Lava brand heavy-duty hand cleaner from Block Drug Company in 1999, and the Solvol brand of heavy-duty hand cleaner from Unilever Australia, Ltd., in 2000, the company expanded its product range to four brands. These products complement each other, providing WDFC with a line of both lubricant and heavy-duty hand-cleaning products aimed at the do-it-yourself hardware, automotive and other retail and industrial markets. In addition, with the April 2001 acquisition of Global Household Brands for $73 million from HPD Holdings, Inc., WDFC added the X-14, 2000 Flushes, and Carpet Fresh household cleaner brands.

The company's revenue comes from three product categories: multipurpose lubricants, which include WD-40 and 3-IN-ONE Oil (79 percent of FY 01, August, sales); hand-cleaning products, which include the Lava and Solvol brands (6 percent); and household products, which include the 2000 Flushes toilet bowl cleaner, X-14 hard surface cleaner, and Carpet Fresh rug and room deodorizer brands (15 percent).

WD-40 is sold in aerosol cans and in liquid form through retail chain stores, warehouse club stores, automotive parts outlets and industrial distributors and suppliers. It has a wide variety of consumer and industrial uses.

3-IN-ONE Oil is a drip-oil lubricant, sold primarily through the same distribution channels as the WD-40 brand. It is a low-cost, entry-level lubricant that is a market share leader among drip oils for household consumers, and it has a variety of industrial applications. In FY 00, WDFC introduced a patented new telescoping spout for 3-IN-ONE that allows precise delivery of oil in tight, hard-to-reach places.

The Lava brand is more than 100 years old and has exceptional awareness among American consumers. Prior to its acquisition, this brand was composed of two sizes of bar soap and one size of liquid cleaner. However, in August 1999, the company augmented the brand with the addition of the Lava Towel, a waterless hand-cleaning towel and two new sizes of Liquid Lava. The company believes that the Lava brand, because of its heavy-duty characteristics, will have greater appeal to consumers who shop in other channels, such as hardware, automotive, and club stores. WDFC intends to develop distribution in these channels where, with its WD-40 and 3-IN-ONE brands, it has considerable marketing experience.

The X-14 brand is a line of hard surface and automatic toilet bowl cleaners. The 2000 Flushes brand is a pioneering line of long-duration automatic toilet bowl cleaners. Carpet Fresh is a rug deodorizer that was introduced in 1978.

In FY 01, the Americas accounted for 72 and 70 percent of sales and operating income, respectively; Europe accounted for 20 and 19 percent of sales and operating income, while Asia/Pacific accounted for 8 and 11 percent, respectively.

McCormick & Company, Inc. (MKC), a diversified specialty food company, is engaged in the manufacture, marketing, and distribution of spices, herbs, seasonings, flavorings, and other specialty food products to the entire food industry. The company also, through subsidiary corporations, manufactures and markets specialty plastic bottles and tubes for food, personal care, and other industries. The company was formed in 1915 as the successor to a business established in 1889.

The company's products are sold through its own sales organization, brokers, and distributors. In the consumer segment, these products are generally resold to consumers through grocery, mass merchandise, drug, and other retail outlets. In the industrial segment, these products are used by food and beverage manufacturers as ingredients for their finished goods and by food-service customers to enhance the flavor of their foods. In the packaging segment, plastic bottles and tubes are sold to pharmaceutical, cosmetics, and other companies in the personal care industry, as well as to the food industry.

McCormick operates in three business segments: consumer, industrial, and packaging. The consumer segment sells spices, herbs, extracts, proprietary seasoning blends, sauces, and marinades to the consumer food market under a variety of brands, including the McCormick brand, and the Club House brand in Canada, the Schwartz brand in the United Kingdom, and the Ducros brand in Europe. The industrial segment sells spices, herbs, extracts, proprietary seasonings, condiments, coatings, and compound flavors to food processors, restaurant chains, distributors, warehouse clubs, and institutional operations. The packaging segment sells plastic packaging products to the food, personal care, and other industries, primarily in the United States.

Many of the spices and herbs purchased by McCormick are imported into the United States from the country of origin, although significant quantities of some materials, such as paprika, dehydrated vegetables, onion and garlic, and food ingredients other than spices and herbs, originate in the United States. The company is a direct importer of certain raw materials, mainly black pepper, vanilla beans, cinnamon, herbs, and seeds from the countries of origin. In addition, McCormick purchases cheese and dairy powders from U.S. sources for use in many industrial products.

Overlooked Company Reviews, Financials Sector

American Capital Strategies (ACAS) originates loans and investments, as well as providing financial assistance to middle-market companies. To identify potential financing opportunities, the company has a dedicated marketing department headed by a senior vice president who manages an extensive referral network composed of private equity and mezzanine funds, investment bankers, unions, attorneys, accountants, commercial bankers, business and financial brokers, and prospective or existing ESOP companies. American Capital also uses its Internet sites and those of its portfolio company, Capital.com, to attract financing opportunities.

The company's financial professionals review informational packages in search of potential financing opportunities and conduct a due-diligence investigation of each applicant that passes an initial screening process. This due-diligence investigation generally includes one or more onsite visits, a review of the target company's historical and prospective financial information, interviews with management, employees, customers, and vendors of the applicant, background investigations on the management team, and research on the applicant's products, services, and industry.

American Capital engages professionals, such as environmental consultants, accountants, lawyers, risk managers, and management consultants, to perform elements of the due-diligence review as it deems appropriate. Upon completion of a due-diligence investigation, one of the company's principals prepares an investment committee report summarizing the target company's historical and projected financial statements, industry, and management team and analyzing its conformity to the company's general investment criteria. The principal then presents this profile to the company's investment committee. The company's investment committee and the company's board of directors must approve each financing.

American Capital attempts to preserve and enhance the earnings quality of its portfolio companies through proactive management of the company's relationships with its clients. This process includes attendance at portfolio company board meetings, management consultation and review, and management of covenant compliance. The company's investment and finance personnel regularly review portfolio company monthly financial statements to assess cash-flow performance and trends, periodically evaluate the operations of the client, seek to identify industry or other economic issues that may adversely affect the client, and prepare quarterly summaries of the aggregate portfolio quality for management review.

ACAS evaluates and classifies all loans based on their current risk profiles. The process requires the director of reporting and compliance to grade a loan on a scale of 1 to 4. Loans graded 4 involve the least amount of risk of loss, while loans graded 1 have the highest risk of loss. The loan grade is then reviewed and approved by the investment committee and the board of directors.

With $246.4 billion in assets under management at the end of FY 01, September, **Franklin Resources, Inc. (BEN),** is one of the largest U.S. money managers. In essence, the company manages the pooled assets of individuals who have sent in their money. U.S. retail assets accounted for $158.1 billion of assets under management, while other assets, including international and institutional assets, accounted for $88.3 billion. At the end of FY 01, equity-based investments accounted for 51 percent of assets under management, fixed-income investments 32 percent, hybrid funds 15 percent, and money funds 2 percent.

Revenues come primarily from fees that BEN charges clients to manage their money. In FY 01, the company earned a fee of 0.58 percent on assets under management, versus 0.61 percent in FY 00. Many factors affect the value of assets under management, including the level of sales of shares of funds compared to redemptions, and the increase or decrease in market value of securities owned by the funds. Through acquisitions, the company has shifted its asset mix from predominantly fixed-income securities to a majority of equity-based investments.

The company's sponsored investment products are distributed under five distinct names: Franklin, Templeton, Mutual Series, Bisset, and Fiduciary. The Templeton funds were acquired in 1992, with the purchase of Templeton Galbraith Hansberger, a firm run by legendary investor Sir John Templeton, who pioneered international investing. These funds boast excellent long-term performance records, although Sir John has retired from active duty.

In April 2001, BEN acquired Fiduciary Trust Company International, another investment management company catering to high-net-worth and institutional clients, for about $775 million in stock. In October 2000, BEN acquired about 98.1 percent of Bisset and Associates Investment Management Ltd, a Canadian mutual fund provider specializing in the growth-at-a-reasonable-price investing style, for about $95 million in cash.

Over the past year, the company continued to expand its market coverage and distribution in the United States and worldwide. Using its broad range of sponsored investment products, BEN covers key market segments: retail, high net worth, separate accounts, and institutional. Its mutual funds have a multiclass share structure to meet varied demands of investors. Although BEN advertises significantly and engages in sales promotion through media sources, fund shares are still sold primarily through a large network of independent securities dealers.

Hudson United Bancorp (HU), Mahwah, New Jersey–based, is the bank holding company for Hudson United Bank, which has over 200 offices in New Jersey, New York, Connecticut, and Pennsylvania. Total assets as of December 31, 2001, were $7.0 billion, up from $6.8 billion on December 31, 2000, but down significantly from $9.7 billion in December 1999.

The reduction in total assets during 2000 was primarily the result of the company's decision to implement a balance sheet deleveraging strategy, under which it sold a significant amount of its lower-yielding investment securities portfolio and used the proceeds from such sale to reduce its borrowings. HU implemented this deleveraging strategy to attempt to increase the company's net interest margin, return on assets, return on equity, and earnings per share while also reducing its exposure to changes in interest rates.

The reduction in total assets during 2000 was also due in part to runoff in certain loan portfolios and deposit categories, primarily related to runoff in loans and deposits of institutions acquired in 1999 and in prior years. Hudson has not completed any acquisitions in recent years, but it had been a frequent acquirer in 1999 and in prior years.

The company began its acquisition program in the fall of 1990. Since that time, the company has completed 31 acquisitions. Through these acquisitions, HU has grown from a $550 million asset banking company to a community banking franchise. The acquisition program has been utilized to achieve efficiencies and to distribute the cost of new products and technologies over a larger asset base. It is the company's philosophy that acquisitions should become accretive to earnings within a short time frame, generally within one year. Through Hudson United, the company owns other subsidiaries engaged in data processing, owning investment securities and real estate assets, and other activities.

St. Petersburg, Florida–based **Raymond James Financial, Inc. (RJF)** is a holding company that, through its subsidiaries, is engaged principally in the securities brokerage business, including the underwriting, distribution, trading, and brokerage of equity and debt securities and the sale of mutual funds and other investment products. In addition, it provides investment management services for retail and institutional clients and banking and trust services for retail clients.

The company's principal subsidiary is Raymond James & Associates (RJA), a full-service broker-dealer. RJA's 79 retail branches and 13 satellites are located primarily in the southeastern United States, with a concentration in Florida and the Midwest. Another subsidiary, Raymond James Financial Services, Inc. (RJFS), participates in the distribution of all the products and services offered by RJA to its retail clients through 3301 independent contractor financial advisers in 1375 offices and 401 satellite offices in all 50 states. Other subsidiaries include Eagle

Asset Management, Inc., Heritage Asset Management, Inc., and Raymond James Bank.

Reportable segments are retail distribution, institutional distribution, investment banking, asset management, and other. The retail distribution segment includes the retail branches of the company's broker-dealer subsidiaries located throughout the United States. These branches provide securities brokerage services including the sale of equities, mutual funds, fixed-income products, and insurance to their retail clients. The institutional distribution segment includes institutional sales offices in the United States and Europe providing securities brokerage services emphasizing the sale of U.S. equities and fixed-income products to institutions.

In FY 00, September, earnings were bolstered by increased commission revenues associated with an increased number of financial advisors, increased net interest associated with increased client balances, growth in assets under management, and improved trading profits. Due to the ongoing investment in back-office capabilities and technology, the company was in a position to handle these increases, and the resultant leverage led to improved margins.

Raymond James has also been successful in its focus on nontransaction-dependent fee revenues, such as investment advisory fees, interest, and asset-based commission alternatives. For FY 00, such fee-based revenues represented about 46 percent of total revenues, up from 36 percent 5 years ago.

In January 2001, the company acquired Goepel McDermid, a private Canadian investment firm, for $48 million in cash and 1 million RJF common shares. As of September 2000, Goepel had 250 investment advisers and 22 branches. The acquisition expanded RJF's presence in Canada, and its retail distribution network. The company expects the acquisition to be slightly dilutive to EPS in the first year, and accretive thereafter.

Seacoast Financial Services Corporation (SCFS) is the holding company for Compass Bank, headquartered in New Bedford, Massachusetts. Compass Bank is a $2.4 billion state-chartered savings bank serving southeastern Massachusetts through a network of 38 full-service offices, six remote ATMs, a customer call center, and online banking at www.compassbank.com.

The bank ranks as the second-largest Massachusetts-based savings bank and one of the largest publicly owned savings banks in Massachusetts. The bank provides a wide array of financial services including consumer banking, mortgage lending, commercial lending, consumer finance, and alternative investments to retail and business customers. The bank's gross loan portfolio totaled $1,747.2 million as of December 31, 1999, representing 82.3 percent of Compass's total assets on that date. Compass primarily makes residential real estate loans secured by one- to four-family residences, indirect auto loans, and commercial real estate loans. Such loans represented 51.3 percent, 24.2 percent, and 12.8 percent, respectively, of Compass's loan portfolio as of December 31, 1999. Compass also makes home equity line-of-credit loans, residential and commercial construction loans, commercial loans, fixed-rate home equity loans, personal installment loans, education loans, and passbook loans. Real estate secures a majority of Compass's loans, including some loans classified as commercial loans.

Compass relies on print, radio, television, and cable advertising, on referrals from existing customers, accountants, attorneys, and real estate professionals, and on relationships with existing borrowers to originate loans. In addition, Compass solicits consumer loans, including home equity loans, by direct mail to existing deposit and residential mortgage loan customers. On December 31, 2000, SCFS completed its acquisition of Home Port Bancorp, Inc., Nantucket, Massachusetts, the holding company for Nantucket Bank, for a total value of approximately $68 million.

Waddell & Reed, Inc. (WDR), was founded in 1937, and it is one of the oldest U.S. mutual fund complexes. The company sells investment products primarily to middle-income Americans through a virtually exclusive sales force. As of June 30, 2001, WDR had $33.9 billion of assets under management, with $28.7 billion of mutual fund assets and $5.2 billion of managed institutional and private accounts. At the same date, the company had 2,066,845 shareholder accounts, up 9.9 percent, year to year.

As of December 31, 2000, WDR had more than 648,000 mutual fund customers, with an average investment of $43,000; and more than 68,000 variable account customers, with an average investment of $54,000.

At the end of 2000, the company was the exclusive underwriter and distributor of 43 mutual funds, including 20 composing the Waddell & Reed Advisors Funds (formerly known as "United Funds"), 12 composing the W&R Funds, and 11 composing the W&R Target Funds. As part of its financial planning services, WDR also distributes variable annuities and life insurance products, underwritten primarily by United Investors Life Insurance Co. (UILIC) and Nationwide Financial Services. WDR sells mutual fund products with a front-end load (sales charges are paid upon purchase of fund shares) and contingent deferred sales charges (sales charges are paid upon redemption within specified periods).

The traditional market for the company has generally been professionals and middle-income families with annual incomes of $40,000 to $100,000 who are saving for retirement. WDR believes demographic trends and shifts in attitudes toward retirement savings will continue to support increased consumer demand for its products. According to U.S. Census Bureau projections, the number of Americans between the ages of 45 and 64 will grow from 53.7 million in 1998 to 76.2 million in 2008, making the preretirement age group the fastest-growing segment of the U.S. population.

WDR distributes funds and other financial products through a network of 2865 financial advisors (as of December 31, 2000), operating from 219 division and district sales offices, and 182 individual advisor offices. The company believes, based on industry data, that its financial advisor sales force was, as of year-end 2000, one of the largest in the United States selling primarily mutual funds. As of year-end 2000, 36 percent of WDR's financial advisors had been with the company for more than 5 years, and 24 percent for more than 10 years. WDR's investment philosophy and financial planning approach emphasize long-term investments.

In March 2001, WDR acquired The Legend Group, a privately held mutual fund distribution and retirement planning company that services primarily employees of school districts and non-for-profit organizations. As of year-end 2000, Legend had 90,000 clients, $2.8 billion in assets under advisement, and 309 advisors located in 22 offices.

Overlooked Company Reviews, Information Technology Sector

Barra, Inc. (BARZ), has clients that include many of the world's largest portfolio managers, fund sponsors, pension and investment consultants, broker-dealers, and master trustees. The company develops, markets, and supports application software and information services used to analyze and manage portfolios of equity, fixed-income, and other financial instruments. In FY 00, March, BARZ reorganized its operations into two business units.

The company's core business unit (accounting for 50 percent of FY 00 revenues) provides portfolio risk management and enterprise risk management systems to investment professionals. These systems consist of three components: data, models, and software applications. Portfolio risk products include the *Aegis System,* a suite of risk management software and applications for managing equity securities and derivatives, and the *Cosmos System,* which allows global fixed-income portfolio managers to manage risk and optimize return in a multicurrency, global bond portfolio. The *Barra Total Risk System* is a platform that addresses both the business and technology issues of delivering a consolidated view of financial risk across an enterprise.

The ventures business unit (50 percent) extends the core business segment's ideas into new markets and consists of several distinct, generally independent companies. *POSIT* (50 percent owned) is an electronic system for low-cost, confidential trade matching during the market day, through which clients enter buy and sell orders to trade single stocks and portfolios of securities among themselves.

On July 16, 2001, BARZ sold its 50 percent–owned Symphony asset management unit to John Nuveen. The company will initially receive net proceeds of $80 million in cash for its stake, after income taxes, with up to $12 million more in future contingency payments.

The other ventures segment of the ventures business includes several properties. Bond Express is an aggregator of bond offerings and is the most widely used bond offering system of its type in the world. BARRA RogersCasey, Inc., offers investment consulting services, a variety of fund-of-funds and private equity products and plans, and the *InvestWorks* system. The Strategic Consulting Group provides consulting services to asset management firms. BARZ also owns a 16 percent stake in Data Downlink Corp., whose flagship product, .xls, aggregates, cross-indexes, and distributes business databases. In addition, BARZ owns a 50 percent interest in Risk Reporting Ltd., which provides quarterly and annual reports that focus on identifying the risk of a pension fund.

As a provider of electronic manufacturing services (EMS), **Jabil Circuit, Inc. (JBL),** seeks to take advantage of the risk aversion of original equipment manufacturers (OEMs). The largest financial risk for OEMs is the construction, maintenance, and ownership of a factory. OEMs are often forced to divest or shut down a factory that is geared specifically for producing a failed product. JBL, which assumes this risk for the OEM, can seek out other OEMs to take the factory space of any product failures. The company produces goods for the international personal computer, computer peripheral, communications, automotive, and consumer markets.

In addition to assuming the risk of factory ownership, JBL reduces inventory by shipping product directly to an OEM's end users and by building products quickly, using advanced automated manufacturing and process control techniques. The company also provides low-total-cost producing through its efficient production methods, through the use of less expensive components, and the low-cost regional locations of its factories.

The company offers customers a complete turnkey (software and

hardware) solution, including circuit and production design; component selection, sourcing, and procurement; automated assembly;
design and implementation of product test; global production, systems assembly, direct-order-fulfillment services; and repair and war-
ranty services. Substantially all net revenue is derived from turnkey
manufacturing.

JBL conducts operations in facilities in the United States, Bel-
gium, Brazil, China, England, Hungary, Ireland, Italy, Malaysia, Mexico, and Scotland. The company's parallel global production strategy
provides customers with improved supply-chain management,
reduced inventory obsolescence, lowered transportation costs and
reduced product fulfillment time. Operations outside North America
accounted for 45 percent of net revenue in FY 01, August, up from 37
percent in FY 00.

The company's strategy is to establish and maintain long-term relationships with leading electronics companies in expanding industries.
A small number of customers have historically accounted for a major
portion of net revenue. In FY 01, 30 customers accounted for over 95
percent of net revenues. Cisco Systems accounted for 23 percent of net
revenues in FY 01, and Dell Computer Corp. 14 percent. In FY 01 the
communications industry accounted for 51 percent of net revenues (44
percent in FY 00), computer peripherals 19 percent (21 percent), personal computers 16 percent (21 percent), and automotive and other 14
percent (14 percent).

In January 2001, JBL agreed to acquire certain manufacturing operations from Marconi Communications for approximately $390 million.
The facilities are located in the United States, United Kingdom, Italy,
and Germany.

Capitalizing on a growing trend for original equipment manufacturers
(OEMs) to outsource production of their products, **Flextronics Corporation (FLEX)** has been growing rapidly. Through a combination of
internal growth and acquisitions, it has become the world's largest
provider of electronic manufacturing services (EMS), with FY 01,
March, pro forma revenues of $12.1 billion. FLEX provides services to
OEMs in the telecom, networking, computer, consumer electronics,
and medical industries.

The company provides a wide range of integrated services, from initial product design to volume production and fulfillment. Manufacturing services range from printed circuit board (PCB) fabrication and assembly to full product assembly and testing. FLEX believes it has strengths in interconnect, miniaturization, and packaging technologies. In addition, it provides engineering services, including design, PCB layout, quick-turn prototyping, and test development, and it also provides logistics services, including materials procurement, inventory management, packaging, and distribution.

FLEX believes its size, global presence, and expertise enable it to win large outsourced manufacturing programs from leading multinational OEMs. An OEM working with the company can achieve accelerated time-to-market and time-to-volume production, as well as reduced total production costs. By working closely with customers through the design, manufacturing, and distribution processes, FLEX believes it becomes an integral part of its customer operations.

Customers include industry leaders such as Alcatel, Cisco, Compaq, Ericsson, Hewlett-Packard, Microsoft, Motorola, Nokia, Palm, Phillips, and Siemens. In FY 01, the 10 largest customers accounted for 59 percent of net sales. No single customer accounted for over 10 percent of sales in FY 01.

The company operates manufacturing centers in 27 countries worldwide, with about 16 million square feet of capacity. In recent years, FLEX has increased overall capacity substantially. FLEX has been active on the acquisition front. In April 2000, it acquired The DII Group, Inc., an EMS company with 1999 revenues of $1.3 billion. In August 2000, Chatham Technologies was acquired, and in November 2000, FLEX acquired JIT Holdings ($562 million in revenues in FY 00).

Pitney Bowes, Inc. (PBI), had its beginnings in the early 1920s, when it introduced its first postage meter devices, and over the years it has built up this business to provide customers with a complete line of mailroom solutions. As mailing and office technology has advanced, the company has moved with the times. It now offers a complete line of digital and networked solutions, leveraging its mailing expertise to offer office equipment and value-added services and solutions that allow businesses to be more efficient and reduce costs. The company also provides lease financing and other financial services to its customers and other businesses.

The global mailing segment, which accounted for 73 percent of 2000 revenues (as restated), includes revenues from the sale and financing of mailing equipment, related supplies, and services. Major products consist of postage meters, parcel registers, mailing machines, manifest systems, letter and parcel scales, mail openers, mailroom furniture, folders and paper handling, and shipping equipment. The latest product is ClickStamp Plus, which allows postage to be printed over the Internet, while combining several software offerings to help improve productivity and decrease customers' mailing costs.

The enterprise solutions segment (22 percent of restated 2000 revenues) includes management services and document messaging technologies. Management services include facilities management contracts for advanced mailing, reprographic, document management, and other services. Document messaging includes the sale, service, and finance of high-speed, software-enabled production mail systems, sortation equipment, incoming mail systems, electronic statement, billing, and payment solutions, and mailing software.

The capital services division (5 percent of restated 2000 revenues) provides large-ticket financing and fee-based programs covering a broad range of products and other financial services. Products financed include aircraft, trucks and trailers, locomotives, railcars, rail and bus facilities, office equipment, and high-technology equipment.

Of total revenues generated in 2000 from the above-mentioned segments, 37 percent came from financing the company's products in the United States and 12 other countries. About 76 percent of total leaseable sales in 2000 were financed, up from 73 percent in 1999.

In December 2000, the company announced plans to spin off the office systems business to stockholders as a separate, publicly traded independent company. The transaction was completed in the fourth quarter of 2001. This segment, which includes the sale, financing, rental, and service of reprographic and facsimile equipment, was accounted for as a discontinued operation.

The mortgage servicing segment was sold in January 2000; it provided billing, collection, and processing services for major investors in residential first mortgages.

Symantec Corporation (SYMC), a world leader in Internet security technology, provides a broad range of content and network security solutions to individuals and enterprises. SYMC is a leading provider of virus protection, firewall, virtual private network, vulnerability management, intrusion detection, remote management technologies and security services to consumers and enterprises around the world.

Symantec is organized in five operating segments: consumer products, enterprise security, enterprise administration, services, and other.

The consumer products segment accounted for 39 percent of total net revenues in FY 01, March. The segment's charter is to ensure that consumers and their information are secure and protected in a connected world. Primary product lines include *Norton AntiVirus* software for the protection, detection, and elimination of computer viruses, and *Norton Internet Security,* a fully integrated suite that provides total Internet protection for the home computer. Others include *Norton SystemWorks, Norton Utilities,* and *Norton CleanSweep.*

The enterprise security and administration segments represented approximately 60 percent of total net revenues in FY 01. The objective of the enterprise security segment is to provide a broad range of security solutions for SYMC's enterprise customers. This segment focuses on two areas: content and network security. The enterprise administration segment offers products that enable companies to be more effective and efficient within their information technology departments. Products include *pcAnywhere* and *Ghost Corporate Edition.*

The services division provides fee-based technical support and consulting services to enterprise customers to assist them with the planning, design, and implementation of enterprise security solutions in the antivirus and Internet-content-filtering technologies.

The other business segment is composed of *sunset products*—that is, products nearing the end of their life cycle—and operations from the *ACT!* and *Visual Cafe* product lines, which were divested on December 31, 1999. SYMC received $75 million in cash for the *Visual Cafe* product line and approximately $20 million of unregistered common stock from Interact Commerce Corporation for the assets of *ACT!* and a four-year license of *ACT!* technology.

International revenues accounted for 45 percent of the total in FY 01, versus 41 percent in FY 00. SYMC has acquired 23 companies since its initial public offering in 1989. In December 2000, SYMC acquired AXENT Technologies in a stock transaction valued at approximately $975 million. SYMC issued approximately 15 million shares to complete the transaction.

Overlooked Company Reviews, Health Care Sector

Medicis Pharmaceutical Corporation (MRX) is a leading developer and marketer of dermatology products. Its growth strategy centers on expanding its market share for its existing products, introducing new products, making synergestic acquisitions, and forming collaborative partnerships. MRX focuses on treating acne, acne-related conditions, fungal infections, skin discoloration, and inflammatory and hyperproliferative skin diseases, such as psoriasis and topical dermatitis.

Principal prescription pharmaceuticals include Dynacin, an oral antibiotic to treat severe acne; Triaz, a topical formulation to treat all forms of acne; Lustra and Lustra-AF topical treatments for ultraviolet-induced skin discolorations and hyperpigmentation associated with oral contraceptive use, pregnancy, hormone replacement therapy, and superficial trauma; Lidex and Synalar topical corticosteroid products to treat inflammatory and hyperoliferative skin disorders, including eczema, psoriasis, and poison ivy; Loprox broad-spectrum topical antifungal treatment; and Topicort topical therapy for psoriasis, eczema, and other skin conditions. Prescription lines also include Ovide, a lotion to treat head lice; Plexion, a topical cleanser for rosacea (a chronic skin condition causing inflammation and redness of the face); Buphenyl, an adjunctive therapy for hyperammonemia in patients with urea cycle disorder; and Omnicef, an oral cephalosporin antibiotic for skin infections, which is being comarketed with Abbott Laboratories.

The company also produces the Esoterica nonprescription line of topical fade creams for treating minor skin discolorations. The leading nonprescription product in its class, Esoterica is used to treat age spots, uneven skin tones, dark patches, and freckles.

In November 2001, the company acquired Ascent Pediatrics for $60 million, plus up to an additional $50 million over the next 5 years contingent upon Ascent's reaching certain sales milestones. A maker of oral liquid drugs used to treat asthma, ear infections, and other pediatric conditions, Ascent also provides MRX entry into the $5 billion pediatric market for established Medicis drugs.

Principal customers consist of leading wholesale pharmaceutical distributors such as McKesson, Cardinal Health, and Quality King, which collectively accounted for over 50 percent of FY 01 total revenues.

Research and development costs totaled $25.5 million in FY 01, equal to 15.3 percent of total revenues. R&D expenses included $17 million paid to Corixa Corporation under a development, commercialization, and license agreement covering Corixa's novel PVAC immunotherapeutic vaccine for psoriasis. Additional future milestone payments of up to $90 million may be paid, based on PVAC's success.

Omnicare, Inc. (OCR) is a leading provider of pharmacy management services to long-term-care institutions such as nursing homes, assisted-living facilities, and other institutional health care facilities. The company also offers consultant pharmacist services and ancillary services, and it operates a contract research organization. At the end of 2001, OCR's pharmacy services unit served 722,000 residents in long-term-care and other settings in 43 states.

The institutional pharmacy segment purchases, repackages, and dispenses prescription and nonprescription medication in accordance with physician orders, and it delivers such prescriptions at least daily to nursing facilities for administration to patients by the facility's nursing staff. OCR typically serves nursing homes in a 150-mile radius of its pharmacies. An on-call pharmacist service is provided 24 hours a day, 365 days a year, for emergency dispensing and delivery or for consultation with the facility's staff or attending physician.

Integral to the company's drug distribution system is its computerized medical records and documentation system. OCR provides the facility with computerized medical administration records and physicians' order sheets and treatment records for each patient. Data extracted from these records is formulated into monthly management reports on patient care and quality assurance. When combined with OCR's unit dose drug delivery system, the computerized system allows greater efficiency in nursing time, improved control, reduced drug waste, and lower error rates both in dispensing and in administration; this can improve drug efficacy and reduce drug-related hospitalizations.

OCR also provides consultant pharmacist services to help clients comply with federal and state regulations related to the quality and standardization of nursing home care. Services include comprehensive, monthly drug regimen reviews for each resident; monthly inspection of medication carts and storage rooms; monitoring and monthly reporting on facility-wide drug usage and drug administration systems and practices; and development and maintenance of pharmaceutical policy and procedures manuals.

The company's *Omnicare Guidelines*, introduced in 1994, are believed to be the first clinically based formulary for the elderly residing in long-term-care institutions. Ancillary offerings provided to nursing facilities include infusion therapy; dialysis services; distribution of disposable medical supplies, including urological, ostomy, nutritional support, and wound care products, and other disposables needed in nursing homes; and direct Medicare billing services for certain product lines for patients eligible under the Medicare Part B program.

The contract research organization unit provides comprehensive product development services to companies in the pharmaceutical, biotechnology, medical device, and diagnostics industries.

Shire Pharmaceutical Group plc (SHPGY) is an international specialty pharmaceutical company with a strategic focus on four therapeutic areas: central nervous system disorders, metabolic diseases, cancer, and gastrointestinal disorders. Revenues are derived from three sources: sales of products by its own sales and marketing operations, licensing and development fees, and royalties. SHPGY has its own direct marketing capability in the United States, Canada, the United Kingdom, the Republic of Ireland, France, Germany, Italy, and Spain. SHPGY has a portfolio of eight key U.S. marketed products, each with significant potential.

The development pipeline has 17 projects in it and includes Reminyl, in registration in the United States and various other markets, SLI 381, a novel once-a-day formulation of Adderall submitted to the U.S. FDA on October 3, 2000, and 8 others that are post Phase II. As the company increases in size, there are likely to be fewer occasions when out-licensing of marketing rights will be appropriate. However, SHPGY remains committed to ongoing collaborations such as that with Janssen Pharmaceutica N.V., the codevelopment and licensing partner for galantamine (Reminyl) in the treatment of Alzheimer's disease.

SHPGY's products for the treatment of central nervous system disorders include Adderall (for attention deficit hyperactivity disorder, or ADHD), DextroStat (ADHD), Carbatrol (epilepsy), and Reminyl (Alzheimer's disease); for metabolic diseases include Calcichew (osteporosis adjunct); for onocology/haematology include Agrylin (elevated blood platelets), Fareston (advanced breast cancer), ProMatine/Amatine (orthostatic hypotension); and for treatments for gastrointestinal disorders Pentasa (ulcerative colitis), Colazide (ulcerative colitis), and Colace/Peri-Colace (constipation). (Company review not provided by *The S&P Stock Guide.*)

Overlooked Company Reviews, Telecommunications Sector

C enturyTel (CTL) plans to pursue acquisitions of underserved incumbent local exchange carrier (ILEC) markets, to promote efficiencies through synergies with its existing network and drive longer-term earnings growth through enhanced service offerings. In 2000, CTL and its affiliates completed the second-largest acquisition in the company's history, purchasing from Verizon Communications more than 490,000 telephone access lines covering four states. As a result of the $1.5 billion cash acquisition, CTL finished 2000 with 1.8 million local access lines, up over 40 percent, year to year. With ILEC operations spanning 21 states, CTL is now the eighth-largest U.S. local exchange telephone company, based on access lines.

To help fund ILEC expansion, CTL has pursued divestitures of its wireless properties. In February 2000, the company sold its remaining Alaska cellular operations, serving 10,600 subscribers, posting an after-tax gain of $5.2 million. In the 2001 second quarter, CTL closed on the sale of 30 PCS licenses to Leap Wireless, posting a $117.7 million after-tax gain. Prompted by a hostile tender offer from Alltel (AT), in August 2001, CTL said it was in discussions with a number of parties to sell its entire wireless business. Management said proceeds would be used for attractive acquisition alternatives developing in the wireline sector, positioning CTL as the leading pure-play rural local exchange carrier in the industry. AT had proposed to acquire CTL for a $21.50 in cash and

0.3467 of an AT share for each CTL share (a value of about $41 a share). CTL's management rejected the bid.

When CTL acquires new local telephone markets, it seeks to deploy value-added calling services that can increase revenues and margins. In the company's legacy markets (pre-Verizon acquisition), CTL had realized year-end 2000 penetration rates of 22.9 percent for caller ID, 39.5 percent for customer calling features, 14.1 percent for voice mail, and 8.6 percent for second telephone lines. In addition, the company is actively deploying digital subscriber line (DSL) service. At the end of 2000, 45 percent of CTL's legacy access lines and 7 percent of its acquired Verizon lines had been made DSL ready. The company antic-ipates rapid growth in its DSL customer base (6000 at year end) over the next few years. CTL also offers long-distance service; it ended 2000 with 363,300 long-distance subscribers. In legacy markets, 24.3 percent of CTL local phone customers also chose CTL for their long-distance service.

During 2000, the company began pursuing selected competitive local exchange (CLEC) operations. As of the 2001 second quarter, it had CLEC operations in two Louisiana markets, and it intended to launch service in two Michigan markets during the second half.

As of the end of 2000, **TDS (TDS)** provided telecommunications ser-vices to 3.8 million customers in 34 states. These services were provided through 82 percent–owned U.S. Cellular (USM), and through incum-bent local exchange carrier (ILEC) and competitive local exchange car-rier (CLEC) businesses.

USM (representing 53 percent of consolidated 2000 revenues) con-sists of 139 majority owned and managed cellular systems in 24 states. The business seeks to strengthen its concentration in regional clusters through acquisitions and trades. USM ended 2000 with 3,061,000 cus-tomers, an increase of 483,000. As the company migrates more cus-tomers onto digital rate plans (with lower per minute fees), it is experiencing much higher call volumes. Following an increase of nearly 1 million digital users, USM's digital subscriber base at the end of 2000 represented about 50 percent of all subscribers nationwide. Average monthly local minutes used per customer increased 37 per-cent during the year. Also during 2000, the company launched a national service plan, SpanAmerica, that offers large amounts of minutes without roaming or long-distance fees for one monthly rate.

At the end of 2000, the company's wholly owned wireline business, TDS Telecom, operated in 28 states with ILEC operations serving 601,200 access lines and two CLEC subsidiaries (TDS Metrocom and USLink) serving 112,100 access lines. In November 2000, TDS announced plans to acquire Chorus Communications Group (CCG) for $195 million and the assumption of $30 million in debt. CCG is an ILEC serving 45,000 access lines and 30,000 Internet customers operating in areas almost entirely contiguous with TDS's existing ILEC territory. During 2000, TDS's new ILEC long-distance product, TDS TrueTalk, signed up 40,500 customers (6.5 percent market share) after 5 months of service. Also during 2000, CLEC operations (primarily based in Minnesota and Wisconsin) expanded into southern Wisconsin and northern Illinois (with plans for a Michigan expansion during 2001).

At the end of 2000, TDS also held a number of minority interests in various telecommunications companies (including holdings owned by USM). These investments included 35.6 million shares of VoiceStream (converted into 131.5 million Deutsche Telekom shares and $570 million in cash in May 2001), 12.9 million ADRs of Vodafone plc (including ADRs owned by USM), 2.5 million shares of Illuminet Holdings, and 0.7 million shares of Rural Cellular.

During 2000, TDS repurchased 2.7 million shares, for $288 million, and USM repurchased 3.5 million shares, for $235 million. Directors of the companies have authorized additional share buybacks.

11 APPENDIX

Overlooked Company Reviews, Utilities Sector

C **inergy Corp. (CIN)** is a holding company serving nearly 1.5 million electric customers and 490,000 gas customers in a 25,000-square-mile area of Ohio, Indiana, and Kentucky. It was formed through the 1994 merger of Cincinnati Gas & Electric Co. and PSI Resources, Inc. The contributions to revenues by the business segment in 2000 were electric, 63.9 percent (72.6 percent in 1999); gas, 34.9 percent (26.9 percent), and other 1.1 percent (0.5 percent).

In its order approving the merger, the SEC reserved jurisdiction over the company's ownership of Cincinnati Gas & Electric's (CG&E) gas operations for 3 years. At the end of the 3-year period, CIN was required to state how its retention of the gas properties met all of the relevant standards of the Public Utility Holding Company Act (PUHCA) of 1935. In February 1998, the company filed with the SEC its rationale on how its retention of the gas operations meets PUHCA requirements. Then, in November 1998, the SEC approved CIN's retention of CG&E's gas operations.

Cincinnati Gas & Electric (CG&E) and its subsidiaries supply electricity and natural gas in the southwestern portion of Ohio and adjacent areas in Kentucky and Indiana. The primary subsidiary of PSI Resources (formerly PSI Holdings) is PSI Energy (formerly Public Service Co. of Indiana), Indiana's largest electric utility, serving a population of about 2.2 million. Consolidated construction expenditures for 2000 were $778 million. For the period from 2001 though 2005, CIN has projected construction expenditures of $6.1 billion. The forecast includes the capital expenditures required (estimated at approximately $1 billion) to comply with proposed nitrogen oxide (NOx) limits.

CIN acquired Producers Energy Marketing, LLC, which has exclusive marketing rights to around 1.1 billion cubic feet per day of natural gas supply. CINergy, Florida Progress Corporation (which was subsequently merged into Progress Energy) and New Century Energies (which was subsequently merged into Xcel Energy) formed Cadence Network LLC, a joint venture that provides energy management services to national accounts. Earlier the company formed a joint venture with Trigen Energy Corporation that builds, owns, and operates cogeneration and trigeneration facilities.

Through Philadelphia Suburban Water and Consumers Water, **Philadelphia Suburban Corporation (PSC)** provides water and waste services in Pennsylvania, Ohio, Illinois, New Jersey, North Carolina, and Maine. Its strategy is to expand its customer base through regional acquisitions. The company seeks to mitigate the impact of adverse weather through geographic diversification; 66 percent of customers were in Pennsylvania in 2000, 14 percent in Ohio, 11 percent in Illinois, 6 percent in New Jersey, 3 percent in Maine, and fewer than 1 percent in North Carolina.

As of early 2002, the company supplied water to more than 602,000 residential, commercial, industrial, and public customers (more than 2.0 million residents, including the Philadelphia Suburban Water unit's 347,000 customers). The service territory consists primarily of residential customers, and it is almost entirely metered for water service, except for fire hydrant service. The water unit customer base grew at a compound annual rate of 1.2 percent in the 3 years through 2000 (3.8 percent, including acquisitions and other growth ventures).

At 2000 year end, the customer base consisted of 88 percent residential; 5 percent commercial; 4.7 percent wastewater and operating contracts; 1.6 percent other; and 0.2 percent industrial. About 64 percent of sales in 2000 came from residential customers.

In April 2000, PSC reached a $17 million rate settlement with the Pennsylvania Public Utility Commission (PUC), equivalent to 9.4 percent of revenues. Water utilities in Pennsylvania are permitted to add a distribution system improvement charge (DSIC) to their water bills, reflecting the capital costs and depreciation related to certain distribution system improvement projects completed and placed into service between rate filings. As a result, the settlement resulted in a 13.5 percent total base rate increase.

In the 5 years through 2000, the company completed 66 acquisitions or growth ventures (excluding Consumers Water), adding 56,000 customers to its base, including the December 1999 acquisition of the water utility assets of Bensalem Township (14,945 customers) for $36.5 million. PSC believes that, with 55,000 community water systems in the United States (85 percent serving fewer than 3300 people), there are many potential acquisition candidates, with the main drivers being economies of scale, increasingly stringent environmental regulations, and the need for investment.

In March 1999, PSC and Consumers Water (CONW) merged in a transaction valued at $463 million in stock and assumed debt. In June 2002, PSC agreed to acquire Pennichuck Corp. in a stock transaction valued at approximately $106 million.

On December 4, 2000, CP&L Energy changed its name to **Progress Energy Ltd.** One week later, on December 11, NYSE trading began under the ticker symbol **PGN.**

On November 30, 2000, the company acquired Florida Progress Corp. (FPC) for about $5.3 billion in cash (65 percent) and stock (35 percent), and the assumption of $2.7 billion in FPC debt. FPC is the holding company for Florida Power, which provides electricity to 1.4 million customers in central, northern, and Gulf Coast Florida.

CP&L Energy was formed on June 20, 2000, as the holding company for Carolina Power & Light Co. (now operating as CP&L), a utility providing electricity to 1.2 million customers in eastern and western North Carolina and central South Carolina, and, following the acquisition of North Carolina Natural Gas (now operating as NCNG), natural gas to 173,000 customers in eastern and southern North Carolina. North Carolina Natural Gas was acquired in July 1999, through the issuance of about $354 million in stock.

Following the FPC acquisition, the holding company was organized into five primary units: energy delivery, which oversees transmission and distribution operations for Carolina Power & Light and Florida Power; energy supply, which oversees generation operations, energy trading and system planning; energy ventures, which focuses on new generation strategies and the wholesale energy marketing and trading operations; energy services, which oversees NCNG and energy management services; and a service company to support the combined company.

Progress Energy's subsidiaries include Electric Fuels Corp., a company that provides energy, marine, rail, and ash-management services; and Progress Telecom, a superregional carrier with a network that stretches across five states, from Washington, D.C., to southeast Florida. The telecom unit also offers access to Latin America through its International Gateways. PGN also has a 100 percent interest in Strategic Resource Solutions Corporation, which specializes in facilities and energy management software, systems, and services.

Southwest Water Company (SWWC) provides a broad range of utility and utility management services, serving more than 1 million people in 30 states from coast to coast. Revenue sources in 2000 were as follows: nonregulated 58 percent and regulated (or utility) the balance. Nonregulated businesses consisted primarily of the following subsidiaries as of year-end 2000: ECO Resources and Master Tek International.

ECO Resources operates and manages water and wastewater treatment facilities owned by cities, municipal utility districts, and private entities. It operates under contract with the facility owners, providing all aspects of water and wastewater operations and maintenance services and performing related services including facility and equipment maintenance and repair, sewer pipeline cleaning, billing and collection, and state-certified laboratory analysis. As a contract operator, ECO does not own any of the water sources, water production facilities, water distribution systems, or any of the wastewater collection systems or wastewater treatment facilities that it operates for clients.

Master Tek International (MTI; 80 percent owned as of year-end 2000) is a nationwide provider of utility submetering, billing, and collection services, serving about 175,000 dwelling units in 24 states. Utility submetering involves the installation of electronic equipment in dwelling units, such as apartments and condominiums, to allow a calculation of each resident's usage of utilities. In addition to installation of submetering devices, MTI provides billing, collection, and customer relations services.

Regulated, or utility, operations consisted of the following as of year-end 2000: Suburban Water Systems, New Mexico Utilities, and Texas Utilities. Suburban Water Systems is a regulated public water utility that produces and supplies water for residential, business, industrial, and public authority use, and for private and public fire protection service under jurisdiction of the California Public Utilities Commission (CPUC). Suburban's service area contains a population of about 297,000 people within Los Angeles and Orange counties, California. New Mexico Utilities (NMU) is a regulated public utility providing water supply and sewage collection services to customers in northwest Albuquerque and in the northern part of Bernalillo County. Texas Utilities (80 percent owned as of year-end 2000) provides water supply and sewage collection and treatment services to approximately 4800 customers for residential, commercial, irrigation, and fire protection under the jurisdiction of the Texas Natural Resource Conservation Commission.

Endnotes

Chapter 3

Fortunate circumstances created an unusually good opportunity to discuss with Kevin Sheehan, CEO and president of Investors Financial Services, company details in a relaxed atmosphere. Mr. Sheehan personally and graciously returned my initial inquiry and request for an interview. I found him to be engaging, knowledgeable, and most informative. As the leader of a small company, one of Mr. Sheehan's goals is to expand coverage of his company in the financial press. By accepting my interview, Mr. Sheehan took another small step in growing shareholder value by increasing the audience of potential investors, mainly readers of this book. More information about Investors Financial Services is readily available from its Web site, annual reports, company press releases, and independent commentary and financial articles. For instance, a combination of the *S&P Stock Report* summary listed above and the information on the company site at ibtco.com gives potential investors a substantial insight into this intriguing and fast-growing company.

Chapter 5

The year's high/low PE range is available at many financial Web sites, such as Zacks.com. Your local public library offers a wealth of financial resources, usually found in its resource center. *The Value Line Investment Survey,* along with *The S&P Stock Reports,* are two mainstays of most library investment resources. Historical financial information, along with an in-depth description and an analysis of current business, is included in both publications.

Chapter 8

According to *BusinessWeek,* "85 percent of original equipment manufacturers (OEM) expect to increase their use of contract manufacturers over the next year. Moreover, in the long run, OEMs expect to outsource 70 percent or more of their manufacturing functions, a far cry from the current penetration of approximately 13 percent." The total value of contract manufacturing is expected to grow by a steady 25 percent annually. The worldwide production of electronic equipment is expected to grow around 7 percent a year, with much of that production increase going to contract manufacturers.

Appendixes

The company reviews were provided by *Standard & Poor's Stock Reports.* S&P provides concise overviews of hundreds of companies, and their analysis is always insightful. I would like to extend my appreciation for S&P's cooperation.

Bibliography and Resources

Adamo, Jack. "The Great Ongoing Stock Option Scam." June 2001, jack-adamo.com.

Bernstein, William. "The Grand Infatuation." fundsinteractive.com. 1999.

Bloomberg Personal Finance, March 2002, pages 33, 86.

Capra, Fritjof, and Gunter Pauli, editors. "New Concepts of Fiduciary Responsibility." *Steering Business Towards Sustainability.* New York: United Nations Publications, 1995, pages 125–141.

Citibank. "ADRs and the Individual Investor." Citibank.com/ADR/DRACADEMY.

Engardio, Pete. "The Barons of Outsourcing." *BusinessWeek* Online, August 28, 2000.

Ericson, Jim. "Outsourcing the Supply Chain: Consultants, Spin-Offs Line Up." Line56.com. November 8, 2001.

Havens, John J., and Paul G. Schervish. "Millionaires and the Millennium: New Estimates of the Forthcoming Wealth Transfer and the Prospects for a Golden Age of Philanthropy." charityamerica.com. October 19, 1999.

Kiplinger's Personal Finance, March 2002, page 34.

Lee, Dwight R., and Richard B. McKenzie. *Getting Rich in America: 8 Simple Rules for Building a Fortune and a Satisfying Life.* New York: HarperBusiness, 2000.

May, John J. "NASDAQ 100 Companies Report Combined Losses of Over $82 billion to SEC While Reporting Profits of $19 billion to Shareholders." SmartStockInvestor.com, January 21, 2002.

msnbc.com. "Stock Option Madness."

Mutual Funds Magazine, March 2002, page 23.

Picerno, James. "Investing: Quality Control." wealth.bloomberg.com/wealth/wealtharticles.com.

Price, John D., Ph.D. "The Three 'Little' Words of Successful Investing." Sherlockinvesting.com. October 1999.

Sheard, Robert. *Money for Life: Build the Wealth You Need to Live Your Dream.* New York: HarperCollins, 2000.

Smith, William J. "The Mystique of Stock Options." *Washington CEO,* September 1999.

Tasch, Edwin, and Stephen Viedeman. "New Concepts of Fiduciary Responsibilities." 1995, noyes.org/admin/concepts.

U.S. News & World Report. "Prices Always Come Back: Lessons of 50 Years in Stocks." Interview with Justin F. Barbour.

Wyatt, Watson. "Finding the Sweet Spot—Stock Options Overhang." 1999, watsonwyatt.com.

Web Sites

inc.com

aaii.com

adlittle.com

andersen.com

DecisionOne.com

finance.yahoo.com

GlobalOutsourcing.org

knowledge.wharton.upenn.edu

marketguide.com

Money.com, Michael Sivy, March 2000

Multex.com

Morningstar.com

nceo.org

pbs.org/newshour

Quicken.com

reis.com

REITNet.com

sec.gov

sia.com

SmartMoney.com

upslogistics.com

Usfilter.com/water/corporateinfo

uswaternews.com

waterinvestments.com

Zacks.com

Index

Letters in **bold** indicate stock sticker symbol

Accounting
  pro forma, 118–120
  stock options, 104–109, 134
Accrued principal, 25
Administer, Inc. **ASF,** 191
ADRs (American depository
    receipts), 149, 167–176
  examples, 173–176
Amateur advice, 17–18
American Capital Strategies **ACFS,**
    261–262
American depository receipts
    (ADRs), 167–176
  examples, 173–176
Apace Oil Corp **APA,** 42, 127, 130,
    204, 238–239
Archer, S. H., 34
Archstone Smith Communities
    Trust **ASN,** 166
Asset allocation, 32–33

AT&T **T,** 49
AvalonBay Communities **AVB,** 166

Barbour, Justin, 144–145
Barra Software **BARZ,** 91–92, 97,
    117, 268–269
Bear market, 143–144
Beginning to invest (*See* Initial con-
    siderations)
Benetton **BNG,** 173
Berkshire Hathaway, 146–148
Bernstein, William, 223
Bonds
  corporate, 26
  diversification, importance of,
    21–26
  vs. stock performance, 11–14
Boon, Robert, 198–199
Boston Properties REIT **BXP,**
    161–162

Buffett, Warren, 105, 107, 146–148
Bull market, 143–144
Business-to-business procurement, 193–194

Campbell, John, 34, 35
Capital gains and mutual funds, 218–222
Capitalization, market, 30–32
   large-cap stocks, 31, 41, 55–56
   mid-cap stocks, 12, 39–46, 55
   small caps, 12, 39–46, 41–46, 54, 56–57
Cascade Natural Gas **CGC,** 122, 205
Case studies
   diversification, 46–50
   management efficiency numbers, 90–93
   overlooked company characteristics, 68–74
   REITs, 159–162
Cash flow, 84–86, 134
Cash flow per share, 120–122
CDs (certificates of deposit), 22
Cemex S.A. de C.V. **CX,** 174
CenturyTel **CTL,** 61, 279–280
Certificates of deposit (CDs), 22
Chicago Bridge & Iron **CBI,** 44–45, 123, 204, 239–240
Cinergy **CIN,** 92, 98, 117, 282–283
Common stock, 26
   (*See also* Stock options)
Computer Sciences **CSC,** 192
Consumer debt payoff, 4–6
Consumer discretionary sector companies, 252–255
Consumer staples sector companies, 256–260
Contract manufacturing, 194–196
Contrarian investing, 111, 123–128
Copart Industries **CPRT,** 89–91, 93–94, 117
Corporate bonds, 26
Corporation life cycle, 53–56

Credit card debt payoff, 4–6
Cristalchile **CGW,** 175

Debt payoff, 4–6
Debt-to-equity calculation, 81–82, 134
Differentiate or Die (Trout), 58
Direct stock purchase plans, 8
Diversification, importance of, 21–50
   asset allocation, 32–33
   bonds, 21–26
   economic sectors, 37–38
   market capitalization, 30–32
   mid-cap stocks, 12, 39–46, 55
   in portfolio, 33–37
   price movements, 28
   small-cap trends, 12, 39–46, 41–46, 54, 56–57
   speculation, 28–30
   stocks, 26–28
Dividend payout ratio, 84, 134
Dividend reinvestment program (DRIP), 141
Dividends and management evaluation, 86–89
Dividends per share, 84
Dollar cost averaging, 140
Donnelley Corporation **DCL,** 136, 253–254
DRIP (dividend reinvestment program), 141
Duke Realty **DRE,** 166

E-procurement, 193–194
Early investing, 8–9
Earnings
   growth of, 62, 134
   reported net earnings, REITs, 157–159
Earnings before interest payments and income taxes (EBITA), 120
Earnings per share, 83–84

EBITA (earnings before interest payments and income taxes), 120

Economic sectors and diversification, 37–38

Energy resources as overlooked trends, 202–210

Energy sector companies, 237–242

Enron, 46–50, 104

Enterprise Products Partners **EPD,** 92, 98, 117, 240–242

Equity Office Properties Trust **EOP,** 63, 165

Equity REITs, 151–152

Equity Residential Properties Trust **EQR,** 165

ETF (exchange-traded fund), 224–226

Ethics and management evaluation, 100–102

Evaluation
of management (*See* Management evaluation)
REITs, 155–157
tools for stock, 80–84
value (*See* Value, evaluating)

Evans, J. L., 34

Exchange-traded fund (ETF), 224–226

Exercisable options, 108

Exercised options, 108

Federal Signal **FSS,** 43, 247–248

Fees
mistakes to avoid, 17
for mutual funds, 213–218

FFO (funds from operations), REITs, 157–159

Financial reports, intelligible, 62–63

Financial sector companies, 261–267

Financing, cash flow from, 85

Fitzgerald, James, 189

Flextronics Corporation **FLEX,** 270–271

Florida Rock Industries **FRK,** 92, 97–98, 117, 243–244

Foregone earnings, 217

Foreign investments and ADRs (American depository receipts), 149, 167–176

Formulas for evaluation tools, 80–84

Forward PEG ratio, 116, 134

401(k) account, 3–4

Francis, Diane, 105–106

Franklin Resources, Inc. **BEN,** 262–263

Free cash flow, 85

Fresenius Medical Care **FMS,** 174

Funds from operations (FFO), REITs, 157–159

GAAP (generally accepted accounting principles), 119

General Electric **GE,** 62, 107

Generally accepted accounting principles (GAAP), 119

Getting Rich in America (Lee & McKenzie), 10, 11

Gibb, Robert, 209

GICS (Global Industry Classification Standard), 37, 231–236

Global accumulation of wealth as overlooked trend, 197–202

Global Industry Classification Standard (GICS), 37, 231–236

Global resources as overlooked trends, 202–210

Graham, Benjamin, 34, 146

Great Lakes REIT **GL,** 159–161

Gross profit margin, 86

Harley-Davidson **HDL,** 45

Havens, John, 201–202

Hawaiian Electric **HE,** 125

Health Care Property investors
HCP, 166–167
Health care sector companies,
275–278
Heineken N.V. **HINKY,** 256–257
Historic returns, 10–12
Hormel Foods Corporation **HRL,**
43, 257–258
Hospitality Properties Trust **HPT,**
167
HSBC Holdings **HBC,** 175
Hudson United Bancorp **HU,** 91,
97, 117, 263–264
Human resources, outsourced,
190–191

Ibbotson Associates, 13, 39,
145–146
ICI **ICI,** 174
Identifying overlooked stocks,
51–74
case studies: overlooked company characteristics
(Investors Financial Ser-
vices), 68–74
corporation life cycle, 53–56
earnings growth, 62
financial reports, intelligible,
62–63
insider stock ownership,
63–65
nimble management, 57–58
overlooked by institutional
investors, 66
overview, 51–53
product and service differentiation, 58–59
product innovation, 59–60
single-market focus, 60–62
small caps, 12, 39–46, 41–46, 54,
56–57
sustainable competitive advantage, 67–68
underdog status, 66

Illinois Tool Works **ITW,** 59–60, 91,
94, 97, 117, 248–249
Immelt, Jeffery, 107
Index mutual funds, 224–226
Individual retirement account
(IRA), 3–4
Industrial sector companies,
247–251
Inflation, 24–26
Information technology, outsourced, 192–193
Information technology sector
companies, 268–274
Initial considerations, 1–19
approach summary, 227–230
consumer debt payoff, 4–6
historic returns, 10–12
importance of individual investing, 1–4
intelligent investing, 9–10
mistakes to avoid, 14–19
pay yourself first, 2, 7–8
start early, 8–9
stock vs. bond performance,
11–14
time and risk, 13
Initial public offering (IPO), 27, 54
Insider stock ownership, 63–65, 134
Intelligent investing, 9–10
The Intelligent Investor (Graham),
34, 146
Interest rates, 13, 125
Intergenerational transfer of
wealth as overlooked trends,
197–202
Investing (*See specific topics*)
Investors Financial Services **IFIN,**
44, 68–74
IPO (initial public offering), 27, 54
IRA (individual retirement
account), 3–4

Jabil Circuit, Inc. **JBL,** 269–270
Johnson & Johnson **JNJ,** 52

Kennametal **KMT,** 43, 249–250
Kimco Realty **KIM,** 166
Kubota Corporation **KUB,** 175

Large-cap stocks, 31, 41, 55–56
Lee, Dwight, 10, 11
Liberty Property Trust **LRY,** 166
Life cycle
    corporate, 53–56
    real estate, 150
Load, mutual funds, 214
Logistics operations, outsourced,
    190
Long-term debt-to-equity calcula-
    tion, 81–82, 134
Luxottica Group **LUX,** 174–175

Malkiel, Burton, 34, 35
Management evaluation, 75–109
    analysis, 93–98
    case studies: management effi-
        ciency numbers, 90–93
    dividends, 86–89
    ethical issues, 100–102
    evaluation tools, 80–86
    management stock ownership,
        63–65, 134
    as nimble, 57–58
    Standard & Poor's Equity Rank-
        ing (Quality Ranking),
        98–100, 134
    stock options, 102–109, 134
    in stock selection, 75–79
    trends, 89–90
Market capitalization (*See* Capital-
    ization, market)
Master limited partnership (MLP),
    207
Material sector companies,
    243–246
Maturity date, 22
May, John, 120
McCormick & Company **MKC,** 92,
    98, 117, 259–260

McKenzie, Richard, 10, 11
Media hype, 17
Medicis Pharmaceuticals **MRX,** 91,
    94, 117, 275–276
Merriman, Paul, 14
Mid-cap stocks, 12, 39–46, 55
Millionaires and the Millennium
    (Havens & Schervish),
    201–202
Mistakes to avoid, 14–19
    about, 14–15
    fees, 17
    focus on wrong things, 18
    following amateur advice,
        17–18
    media hype, 17
    performance expectations,
        18–19
    procrastinating, 15
    risk, 16–17
    written plan lacking, 15–16
MLP (master limited partnership),
    207
Momentum investing, 112
Money for Life (Sheard), 7–8
Morningstar, Inc., 215
Mortgage REITs, 151–152
Motorola **MOT,** 130–131
Mutual funds, 211–230
    about, 211–212
    capital gains taxes, 218–222
    defined, 212–213
    exchange-traded and index
        funds, 224–226
    fees, 213–218
    fund portfolio analysis, 222–223
    performance, 223–224
    tax-deferred accounts, 222

National Fuel Gas **NFG,** 205
Natural gas resources, 204–205
NAV (net asset value), 212
Net asset value (NAV), 212
Net earnings, REITs, 157–159

*New Concepts of Fiduciary Respon-
sibilities* (Tasch & Viede-
man), 77
No-load, mutual funds, 214
Nokia **NOK,** 35
Nonlease services, REITs, 164

Offering, 26–27
Oil resources, 202–204
Omnicare **OCR,** 43, 126–127,
276–277
Operating cash flow, 85, 134
O'Shaughnessy, James, 122
Outsourcing as overlooked trend,
188–196
Outstanding shares, 30
Overlooked stocks, defined, 51–53
(*See also specific topics*)
Overlooked trends, 177–210
about, 177–178
global accumulation of wealth,
197–202
global resources, 202–210
intergenerational transfer of
wealth, 197–202
outsourcing, 188–196
water, 178–188

Pass-through securities and REITs,
150–151
Pay yourself first, 2, 7–8
Paychex, Inc. **PAYX,** 191, 250–251
Payout ratio, 84
Payroll, outsourced, 190
PE (price-to-earnings) ratio, 112–114
PEG ratio, 114–116, 117–118, 134
Pennichuck **PNNW,** 186
Performance
historic returns, 10–12
mistakes to avoid, 18–19
mutual funds, 223–224
of REITs, 153–155
stock vs. bond performance,
11–14

Perot Systems Corporation **PER,** 193
Perry, Roland, 112
Peters, Tom, 188
Philadelphia Suburban Corporation **PSC,** 44, 185, 283–284
Pitney Bowes, Inc. **PBI,** 271–272
Plum Creek Timber **PCL,** 43,
127–128, 130, 154, 206–207,
244–245
P&O Princess **POC,** 173
Portfolio building, 133–148
bulls vs. bears, 143–144
diversification, 33–37
Graham and Buffett, 146–148
lessons learned, 144–146
with mutual funds, 222–223
opportunity awareness, 135–137
process, 137–140
small-cap, 12, 39–46, 41–46, 54,
56–57
stock picking summary,
134–135
stocks added to an index,
142–143
volatility management, 140–141
Price, John, 67
Price-to-cash flow, 121, 135
Price-to-earnings (PE) ratio,
112–114
Pro forma, 118–120
Product differentiation, 58–59
Product innovation, 59–60
Profit taking, 129–132
Progress Energy Ltd. **PGN,**
284–286
ProLogis Trust **PLD,** 165
Public Storage **PSA,** 166

Raymond James Financial, Inc.
RJF, 264–265
Rayonier **RYN,** 207–208
Real estate investment trusts (*See*
REITs [real estate investment
trusts])

Real estate life cycle, 50
REIT Modification Act of 2001
    (RMA), 164
REITs (real estate investment
    trusts), 149–167
  case studies, 63, 159–162
  defined, 149–150
  evaluation, 155–157
  examples of, 165–167
  funds from operations (FFO),
    157–159
  historic performance, 153–155
  pass-through securities,
    150–151
  reported net earnings, 157–159
  risks in, 164–165
  transition in, 162–164
  types of, 151–152
Reported net earnings, REITs,
    157–159
Repriced options, 106, 134
Retirement cost calculators, 2–3
Return on assets (ROA), 80–81
Return on capital (ROC), 80, 134
Return on equity (ROE), 80, 134
Returns, historic, 10–12
Revenues, 85–86, 134
Risk
  mistakes to avoid, 16–17
  REITs, 164–165
  as time mitigated, 13
  volatility management, 140–142
ROA (return on assets), 80–81
ROC (return on capital), 80, 134
ROE (return on equity), 80, 134
Roth IRA, 3

Savings, pay yourself first, 2–8
SBBI (Stocks, Bonds, Bills and Infla-
    tion, Edition 2000), 11
Schervish, Paul, 201–202
The Scott Company SMG, 245
Seacoast Financial Corporation
    SCFS, 58, 265–266

Secondary public offering, 27
Senior Housing Properties SNH,
    167
Service differentiation, 58–59
Share-price-to-sales ratio, 122–123,
    135
Shareholder equity calculation, 80
Shareholders, 26, 134
Shares, 26
    (See also Stocks)
Sheard, Robert, 7–8
Sheehan, Kevin, 68–74, 197
Shire Pharmaceuticals SHPGY, 52,
    277–278
Single-market focus, 60–62
Sivy, Michael, 83
Small-cap stocks, 12, 39–46, 41–46,
    54, 56–57
Sony SNE, 174
Southwest Water SWWC, 285–286
Speculation, 28–30
Standard & Poor's Equity Ranking
    (Quality Ranking), 98–100,
    134
  Global Industry Classification
    Standard (GICS), 37, 231–236
Standard reflex stock movements,
    124
Starting out (See Initial considera-
    tions)
Stock options, 102–109, 134
Stockholders, 26
Stocks
  vs. bond performance, 11–14
  diversification, 26–28
  and management evaluation,
    75–79
  price movements, 28
    (See also specific topics)
Stocks, Bonds, Bills and Inflation,
    Edition 2000 (SBBI), 11
Suez SA SZE, 176, 186–187
Sustainable competitive advan-
    tage, 67–68

Swire Pacific Ltd. **SWRAY,** 175–176
Symantec **SYMC,** 44, 273–274

Tasch, Edward, 77
Tax-advantaged funds, 220
Tax-deferred accounts, 222
Taxable REIT subsidiary (TRS), 164
Taxes
    capital gains and mutual funds,
        218–222
    dividends, 87
    pass-through securities and
        REITs, 150–151
TDS **TDS,** 280–281
Tecumseh Products Company
    TECUA, 64–65
Telecommunications sector com-
    panies, 279–281
Telephone and Data Systems **TDS,**
    44
Templeton, John, 111
Timber resources, 205–209
TIPS (treasury inflation protected
    security), 24–26
The Toro Company **TTC,** 254–255
Treasury inflation protected secu-
    rity (TIPS), 24–26
Trends
    in management evaluation,
        89–90
    overlooked (See Overlooked
        trends)
Trout, AL, 58
TRS (taxable REIT subsidiary), 164
Turner, Lynn, 119
12(b)-1 fee, 214
Tyson, Don, 64
Tyson Foods **TSN,** 63–64

Underdog status, 66
Undistributed capital gains, 218
Unexercised options, 108
United Parcel Services (UPS), 190

UPS (United Parcel Services), 190
U.S. savings bonds, 22
U.S. treasury bonds, 22
Utilities sector companies, 282–286

Value, evaluating, 111–132
    cash flow per share, 120–122
    contrarian investing, 111,
        123–128
    finding value, 112
    PEG ratio, 114–118, 134
    price-to-earnings (PE) ratio,
        112–114, 135
    pro forma, 118–120
    profit taking, 129–132
    share-price-to-sales ratio,
        122–123
    value investing, 128–129
Value investing, 128–129
Vesting, 102
Viedeman, Stephen, 77
Vivendi Environmental, 186–187

Waddell & Reed Financial **WDR,**
    113, 115, 116, 117, 266–267
Water as overlooked trend,
    178–188
WD-40 Company **WDFC,** 258–259
Welch, Jack, 101
What Works on Wall Street
    (O'Shaughnessy), 122
Whitmore, C., 195
World Trade Center attacks (2001),
    107
Written plan, lack of, 15–16
Wyatt, Watson, 104

Xu, Yexiao, 34, 35

Yield, 125

Zell, Bill, 63
Zuckerman, Mortimer, 161

About the Author

George Fisher is the publisher of the popular newsletter *Power Investing with DRIPs.* The author of *All about DRIPs and DSPs,* Fisher has been featured in a variety of major media including *Your Money,* the *Christian Science Monitor,* Bloomberg Finance, the *International Herald Tribune,* the *Washington Post,* CNBC, CBSMarketWatch.com, and Foxwire. He is a regular contributor to NetStockDirect.com, *Dick Davis Digest,* and *Bulls and Bears Newsletter.*